W9-CKQ-732

Euclid Public Library
631 E. 222nd Street
Euclid, Ohio 44123
216-261-5300

God Is in
the Manger

DIETRICH BONHOEFFER

God Is in the Manger

Reflections on Advent and Christmas

TRANSLATED BY O. C. DEAN JR.

COMPILED AND EDITED BY JANA RIESS

WJK WESTMINSTER JOHN KNOX PRESS LOUISVILLE · KENTUCKY

© 2010 Westminster John Knox Press

2012 hardback edition
Originally published in paperback in the United States
by Westminster John Knox Press in 2010
Louisville, KY

Devotional text herein originally appeared in
Dietrich Bonhoeffer's *I Want to Live These Days with You: A Year of Daily Devotions*
(Louisville, KY: Westminster John Knox Press, 2007). Translated by O. C. Dean Jr.
from the German *So will ich diese Tage mit euch leben* by Dietrich Bonhoeffer
Jahreslesebuch published in 2005 by Gütersloher Verlagshaus, Gütersloh, Germany.

12 13 14 15 16 17 18 19 20 21 — 10 9 8 7 6 5 4 3 2 1

All rights reserved. No part of this book may be reproduced or transmitted in any
form or by any means, electronic or mechanical, including photocopying, recording,
or by any information storage or retrieval system, without permission in writing
from the publisher. For information, address Westminster John Knox Press,
100 Witherspoon Street, Louisville, Kentucky 40202-1396. Or contact us
online at www.wjkbooks.com.

Scripture quotations from the New Revised Standard Version
of the Bible are copyright © 1989 by the Division of Christian Education of the
National Council of the Churches of Christ in the U.S.A. and are used by permission.

Scripture quotations from the Revised Standard Version of the Bible are
copyright © 1946, 1952, 1971, and 1973 by the Division of Christian Education of the
National Council of the Churches of Christ in the U.S.A. and are used by permission.

Book design by Drew Stevens
Cover design by designpointinc.com

Library of Congress Cataloging-in-Publication Data

Bonhoeffer, Dietrich, 1906–1945.
  [Selections. English. 2010]
  God is in the manger : reflections on Advent and Christmas / by Dietrich
Bonhoeffer ; translated by O. C. Dean Jr. ; compiled and edited by Jana Riess.
 — 1st ed.
     p. cm.
  Includes bibliographical references and index.
  ISBN 978-0-664-23429-4 (alk. paper)
  1. Advent — Meditations. 2. Christmas — Meditations I. Riess, Jana. II. Title.
  BV40.B66513 2010
  242'.33 — dc22   2010003667
  ISBN: 978-0-664-23887-2 (hardback edition)

PRINTED IN THE UNITED STATES OF AMERICA

♾ The paper used in this publication meets the minimum requirements of the
American National Standard for Information Sciences — Permanence of Paper for
Printed Library Materials, ANSI Z39.48-1992.

Westminster John Knox Press advocates the responsible use of our natural resources.
The text paper of this book is made from at least 30% post-consumer waste.

Most Westminster John Knox Press books are available at special quantity
discounts when purchased in bulk by corporations, organizations, and special-
interest groups. For more information, please e-mail SpecialSales@wjkbooks.com.

CONTENTS

TRANSLATOR'S PREFACE

Since Dietrich Bonhoeffer wrote before the days of inclusive gender, his works reflect a male-oriented world in which, for example, the German words for "human being" and "God" are masculine, and male gender was understood as common gender. In this respect, his language has, for the most part, been updated in accordance with the practices of the New Revised Standard Version of the Bible (NRSV); that is, most references to human beings have become gender-inclusive, whereas references to the Deity have remained masculine.

While scriptural quotations are mostly from the NRSV, it was necessary at times to substitute the King James Version (KJV), the Revised Standard Version (RSV), or a literal translation of Luther's German version, as quoted by Bonhoeffer, in order to allow the author to make his point. In a few other cases, the translation was adjusted to reflect the wording of the NRSV.

O. C. Dean Jr.

EDITOR'S PREFACE

This devotional brings together daily reflections from one of the twentieth century's most beloved theologians, Dietrich Bonhoeffer (1906–1945). These reflections have been chosen especially for the seasons of Advent and Christmas, a time when the liturgical calendar highlights several themes of Bonhoeffer's beliefs and teachings: that Christ expresses strength best through weakness, that faith is more important than the beguiling trappings of religion, and that God is often heard most clearly by those in poverty and distress.[1]

Although he came from a well-to-do family, by the time he wrote most of the content in this book, Bonhoeffer was well acquainted with both poverty and distress. Just two days after Adolf Hitler had seized control of Germany in early 1933, Bonhoeffer delivered a radio sermon in which he criticized the new regime and warned Germans that "the Führer concept" was dangerous and wrong. "Leaders of offices which set themselves up as gods mock God," his address concluded. But Germany never got to hear those final statements, because Bonhoeffer's microphone had been switched off mid-transmission.[2] This began a twelve-year struggle against Nazism in Germany, with Bonhoeffer running afoul of authorities and being arrested in 1943. Much of the content of this book was written during the two years he spent in prison.

For Bonhoeffer, waiting—one of the central themes of the Advent experience—was a fact of life during the war: waiting to be released from prison; waiting to be able to spend more than an hour a month in the company of his young fiancée, Maria von Wedemeyer; waiting for the end of the war. In his absence, friends and former students were killed in battle and his parents' home was bombed; there was little he could do about any of this except pray and wield a powerful pen. There was a helplessness in his situation that he recognized as a parallel to Advent, Christians' time of waiting for redemption in Christ. "Life in a prison cell may well be compared to Advent," Bonhoeffer wrote his best friend Eberhard Bethge as the holidays approached in 1943. "One waits, hopes, and does this, that, or the other—things that are really of no consequence—the door is shut, and can only be opened *from the outside*."[3]

But the prison door was never opened for Bonhoeffer, not in life at least. As the Third Reich crumbled in April 1945, Hitler ordered the execution of some political prisoners who had conspired to overthrow him. Since papers had recently been discovered that confirmed Bonhoeffer's involvement in this anti-Nazi plot, the theologian was among those scheduled to be executed in one of Hitler's final executive decrees.[4] Bonhoeffer was hanged on April 8, 1945, just ten days before German forces began to surrender and less than three weeks before Hitler's own death by suicide. Bonhoeffer was just thirty-nine years old.

Although Bonhoeffer's death (and the narrow timing of it) is tragic, we are fortunate that he was a prolific writer who left behind so many lectures, papers, letters, and diary entries from which we may piece together his theology.

HOW TO USE THIS BOOK

Advent is rarely exactly four weeks long, and can in fact vary in length from year to year. It always begins four Sundays before Christmas (December 25), but since Christmas falls on a different day of the week each year, Advent can begin anywhere between November 27 on the early side and December 3 on the late side. The first four weeks of this devotional assume the earliest possible start date, so that if Advent falls on or around November 27, you will have four full weeks of devotions to see you through to Christmas Day. If you're using the book in a year when Advent is slightly shorter, feel free to skip a few devotions in the first or last week.

The four Advent weeks are arranged by theme—waiting, mystery, redemption, and incarnation—and are followed by devotions for the twelve days of Christmas, which stretch from Christmas Day until January 5, just before the liturgical feast of Epiphany. These last entries are dated, since the twelve days of Christmas always begin on December 25 and end on January 5, unlike the varying days of Advent. This book also includes a final reflection for January 6, the feast of Epiphany.

Each day's devotion has a reflection from Dietrich Bonhoeffer, a Scripture to contemplate, and some bonus material. Most of the latter material is drawn from Bonhoeffer's own letters, sermons, and poetry, showing how he celebrated Christmas even when imprisoned and separated from family and beloved friends. It's important to remember how Bonhoeffer's beliefs were forged in the crucible of war and protest, and did not simply fall from the sky; it's equally important to recognize how intimately connected he was to those he loved. He did not exist in a vacuum. His legacy has also been profound, so a few of the bonus entries are taken from thinkers who might be called "heirs of Bonhoeffer"—contemporary Christian writers like Eugene Peterson, Luci Shaw, and Frederica Mathewes-Green, who reflect on some of the same issues that he did.

WAITING

The Advent Season Is a Season of Waiting

Jesus stands at the door knocking (Rev. 3:20). In total reality, he comes in the form of the beggar, of the dissolute human child in ragged clothes, asking for help. He confronts you in every person that you meet. As long as there are people, Christ will walk the earth as your neighbor, as the one through whom God calls you, speaks to you, makes demands on you. That is the great seriousness and great blessedness of the Advent message. Christ is standing at the door; he lives in the form of a human being among us. Do you want to close the door or open it?

It may strike us as strange to see Christ in such a near face, but he said it, and those who withdraw from the serious reality of the Advent message cannot talk of the coming of Christ in their heart, either. . . .

Christ is knocking. It's still not Christmas, but it's also still not the great last Advent, the last coming of Christ. Through all the Advents of our life that we celebrate runs the longing for the last Advent, when the word will be: "See, I am making all things new" (Rev. 21:5).

The Advent season is a season of waiting, but our whole life is an Advent season, that is, a season of waiting for the last Advent, for the time when there will be a new heaven and a new earth.

We can, and should also, celebrate Christmas despite the ruins around us. . . . I think of you as you now sit together with the children and with all the Advent decorations—as in earlier years you did with us. We must do all this, even more intensively because we do not know how much longer we have.[1]

Letter to Bonhoeffer's parents, November 29, 1943,
written from Tegel prison camp

Listen! I am standing at the door, knocking; if you hear my voice and open the door, I will come in to you and eat with you, and you with me.

Revelation 3:20

Waiting Is an Art

Celebrating Advent means being able to wait. Waiting is an art that our impatient age has forgotten. It wants to break open the ripe fruit when it has hardly finished planting the shoot. But all too often the greedy eyes are only deceived; the fruit that seemed so precious is still green on the inside, and disrespectful hands ungratefully toss aside what has so disappointed them. Whoever does not know the austere blessedness of waiting—that is, of hopefully doing without—will never experience the full blessing of fulfillment.

Those who do not know how it feels to struggle anxiously with the deepest questions of life, of their life, and to patiently look forward with anticipation until the truth is revealed, cannot even dream of the splendor of the moment in which clarity is illuminated for them. And for those who do not want to win the friendship and love of another person—who do not expectantly open up their soul to the soul of the other person, until friendship and love come, until they make their entrance—for such people the deepest blessing of the one life of two intertwined souls will remain forever hidden.

For the greatest, most profound, tenderest things in the world, we must wait. It happens not here in a storm but according to the divine laws of sprouting, growing, and becoming.

❖ ❖ ❖

Be brave for my sake, dearest Maria, even if this letter is
your only token of my love this Christmas-tide. We shall
both experience a few dark hours —why should we disguise
that from each other? We shall ponder the incomprehensibility of our lot and be assailed by the question of why, over
and above the darkness already enshrouding humanity, we
should be subjected to the bitter anguish of a separation
whose purpose we fail to understand. . . . And then, just
when everything is bearing down on us to such an extent
that we can scarcely withstand it, the Christmas message
comes to tell us that all our ideas are wrong, and that what
we take to be evil and dark is really good and light because
it comes from God. Our eyes are at fault, that is all. God is
in the manger, wealth in poverty, light in darkness, succor
in abandonment. No evil can befall us; whatever men may
do to us, they cannot but serve the God who is secretly
revealed as love and rules the world and our lives.[2]

Letter to fiancée Maria von Wedemeyer
from prison, December 13, 1943

A shoot shall come out from the stump of Jesse,
    and a branch shall grow out of his roots.
The spirit of the LORD shall rest on him,
    the spirit of wisdom and understanding,
    the spirit of counsel and might,
    the spirit of knowledge and the fear of the LORD.
His delight shall be in the fear of the LORD.

He shall not judge by what his eyes see,
    or decide by what his ears hear;
but with righteousness he shall judge the poor.
                            Isaiah 11:1–4a

Not Everyone Can Wait

Not everyone can wait: neither the sated nor the satisfied nor those without respect can wait. The only ones who can wait are people who carry restlessness around with them and people who look up with reverence to the greatest in the world. Thus Advent can be celebrated only by those whose souls give them no peace, who know that they are poor and incomplete, and who sense something of the greatness that is supposed to come, before which they can only bow in humble timidity, waiting until he inclines himself toward us—the Holy One himself, God in the child in the manger. God is coming; the Lord Jesus is coming; Christmas is coming. Rejoice, O Christendom!

I think we're going to have an exceptionally good Christmas. The very fact that every outward circumstance precludes our making provision for it will show whether we can be content with what is truly essential. I used to be very fond of thinking up and buying presents, but now that we have nothing to give, the gift God gave us in the birth of Christ will seem all the more glorious; the emptier our hands, the better we understand what Luther meant by his dying words: "We're beggars; it's true." The poorer our quarters, the more clearly we perceive that our hearts should be Christ's home on earth.[3]

Letter to fiancée Maria von Wedemeyer,
December 1, 1943

❖ ❖ ❖

Then he looked up at his disciples and said:
"Blessed are you who are poor,
　　for yours is the kingdom of God.
"Blessed are you who are hungry now,
　　for you will be filled.
"Blessed are you who weep now,
　　for you will laugh.
"Blessed are you when people hate you, and
when they exclude you, revile you, and defame you
on account of the Son of Man. Rejoice in that day
and leap for joy, for surely your reward is great in
heaven; for that is what their ancestors did to the
prophets.
"But woe to you who are rich,
　　for you have received your consolation.
"Woe to you who are full now,
　　for you will be hungry.
"Woe to you who are laughing now,
　　for you will mourn and weep.
"Woe to you when all speak well of you, for that
is what their ancestors did to the false prophets."

Luke 6:20–26

An Un-Christmas-Like Idea

When the old Christendom spoke of the coming again of the Lord Jesus, it always thought first of all of a great day of judgment. And as un-Christmas-like as this idea may appear to us, it comes from early Christianity and must be taken with utter seriousness. . . . The coming of God is truly not only a joyous message, but is, first, frightful news for anyone who has a conscience. And only when we have felt the frightfulness of the matter can we know the incomparable favor. God comes in the midst of evil, in the midst of death, and judges the evil in us and in the world. And in judging it, he loves us, he purifies us, he sanctifies us, he comes to us with his grace and love. He makes us happy as only children can be happy.

We have become so accustomed to the idea of divine love and of God's coming at Christmas that we no longer feel the shiver of fear that God's coming should arouse in us. We are indifferent to the message, taking only the pleasant and agreeable out of it and forgetting the serious aspect, that the God of the world draws near to the people of our little earth and lays claim to us.[4]

Dietrich Bonhoeffer, "The Coming of Jesus in Our Midst"

❖ ❖ ❖

In that region there were shepherds living in the fields, keeping watch over their flock by night. Then an angel of the Lord stood before them, and the glory of the Lord shone around them, and they were terrified. But the angel said to them, "Do not be afraid; for see — I am bringing you good news of great joy for all the people: to you is born this day in the city of David a Savior, who is the Messiah, the Lord. This will be a sign for you: you will find a child wrapped in bands of cloth and lying in a manger." And suddenly there was with the angel a multitude of the heavenly host, praising God and saying,

> "Glory to God in the highest heaven,
>   and on earth peace among those whom
>   he favors!"

Luke 2:8–14

A Soft, Mysterious Voice

In the midst of the deepest guilt and distress of the people, a voice speaks that is soft and mysterious but full of the blessed certainty of salvation through the birth of a divine child (Isa. 9:6–7). It is still seven hundred years until the time of fulfillment, but the prophet is so deeply immersed in God's thought and counsel that he speaks of the future as if he saw it already, and he speaks of the salvific hour as if he already stood in adoration before the manger of Jesus. "For a child has been born for us." What will happen one day is already real and certain in God's eyes, and it will be not only for the salvation of future generations but already for the prophet who sees it coming and for his generation, indeed, for all generations on earth. "For a child has been born *for us*." No human spirit can talk like this on its own. How are we who do not know what will happen next year supposed to understand that someone can look forward many centuries? And the times then were no more transparent than they are today. Only the Spirit of God, who encompasses the beginning and end of the world, can in such a way reveal to a chosen person the mystery of the future, so that he must prophesy for strengthening believers and warning unbelievers. This individual voice ultimately enters into the nocturnal adoration of the shepherds (Luke 2:15–20) and into the full jubilation of the Christ-believing community: "For a child has been born for us, a son given to us."

❖ ❖ ❖

A shaking of heads, perhaps even an evil laugh, must go through our old, smart, experienced, self-assured world, when it hears the call of salvation of believing Christians: "For a child has been born for us, a son given to us."[5]

Dietrich Bonhoeffer

❖ ❖ ❖

For a child has been born for us,
    a son given to us;
authority rests upon his shoulders;
    and he is named
Wonderful Counselor, Mighty God,
    Everlasting Father, Prince of Peace.
His authority shall grow continually,
    and there shall be endless peace
for the throne of David and his kingdom.
    He will establish and uphold it
with justice and with righteousness
    from this time onward and forevermore.
The zeal of the LORD of hosts will do this.

Isaiah 9:6–7

Silence: Waiting for God's Word

We are silent in the early hours of each day, because God is supposed to have the first word, and we are silent before going to sleep, because to God also belongs the last word. We are silent solely for the sake of the word, not in order to show dishonor to the word but in order to honor and receive it properly. Silence ultimately means nothing but waiting for God's word and coming away blessed by God's word. . . . Silence before the word, however, will have its effect on the whole day. If we have learned to be silent before the word, we will also learn to be economical with silence and speech throughout the day. There is an impermissible self-satisfied, prideful, offensive silence. This teaches us that what is important is never silence in itself. The silence of the Christian is a listening silence, a humble silence that for the sake of humility can also be broken at any time. It is a silence in connection with the word. . . . In being quiet there is a miraculous power of clarification, of purification, of bringing together what is important. This is a purely profane fact. Silence before the word, however, leads to the right hearing and thus also to the right speaking of the word of God at the right time. A lot that is unnecessary remains unsaid.

Today is Remembrance Sunday. Will you have a memorial service for B. Riemer? It would be nice, but difficult. Then comes Advent, with all its happy memories for us. It was you who really opened up to me the world of music-making that we have carried on during the weeks of Advent. Life in a prison cell may well be compared to Advent: one waits, hopes, and does this, that, or the other—things that are really of no consequence—the door is shut, and can only be opened *from the outside.*[6]

> Letter from Bonhoeffer at Tegel prison to
> Eberhard Bethge, November 21, 1943

For God alone my soul waits in silence,
    for my hope is from him.
He alone is my rock and my salvation,
    my fortress; I shall not be shaken.
On God rests my deliverance and my honor;
    my mighty rock, my refuge is in God.
Trust in him at all times, O people;
    pour out your heart before him;
    God is a refuge for us.

Psalm 62:5–8

God's Holy Present

S erve the opportune time." The most profound matter will be revealed to us only when we consider that not only does the world have its time and its hours, but also that our own life has its time and its hour of God, and that behind these times of our lives traces of God become visible, that under our paths are the deepest shafts of eternity, and every step brings back a quiet echo from eternity. It is only a matter of understanding the deep, pure form of these times and representing them in our conduct of life. Then in the middle of our time we will also encounter God's holy present. "My times are in your hand" (Ps. 31:15). Serve your times, God's present in your life. God has sanctified your time. Every time, rightly understood, is immediate to God, and God wants us to be fully what we are. . . . Only those who stand with both feet on the earth, who are and remain totally children of earth, who undertake no hopeless attempts at flight to unreachable heights, who are content with what they have and hold on to it thankfully—only they have the full power of the humanity that serves the opportune time and thus eternity. . . . The Lord of the ages is God. The turning point of the ages is Christ. The right spirit of the ages is the Holy Spirit.

Dear parents . . . I don't need to tell you how much I long for freedom and for you all. But over the decades you have provided for us such incomparably beautiful Christmases that my thankful remembrance of them is strong enough to light up one dark Christmas. Only such times can really reveal what it means to have a past and an inner heritage that is independent of chance and the changing of the times. The awareness of a spiritual tradition that reaches through the centuries gives one a certain feeling of security in the face of all transitory difficulties. I believe that those who know they possess such reserves of strength do not need to be ashamed even of softer feelings—which in my opinion are still among the better and nobler feelings of humankind—when remembrance of a good and rich past calls them forth. Such feelings will not overwhelm those who hold fast to the values that no one can take from them.[7]

Letter to Bonhoeffer's parents, written from
Tegel prison, December 17, 1943

For I hear the whispering of many—
    terror all around!—
as they scheme together against me,
    as they plot to take my life.

But I trust in you, O LORD;
    I say, "You are my God."
My times are in your hand;
    deliver me from the hand of my enemies
        and persecutors.
Let your face shine upon your servant;
    save me in your steadfast love.

Psalm 31:13–16

MYSTERY

Respect for the Mystery

The lack of mystery in our modern life is our downfall and our poverty. A human life is worth as much as the respect it holds for the mystery. We retain the child in us to the extent that we honor the mystery. Therefore, children have open, wide-awake eyes, because they know that they are surrounded by the mystery. They are not yet finished with this world; they still don't know how to struggle along and avoid the mystery, as we do. We destroy the mystery because we sense that here we reach the boundary of our being, because we want to be lord over everything and have it at our disposal, and that's just what we cannot do with the mystery. . . . Living without mystery means knowing nothing of the mystery of our own life, nothing of the mystery of another person, nothing of the mystery of the world; it means passing over our own hidden qualities and those of others and the world. It means remaining on the surface, taking the world seriously only to the extent that it can be *calculated* and *exploited*, and not going beyond the world of calculation and exploitation. Living without mystery means not seeing the crucial processes of life at all and even denying them.

Ascension joy—inwardly we must become very quiet to hear the soft sound of this phrase at all. Joy lives in its quietness and incomprehensibility. This joy is in fact incomprehensible, for the comprehensible never makes for joy.[1]

Dietrich Bonhoeffer

❖   ❖   ❖

I want their hearts to be encouraged and united in love, so that they may have all the riches of assured understanding and have the knowledge of God's mystery, that is, Christ himself, in whom are hidden all the treasures of wisdom and knowledge.

Colossians 2:2–3

DAY TWO

The Mystery of Love

The mystery remains a mystery. It withdraws from our grasp. Mystery, however, does not mean simply not knowing something.

The greatest mystery is not the most distant star; on the contrary, the closer something comes to us and the better we know it, then the more mysterious it becomes for us. The greatest mystery to us is not the most distant person, but the one next to us. The mystery of other people is not reduced by getting to know more and more about them. Rather, in their closeness they become more and more mysterious. And the final depth of all mystery is when two people come so close to each other that they *love* each other. Nowhere in the world does one feel the might of the mysterious and its wonder as strongly as here. When two people know everything about each other, the mystery of the love between them becomes infinitely great. And only in this love do they understand each other, know everything about each other, know each other completely. And yet, the more they love each other and know about each other in love, the more deeply they know the mystery of their love. Thus, knowledge about each other does not remove the mystery, but rather makes it more profound. *The very fact* that the other person is so near to me is the greatest mystery.

❖   ❖   ❖

All that is Christmas originates in heaven and comes from there to us all, to you and me alike, and forms a stronger bond between us than we could ever forge by ourselves.[2]

Maria von Wedemeyer to Dietrich Bonhoeffer,
December 19, 1943, from Pätzig

❖   ❖   ❖

I thank my God every time I remember you, constantly praying with joy in every one of my prayers for all of you, because of your sharing in the gospel from the first day until now. I am confident of this, that the one who began a good work among you will bring it to completion by the day of Jesus Christ. It is right for me to think this way about all of you, because you hold me in your heart, for all of you share in God's grace with me, both in my imprisonment and in the defense and confirmation of the gospel. For God is my witness, how I long for all of you with the compassion of Christ Jesus. And this is my prayer, that your love may overflow more and more with knowledge and full insight to help you to determine what is best, so that in the day of Christ you may be pure and blameless, having produced the harvest of righteousness that comes through Jesus Christ for the glory and praise of God. I want you to know, beloved, that what has happened to me has actually helped to spread the gospel, so that it has become known throughout the whole imperial guard and to everyone else that my imprisonment is for Christ; and most of the brothers and sisters, having been made confident in the Lord by my imprisonment, dare to speak the word with greater boldness and without fear.

Philippians 1:3–14

The Wonder of All Wonders

God travels wonderful ways with human beings, but he does not comply with the views and opinions of people. God does not go the way that people want to prescribe for him; rather, his way is beyond all comprehension, free and self-determined beyond all proof.

Where reason is indignant, where our nature rebels, where our piety anxiously keeps us away: that is precisely where God loves to be. There he confounds the reason of the reasonable; there he aggravates our nature, our piety—that is where he wants to be, and no one can keep him from it. Only the humble believe him and rejoice that God is so free and so marvelous that he does wonders where people despair, that he takes what is little and lowly and makes it marvelous. And that is the wonder of all wonders, that God loves the lowly. . . . God is not ashamed of the lowliness of human beings. God marches right in. He chooses people as his instruments and performs his wonders where one would least expect them. God is near to lowliness; he loves the lost, the neglected, the unseemly, the excluded, the weak and broken.

That . . . is the unrecognized mystery of this world: Jesus Christ. That this Jesus of Nazareth, the carpenter, was himself the Lord of glory: that was the mystery of God. It was a mystery because God became poor, low, lowly, and weak out of love for humankind, because God became a human being like us, so that we would become divine, and because he came to us so that we would come to him. God as the one who becomes low for our sakes, *God in Jesus of Nazareth—that is the secret, hidden wisdom* . . . that "no eye has seen nor ear heard nor the human heart conceived" (1 Cor. 2:9). . . . That is the *depth of the Deity,* whom *we worship as mystery* and *comprehend as mystery.*[3]

Dietrich Bonhoeffer

None of the rulers of this age understood this; for if they had, they would not have crucified the Lord of glory. But, as it is written,

> "What no eye has seen, nor ear heard,
>   nor the human heart conceived,
> what God has prepared for those who love
>   him" —

these things God has revealed to us through the Spirit; for the Spirit searches everything, even the depths of God.

1 Corinthians 2:8–10

The Scandal of Pious People

The lowly God-man is the scandal of pious people and of people in general. This scandal is his
historical ambiguity. The most incomprehensible
thing for the pious is this man's claim that he is not
only a pious human being but also the Son of God.
Whence his authority: "But I say to you" (Matt. 5:22)
and "Your sins are forgiven" (Matt. 9:2). If Jesus'
nature had been deified, this claim would have been
accepted. If he had given signs, as was demanded of
him, they would have believed him. But at the point
where it really mattered, he held back. And that created the scandal. Yet everything depends on this fact.
If he had answered the Christ question addressed to
him through a miracle, then the statement would no
longer be true that he became a human being like us,
for then there would have been an exception at the
decisive point. . . . If Christ had documented himself with miracles, we would naturally believe, but
then Christ would not be our salvation, for then there
would not be faith in the God who became human,
but only the recognition of an alleged supernatural
fact. But that is not faith. . . . Only when I forgo visible proof, do I believe in God.

The kingdom belongs to people who aren't trying to look good or impress anybody, even themselves. They are not plotting how they can call attention to themselves, worrying about how their actions will be interpreted or wondering if they will get gold stars for their behavior. Twenty centuries later, Jesus speaks pointedly to the preening ascetic trapped in the fatal narcissism of spiritual perfectionism, to those of us caught up in boasting about our victories in the vineyard, to those of us fretting and flapping about our human weaknesses and character defects. The child doesn't have to struggle to get himself in a good position for having a relationship with God; he doesn't have to craft ingenious ways of explaining his position to Jesus; he doesn't have to create a pretty face for himself; he doesn't have to achieve any state of spiritual feeling or intellectual understanding. All he has to do is happily accept the cookies, the gift of the kingdom.[4]

Brennan Manning, *The Ragamuffin Gospel*

But we proclaim Christ crucified, a stumbling block to Jews and foolishness to Gentiles, but to those who are the called, both Jews and Greeks, Christ the power of God and the wisdom of God. For God's foolishness is wiser than human wisdom, and God's weakness is stronger than human strength.

1 Corinthians 1:23–25

The Power and Glory of the Manger

For the great and powerful of this world, there are only two places in which their courage fails them, of which they are afraid deep down in their souls, from which they shy away. These are the manger and the cross of Jesus Christ. No powerful person dares to approach the manger, and this even includes King Herod. For this is where thrones shake, the mighty fall, the prominent perish, because God is with the lowly. Here the rich come to nothing, because God is with the poor and hungry, but the rich and satisfied he sends away empty. Before Mary, the maid, before the manger of Christ, before God in lowliness, the powerful come to naught; they have no right, no hope; they are judged. . . .

Who among us will celebrate Christmas correctly? Whoever finally lays down all power, all honor, all reputation, all vanity, all arrogance, all individualism beside the manger; whoever remains lowly and lets God alone be high; whoever looks at the child in the manger and sees the glory of God precisely in his lowliness.[5]

Dietrich Bonhoeffer

And Mary said,
"My soul magnifies the Lord,
    and my spirit rejoices in God my Savior,
for he has looked with favor on the lowliness of his
        servant.
    Surely, from now on all generations will call me
    blessed;
for the Mighty One has done great things for me,
    and holy is his name.
His mercy is for those who fear him
    from generation to generation.
He has shown strength with his arm;
    he has scattered the proud in the thoughts of
        their hearts.
He has brought down the powerful from their
        thrones,
    and lifted up the lowly;
he has filled the hungry with good things,
    and sent the rich away empty.
He has helped his servant Israel,
    in remembrance of his mercy,
    according to the promise he made to our
        ancestors,
    to Abraham and to his descendants forever."

Luke 1:46–55

The Mysteries of God

No priest, no theologian stood at the manger of Bethlehem. And yet all Christian theology has its origin in the wonder of all wonders: that God became human. Holy theology arises from knees bent before the mystery of the divine child in the stable. Without the holy night, there is no theology. "God is revealed in flesh," the God-human Jesus Christ — that is the holy mystery that theology came into being to protect and preserve. How we fail to understand when we think that the task of theology is to solve the mystery of God, to drag it down to the flat, ordinary wisdom of human experience and reason! Its sole office is to preserve the miracle as miracle, to comprehend, defend, and glorify God's mystery precisely as mystery. This and nothing else, therefore, is what the early church meant when, with never flagging zeal, it dealt with the mystery of the Trinity and the person of Jesus Christ. . . . If Christmas time cannot ignite within us again something like a love for holy theology, so that we — captured and compelled by the wonder of the manger of the Son of God — must reverently reflect on the mysteries of God, then it must be that the glow of the divine mysteries has also been extinguished in our heart and has died out.

Wonder is the only adequate launching pad for exploring this fullness, this wholeness, of human life. Once a year, each Christmas, for a few days at least, we and millions of our neighbors turn aside from our preoccupations with life reduced to biology or economics or psychology and join together in a community of wonder. The wonder keeps us open-eyed, expectant, alive to life that is always more than we can account for, that always exceeds our calculations, that is always beyond anything we can make.[6]

Eugene Peterson

When the angels had left them and gone into heaven, the shepherds said to one another, "Let us go now to Bethlehem and see this thing that has taken place, which the Lord has made known to us." So they went with haste and found Mary and Joseph, and the child lying in the manger. When they saw this, they made known what had been told them about this child; and all who heard it were amazed at what the shepherds told them. But Mary treasured all these words and pondered them in her heart. The shepherds returned, glorifying and praising God for all they had heard and seen, as it had been told them.

Luke 2:15–20

An Unfathomable Mystery

In an incomprehensible reversal of all righteous and pious thinking, God declares himself guilty to the world and thereby extinguishes the guilt of the world. God himself takes the humiliating path of reconciliation and thereby sets the world free. God wants to be guilty of our guilt and takes upon himself the punishment and suffering that this guilt brought to us. God stands in for godlessness, love stands in for hate, the Holy One for the sinner. Now there is no longer any godlessness, any hate, any sin that God has not taken upon himself, suffered, and atoned for. Now there is no more reality and no more world that is not reconciled with God and in peace. That is what God did in his beloved Son Jesus Christ. *Ecce homo* — see the incarnate God, the unfathomable mystery of the love of God for the world. God loves human beings. God loves the world — not ideal human beings but people as they are, not an ideal world but the real world.

We prepare to witness a mystery. More to the point, we prepare to witness *the* Mystery, the *God made flesh*. While it is good that we seek to know the Holy One, it is probably not so good to presume that we ever complete the task, to suppose that we ever know anything about him except what he has *made known* to us. The prophet Isaiah helps us to remember our limitations when he writes, "To whom then will you compare me . . . ? says the Holy One. . . ." Think of it like this: he cannot be exhausted by our ideas about him, but he is everywhere suggested. He cannot be comprehended, but he can be touched. His coming in the flesh—this Mystery we prepare to glimpse again—confirms that he is to be touched.[7]

Scott Cairns, in *God with Us*

To whom then will you liken God,
    or what likeness compare with him? . . .
. . . .
Have you not known? Have you not heard?
    Has it not been told you from the beginning?
    Have you not understood from the foundations of
        the earth?
It is he who sits above the circle of the earth,
    and its inhabitants are like grasshoppers;
who stretches out the heavens like a curtain,
    and spreads them like a tent to live in;
who brings princes to naught,
    and makes the rulers of the earth as nothing.

Isaiah 40:18, 21–23

ADVENT WEEK THREE

REDEMPTION

Jesus Enters into the
Guilt of Human Beings

Jesus does not want to be the only perfect human being at the expense of humankind. He does not want, as the only guiltless one, to ignore a humanity that is being destroyed by its guilt; he does not want some kind of human ideal to triumph over the ruins of a wrecked humanity. Love for real people leads into the fellowship of human guilt. Jesus does not want to exonerate himself from the guilt in which the people he loves are living. A love that left people alone in their guilt would not have real people as its object. So, in vicarious responsibility for people and in his love for real human beings, Jesus becomes the one burdened by guilt—indeed, the one upon whom all human guilt ultimately falls and the one who does not turn it away but bears it humbly and in eternal love. As the one who acts responsibly in the historical existence of humankind, as the human being who has entered reality, Jesus becomes guilty. But because his historical existence, his incarnation, has its sole basis in God's love for human beings, it is the love of God that makes Jesus become guilty. Out of selfless love for human beings, Jesus leaves his state as the one without sin and enters into the guilt of human beings. He takes it upon himself.

❖ ❖ ❖

We have something to hide. We have secrets, worries, thoughts, hopes, desires, passions which no one else gets to know. We are sensitive when people get near those domains with their questions. And now, against all rules of tact the Bible speaks of the truth that in the end we will appear before Christ with everything we are and were. . . . And we all know that we could justify ourselves before any human court, but not before this one. Lord, who can justify themselves?[1]

Bonhoeffer's sermon for Repentance
Sunday, November 19, 1933

For all of us must appear before the judgment seat of Christ, so that each may receive recompense for what has been done in the body, whether good or evil.

2 Corinthians 5:10

Taking on Guilt

B ecause what is at stake for Jesus is not the proclamation and realization of new ethical ideals,
and thus also not his own goodness (Matt. 19:17),
but solely his love for real human beings, he can
enter into the communication of their guilt; he can be
loaded down with their guilt. . . . It is his love alone
that lets him become guilty. Out of his selfless love,
out of his sinless nature, Jesus enters into the guilt
of human beings; he takes it upon himself. A sinless
nature and guilt bearing are bound together in him
indissolubly. As the sinless one Jesus takes guilt upon
himself, and under the burden of this guilt, he shows
that he is the sinless one.

Lord Jesus, come yourself, and dwell with us, be human as we are, and overcome what overwhelms us. Come into the midst of my evil, come close to my unfaithfulness. Share my sin, which I hate and which I cannot leave. Be my brother, Thou Holy God. Be my brother in the kingdom of evil and suffering and death.[2]

Sermon for Advent Sunday,
December 2, 1928

❖ ❖ ❖

Then someone came to him and said, "Teacher, what good deed must I do to have eternal life?" And he said to him, "Why do you ask me about what is good? There is only one who is good. If you wish to enter into life, keep the commandments." He said to him, "Which ones?" And Jesus said, "You shall not murder; You shall not commit adultery; You shall not steal; You shall not bear false witness; Honor your father and mother; also, You shall love your neighbor as yourself."

Matthew 19:16–19

Becoming Guilty

B ecause Jesus took upon himself the guilt of all people, everyone who acts responsibly becomes guilty. Those who want to extract themselves from the responsibility for this guilt, also remove themselves from the ultimate reality of human existence. Moreover, they also remove themselves from the redeeming mystery of the sinless guilt bearing of Jesus Christ and have no share in the divine justification that covers this event. They place their personal innocence above their responsibility for humankind, and they are blind to the unhealed guilt that they load on themselves in this very way. They are also blind to the fact that real innocence is revealed in the very fact that for the sake of other people it enters into the communion of their guilt. Through Jesus Christ, the nature of responsible action includes the idea that the sinless, the selflessly loving become the guilty.

In eight days, we shall celebrate Christmas and now for once let us make it really a festival of Christ in our world. . . . It is not a light thing to God that every year we celebrate Christmas and do not take it seriously. His word holds and is certain. When he comes in his glory and power into the world in the manger, he will put down the mighty from their seats, unless ultimately, ultimately they repent.[3]

> Sermon to a London church on the third
> Sunday of Advent, December 17, 1933

> Come now, let us argue it out,
>   says the LORD:
> though your sins are like scarlet,
>   they shall be like snow;
> though they are red like crimson,
>   they shall become like wool.
>   *Isaiah 1:18*

DAY FOUR

Look Up, Your Redemption Is Drawing Near

Let's not deceive ourselves. "Your redemption is drawing near" (Luke 21:28), whether we know it or not, and the only question is: Are we going to let it come to us too, or are we going to resist it? Are we going to join in this movement that comes down from heaven to earth, or are we going to close ourselves off? Christmas is coming—whether it is with us or without us depends on each and every one of us.

Such a true Advent happening now creates something different from the anxious, petty, depressed, feeble Christian spirit that we see again and again, and that again and again wants to make Christianity contemptible. This becomes clear from the two powerful commands that introduce our text: "Look up and raise your heads" (Luke 21:28 RSV). Advent creates people, new people. We too are supposed to become new people in Advent. Look up, you whose gaze is fixed on this earth, who are spellbound by the little events and changes on the face of the earth. Look up to these words, you who have turned away from heaven disappointed. Look up, you whose eyes are heavy with tears and who are heavy and who are crying over the fact that the earth has gracelessly torn us away. Look up, you who, burdened with guilt, cannot lift your eyes. Look up, your redemption is drawing near. Something different from what you see daily will happen. Just be aware, be watchful, wait just another short moment. Wait and something quite new will break over you: God will come.

You know what a mine disaster is. In recent weeks we have had to read about one in the newspapers.

The moment even the most courageous miner has dreaded his whole life long is here. It is no use running into the walls; the silence all around him remains. . . . The way out for him is blocked. He knows the people up there are working feverishly to reach the miners who are buried alive. Perhaps someone will be rescued, but here in the last shaft? An agonizing period of waiting and dying is all that remains.

But suddenly a noise that sounds like tapping and breaking in the rock can be heard. Unexpectedly, voices cry out, "Where are you, help is on the way!" Then the disheartened miner picks himself up, his heart leaps, he shouts, "Here I am, come on through and help me! I'll hold out until you come! Just come soon!" A final, desperate hammer blow to his ear, now the rescue is near, just one more step and he is free.

We have spoken of Advent itself. That is how it is with the coming of Christ: "Look up and raise your heads, because your redemption is drawing near."[4]

> Bonhoeffer's Advent sermon in a London
> church, December 3, 1933

Now when these things begin to take place, stand up and raise your heads, because your redemption is drawing near.

Luke 21:28

DAY FIVE

World Judgment and World Redemption

When God chooses Mary as the means when God himself wants to come into the world in the manger of Bethlehem, this is not an idyllic family affair. It is instead the beginning of a complete reversal, a new ordering of all things on this earth. If we want to participate in this Advent and Christmas event, we cannot simply sit there like spectators in a theater and enjoy all the friendly pictures. Rather, we must join in the action that is taking place and be drawn into this reversal of all things ourselves. Here we too must act on the stage, for here the spectator is always a person acting in the drama. We cannot remove ourselves from the action.

With whom, then, are we acting? Pious shepherds who are on their knees? Kings who bring their gifts? What is going on here, where Mary becomes the mother of God, where God comes into the world in the lowliness of the manger? World judgment and world redemption—that is what's happening here. And it is the Christ child in the manger himself who holds world judgment and world redemption. He pushes back the high and mighty; he overturns the thrones of the powerful; he humbles the haughty; his arm exercises power over all the high and mighty; he lifts what is lowly, and makes it great and glorious in his mercy.

❖　❖　❖

Close to you I waken in the dead of night,
And start with fear—are you lost to me once more?
　　Is it always vainly that I seek you, you, my past?
I stretch my hands out,
and I pray—
and a new thing now I hear;
"The past will come to you once more,
and be your life's enduring part,
through thanks and repentance.
Feel in the past God's deliverance and goodness,
Pray him to keep you today and tomorrow."[5]
Poem written in Tegel prison, 1944

"For God so loved the world that he gave his only Son, so that everyone who believes in him may not perish but may have eternal life.

"Indeed, God did not send the Son into the world to condemn the world, but in order that the world might be saved through him. Those who believe in him are not condemned; but those who do not believe are condemned already, because they have not believed in the name of the only Son of God. And this is the judgment, that the light has come into the world, and people loved darkness rather than light because their deeds were evil. For all who do evil hate the light and do not come to the light, so that their deeds may not be exposed. But those who do what is true come to the light, so that it may be clearly seen that their deeds have been done in God."

John 3:16–21

Overcoming Fear

Human beings are dehumanized by fear. . . . But they should not be afraid. We should not be afraid! That is the difference between human beings and the rest of creation, that in all hopelessness, uncertainty, and guilt, they know a hope, and this hope is: Thy will be done. Yes. Thy will be done. . . . We call the name of the One before whom the evil in us cringes, before whom fear and anxiety must themselves be afraid, before whom they shake and take flight; the name of the One who alone conquered fear, captured it and led it away in a victory parade, nailed it to the cross and banished it to nothingness; the name of the One who is the victory cry of the humanity that is redeemed from the fear of death—Jesus Christ, the one who was crucified and lives. He alone is the Lord of fear; it knows him as its Lord and yields to him alone. Therefore, look to him in your fear. Think about him, place him before your eyes, and call him. Pray to him and believe that he is now with you and helps you. The fear will yield and fade, and you will become free through faith in the strong and living Savior Jesus Christ (Matt. 8:23–27).

Only when we have felt the terror of the matter, can we recognize the incomparable kindness. God comes into the very midst of evil and death, and judges the evil in us and in the world. And by judging us, God cleanses and sanctifies us, comes to us with grace and love. . . . God wants to always be with us, wherever we may be—in our sin, suffering, and death. We are no longer alone; God is with us.[6]

"The Coming of Jesus in Our Midst"

And when he got into the boat, his disciples followed him. A windstorm arose on the sea, so great that the boat was being swamped by the waves; but he was asleep. And they went and woke him up, saying, "Lord, save us! We are perishing!" And he said to them, "Why are you afraid, you of little faith?" Then he got up and rebuked the winds and the sea; and there was a dead calm. They were amazed, saying, "What sort of man is this, that even the winds and the sea obey him?"

Matthew 8:23–27

God Does Not Want to Frighten People

The Bible never wants to make us fearful. God does not want people to be afraid—not even of the last judgment. Rather, he wants to let human beings know everything, so that they will know all about life and its meaning. He lets people know even today, so that they may already live their lives openly and in the light of the last judgment. He lets us know solely for one reason: so that we may find the way to Jesus Christ, so that we may turn away from our evil way and try to find him, Jesus Christ. God does not want to frighten people. He sends us the word of judgment only so that we will reach all the more passionately, all the more avidly, for the promise of grace, so that we will know that we cannot prevail before God on our own strength, that before him we would have to pass away, but that in spite of every-thing he does not want our death, but our life. . . . Christ judges, that is, grace is judge and forgiveness and love—whoever clings to it is already set free.

Repentance means turning away from one's own work to the mercy of God. The whole Bible calls to us and cheers us: Turn back, turn back! Return—where to? To the everlasting grace of God, who does not leave us. . . . God will be merciful—so come, judgment day! Lord Jesus, make us ready. We rejoice. Amen.[7]

Bonhoeffer's sermon for Repentance
Sunday, November 19, 1933

From that time Jesus began to proclaim, "Repent, for the kingdom of heaven has come near."

Matthew 4:17

INCARNATION

DAY ONE

God Becomes Human

God becomes human, really human. While we endeavor to grow out of our humanity, to leave our human nature behind us, God becomes human, and we must recognize that God wants us also to become human—really human. Whereas we distinguish between the godly and the godless, the good and the evil, the noble and the common, God loves real human beings without distinction. . . . God takes the side of real human beings and the real world against all their accusers. . . . But it's not enough to say that God takes care of human beings. This sentence rests on something infinitely deeper and more impenetrable, namely, that in the conception and birth of Jesus Christ, God took on humanity in bodily fashion. God raised his love for human beings above every reproach of falsehood and doubt and uncertainty by himself entering into the life of human beings as a human being, by bodily taking upon himself and bearing the nature, essence, guilt, and suffering of human beings. Out of love for human beings, God becomes a human being. He does not seek out the most perfect human being in order to unite with that person. Rather, he takes on human nature as it is.

❖ ❖ ❖

This is about the birth of a child, not of the astonishing work of a strong man, not of the bold discovery of a wise man, not of the pious work of a saint. It really is beyond all our understanding: the birth of a child shall bring about the great change, shall bring to all mankind salvation and deliverance.[1]

"The Government upon the Shoulders
of a Child," Christmas 1940

In the beginning was the Word, and the Word was with God, and the Word was God. He was in the beginning with God. All things came into being through him, and without him not one thing came into being. What has come into being in him was life, and the life was the light of all people. The light shines in the darkness, and the darkness did not overcome it.

John 1:1–5

DAY TWO

Human Beings Become Human Because God Became Human

The figure of Jesus Christ takes shape in human beings. Human beings do not take on an independent form of their own. Rather, what gives them form and maintains them in their new form is always and only the figure of Jesus Christ himself. It is therefore not an imitation, not a repetition of his form, but their own form that takes shape in human beings. Human beings are not transformed into a form that is foreign to them, not into the form of God, but into their own form, a form that belongs to them and is essential to them. Human beings become human because God became human, but human beings do not become God. They could not and cannot bring about that change in their form, but God himself changes his form into human form, so that human beings—though not becoming God—can become human.

In Christ the form of human beings before God was created anew. It was not a matter of place, of time, of climate, of race, of the individual, of society, of religion, or of taste, but rather a question of the life of humanity itself that it recognized in Christ its image and its hope. What happened to Christ happened to humanity.

❖ ❖ ❖

The whole Christian story is strange. Frederick Buechner describes the Incarnation as "a kind of vast joke whereby the creator of the ends of the earth comes among us in diapers." He concludes, "Until we too have taken the idea of the God-man seriously enough to be scandalized by it, we have not taken it as seriously as it demands to be taken."

But we have taken the idea as seriously as a child can. America is far from spiritually monolithic, but the vast backdrop of our culture is Christian, and for most of us it is the earliest faith we know. The "idea of the God-man" is not strange or scandalous, because it first swam in milk and butter on the top of our oatmeal decades ago. At that age, many things were strange, though most were more immediately palpable. A God-filled baby in a pile of straw was a pleasant image, but somewhat theoretical compared with the heart-stopping exhilaration of a visit from Santa Claus. The way a thunderstorm ripped the night sky, the hurtling power of the automobile Daddy drove so bravely, the rapture of ice cream—how could the distant Incarnation compete with those?

We grew up with the Jesus story, until we outgrew it. The last day we walked out of Sunday School may be the last day we seriously engaged this faith.[2]

Frederica Mathewes-Green,
At the Corner of East and Now

When I was a child, I spoke like a child, I thought like a child, I reasoned like a child; when I became an adult, I put an end to childish ways. For now we see in a mirror, dimly, but then we will see face to face. Now I know only in part; then I will know fully, even as I have been fully known.

1 Corinthians 13:11–12

Christmas, Fulfilled Promise

Moses died on the mountain from which he was permitted to view from a distance the promised land (Deut. 32:48–52). When the Bible speaks of God's promises, it's a matter of life and death. . . . The language that reports this ancient history is clear. Anyone who has seen God must die; the sinner dies before the promise of God. Let's understand what that means for us so close to Christmas. The great promise of God—a promise that is infinitely more important than the promise of the promised land—is supposed to be fulfilled at Christmas. . . . The Bible is full of the proclamation that the great miracle has happened as an act of God, without any human doing. . . . What happened? God had seen the misery of the world and had come himself in order to help. Now he was there, not as a mighty one, but in the obscurity of humanity, where there is sinfulness, weakness, wretchedness, and misery in the world. That is where God goes, and there he lets himself be found by everyone. And this proclamation moves through the world anew, year after year, and again this year also comes to us.

We all come with different personal feelings to the Christmas festival. One comes with pure joy as he looks forward to this day of rejoicing, of friendships renewed, and of love. . . . Others look for a moment of peace under the

Christmas tree, peace from the pressures of daily work. . . . Others again approach Christmas with great apprehension. It will be no festival of joy to them. Personal sorrow is painful especially on this day for those whose loneliness is deepened at Christmastime. . . . And despite it all, Christmas comes. Whether we wish it or not, whether we are sure or not, we must hear the words once again: Christ the Savior is here! The world that Christ comes to save is our fallen and lost world. None other.[3]

Sermon to a German-speaking church in
Havana, Cuba, December 21, 1930

In the sixth month the angel Gabriel was sent by God to a town in Galilee called Nazareth, to a virgin engaged to a man whose name was Joseph, of the house of David. The virgin's name was Mary. And he came to her and said, "Greetings, favored one! The Lord is with you." But she was much perplexed by his words and pondered what sort of greeting this might be. The angel said to her, "Do not be afraid, Mary, for you have found favor with God. And now, you will conceive in your womb and bear a son, and you will name him Jesus. He will be great, and will be called the Son of the Most High, and the Lord God will give to him the throne of his ancestor David. He will reign over the house of Jacob forever, and of his kingdom there will be no end."

Luke 1:26–33

The Great Turning Point of All Things

What kings and leaders of nations, philosophers and artists, founders of religions and teachers of morals have tried in vain to do—that now happens through a newborn child. Putting to shame the most powerful human efforts and accomplishments, a child is placed here at the midpoint of world history—a child born of human beings, a son given by God (Isa. 9:6). That is the mystery of the redemption of the world; everything past and everything future is encompassed here. The infinite mercy of the almighty God comes to us, descends to us in the form of a child, his Son. That this child is born *for us*, this son is given *to us*, that this human child and Son of God belongs to me, that I know him, have him, love him, that I am his and he is mine—on this alone my life now depends. A child has our life in his hands. . . .

How shall we deal with such a child? Have our hands, soiled with daily toil, become too hard and too proud to fold in prayer at the sight of this child? Has our head become too full of serious thoughts . . . that we cannot bow our head in humility at the wonder of this child? Can we not forget all our stress and struggles, our sense of importance, and for once worship the child, as did the shepherds and the wise men from the East, bowing before the divine child in the manger like children?[4]

"The Government upon the Shoulders
of the Child," Christmas 1940

What then are we to say about these things? If God is for us, who is against us? He who did not withhold his own Son, but gave him up for all of us, will he not with him also give us everything else? Who will bring any charge against God's elect? It is God who justifies. Who is to condemn? It is Christ Jesus, who died, yes, who was raised, who is at the right hand of God, who indeed intercedes for us.

Romans 8:31–34

God Became a Child

"Mighty God" (Isa. 9:6) is the name of this child. The child in the manger is none other than God himself. Nothing greater can be said: God became a child. In the Jesus child of Mary lives the almighty God. Wait a minute! Don't speak; stop thinking! Stand still before this statement! God became a child! Here he is, poor like us, miserable and helpless like us, a person of flesh and blood like us, our brother. And yet he is God; he is might. Where is the divinity, where is the might of the child? In the divine love in which he became like us. His poverty in the manger is his might. In the might of love he overcomes the chasm between God and humankind, he overcomes sin and death, he forgives sin and awakens from the dead. Kneel down before this miserable manger, before this child of poor people, and repeat in faith the stammering words of the prophet: "Mighty God!" And he will be your God and your might.

And now Christmas is coming and you won't be there. We shall be apart, yes, but very close together. My thoughts will come to you and accompany you. We shall sing "Friede auf Erden" [Peace on Earth] and pray together, but we shall sing "Ehre sei Gott in der Höhe!" [Glory be to God on high] even louder. That is what I pray for you and for all of us, that the Savior may throw open the gates of heaven for us at darkest night on Christmas Eve, so that we can be joyful in spite of everything.[7]

Maria von Wedemeyer to Bonhoeffer,
December 10, 1943

In those days a decree went out from Emperor Augustus that all the world should be registered. This was the first registration and was taken while Quirinius was governor of Syria. All went to their own towns to be registered. Joseph also went from the town of Nazareth in Galilee to Judea, to the city of David called Bethlehem, because he was descended from the house and family of David. He went to be registered with Mary, to whom he was engaged and who was expecting a child. While they were there, the time came for her to deliver her child. And she gave birth to her firstborn son and wrapped him in bands of cloth, and laid him in a manger, because there was no place for them in the inn.

Luke 2:1–7

THE TWELVE
DAYS OF
CHRISTMAS
AND EPIPHANY

Living by God's Mercy

We cannot approach the manger of the Christ child in the same way we approach the cradle of another child. Rather, when we go to his manger, something happens, and we cannot leave it again unless we have been judged or redeemed. Here we must either collapse or know the mercy of God directed toward us.

What does that mean? Isn't all of this just a way of speaking? Isn't it just pastoral exaggeration of a pretty and pious legend? What does it mean that such things are said about the Christ child? Those who want to take it as a way of speaking will do so and continue to celebrate Advent and Christmas as before, with pagan indifference. For us it is not just a way of speaking. For that's just it: it is God himself, the Lord and Creator of all things, who is so small here, who is hidden here in the corner, who enters into the plainness of the world, who meets us in the help-lessness and defenselessness of a child, and wants to be with us. And he does this not out of playfulness or sport, because we find that so touching, but in order to show us where he is and who he is, and in order from this place to judge and devalue and dethrone all human ambition.

The throne of God in the world is not on human thrones, but in human depths, in the manger. Stand-ing around his throne there are no flattering vassals but dark, unknown, questionable figures who cannot get their fill of this miracle and want to live entirely by the mercy of God.

"Joy to the world!" Anyone for whom this sound is foreign, or who hears in it nothing but weak enthusiasm, has not yet really heard the gospel. For the sake of humankind, Jesus Christ became a human being in a stable in Bethlehem: Rejoice, O Christendom! For sinners, Jesus Christ became a companion of tax collectors and prostitutes: Rejoice, O Christendom! For the condemned, Jesus Christ was condemned to the cross on Golgotha: Rejoice, O Christendom! For all of us, Jesus Christ was resurrected to life: Rejoice, O Christendom! . . . All over the world today people are asking: Where is the path to joy? The church of Christ answers loudly: Jesus is our joy! (1 Pet. 1:7–9). Joy to the world!

Dietrich Bonhoeffer

In this you rejoice, even if now for a little while you have had to suffer various trials, so that the genuineness of your faith—being more precious than gold that, though perishable, is tested by fire—may be found to result in praise and glory and honor when Jesus Christ is revealed. Although you have not seen him, you love him; and even though you do not see him now, you believe in him and rejoice with an indescribable and glorious joy, for you are receiving the outcome of your faith, the salvation of your souls.

1 Peter 1:6–9

The Great Kingdom of Peace Has Begun

The authority of this poor child will grow (Isa. 9:7). It will encompass all the earth, and knowingly or unknowingly, all human generations until the end of the ages will have to serve it. It will be an authority over the hearts of people, but thrones and great kingdoms will also grow strong or fall apart with this power. The mysterious, invisible authority of the divine child over human hearts is more solidly grounded than the visible and resplendent power of earthly rulers. Ultimately all authority on earth must serve only the authority of Jesus Christ over humankind.

With the birth of Jesus, the great kingdom of peace has begun. Is it not a miracle that where Jesus has really become Lord over people, peace reigns? That there is one Christendom on the whole earth, in which there is peace in the midst of the world? Only where Jesus is not allowed to reign—where human stubbornness, defiance, hate, and avarice are allowed to live on unbroken—can there be no peace. Jesus does not want to set up his kingdom of peace by force, but where people willingly submit themselves to him and let him rule over them, he will give them his wonderful peace.

I'm in the dark depths of night, and my thoughts are roaming far afield. Now that all the merry-making and rejoicing and candlelight are over and the noise and commotion of the day have been replaced by silence, inside and out, other voices can be heard. . . . The chill night wind and the mysterious darkness can open hearts and release forces that are unfathomable, but good and consoling. . . . Can you think of a better time than night-time? That's why Christ, too, chose to come to us — with his angels — at night.[1]

Maria von Wedemeyer to Bonhoeffer,
December 25, 1943

❖　❖　❖

Now the birth of Jesus the Messiah took place in this way. When his mother Mary had been engaged to Joseph, but before they lived together, she was found to be with child from the Holy Spirit. Her husband Joseph, being a righteous man and unwilling to expose her to public disgrace, planned to dismiss her quietly. But just when he had resolved to do this, an angel of the Lord appeared to him in a dream and said, "Joseph, son of David, do not be afraid to take Mary as your wife, for the child conceived in her is from the Holy Spirit. She will bear a son, and you are to name him Jesus, for he will save his people from their sins." All this took place to fulfill what had been spoken by the Lord through the prophet:

> "Look, the virgin shall conceive and bear a son,
>   and they shall name him Emmanuel,"

which means, "God is with us." When Joseph awoke from sleep, he did as the angel of the Lord commanded him; he took her as his wife, but had no marital relations with her until she had borne a son; and he named him Jesus.

Matthew 1:18–25

On the Weak Shoulders of a Child

Authority rests upon his shoulders" (Isa. 9:6). Authority over the world is supposed to lie on the weak shoulders of this newborn child! One thing we know: these shoulders will come to carry the entire burden of the world. With the cross, all the sin and distress of this world will be loaded on these shoulders. But authority consists in the fact that the bearer does not collapse under the burden but carries it to the end. The authority that lies on the shoulders of the child in the manger consists in the patient bearing of people and their guilt. This bearing, however, begins in the manger; it begins where the eternal word of God assumes and bears human flesh. The authority over all the world has its beginning in the very lowliness and weakness of the child. . . . He accepts and carries the humble, the lowly, and sinners, but he rejects and brings to nothing the proud, the haughty, and the righteous (Luke 1:51–52).

From the Christian point of view there is no special problem about Christmas in a prison cell. For many people in this building it will probably be a more sincere and genuine occasion than in places where nothing but the name is kept. The misery, suffering, poverty, loneliness, helplessness, and guilt mean something quite different in the eyes of God from what they mean in the judgment of man, that

God will approach where men turn away, that Christ was born in a stable because there was no room for him in the inn—these are things that a prisoner can understand better than other people; for him they really are glad tidings.[2]

Bonhoeffer's letter to his parents from
Tegel prison, December 17, 1943

❖   ❖   ❖

Let the same mind be in you that was in Christ Jesus,
who, though he was in the form of God,
did not regard equality with God
as something to be exploited,
but emptied himself,
taking the form of a slave,
being born in human likeness.
And being found in human form,
he humbled himself
and became obedient to the point of death—
even death on a cross.

Therefore God also highly exalted him
and gave him the name
that is above every name,
so that at the name of Jesus
every knee should bend,
in heaven and on earth and under the earth,
and every tongue should confess
that Jesus Christ is Lord,
to the glory of God the Father.

Philippians 2:5–11

THE TWELVE DAYS OF CHRISTMAS / 71

With God There Is Joy

Everlasting joy shall be upon their heads" (Isa. 35:10). Since ancient times, in the Christian church, acedia—sadness of heart, resignation—has been considered a mortal sin. "Serve the LORD with gladness!" (Ps. 100:2 RSV), urges the Scripture. For this, our life has been given to us, and for this, it has been sustained for us to this present hour. The joy that no one can take from us belongs not only to those who have been called home, but also to us who are still living. In this joy we are one with them, but never in sadness. How are we supposed to be able to help those who are without joy and courage, if we ourselves are not borne by courage and joy? What is meant here is not something made or forced, but something given and free. With God there is joy, and from him it comes down and seizes spirit, soul, and body. And where this joy has seized a person, it reaches out around itself, it pulls others along, it bursts through closed doors. There is a kind of joy that knows nothing at all of the pain, distress, and anxiety of the heart. But it cannot last; it can only numb for a time. The joy of God has gone through the poverty of the manger and the distress of the cross; therefore it is invincible and irrefutable.

Acedia may be an unfamiliar term to those not well versed in monastic history or medieval literature. But that does not mean it has no relevance for contemporary readers. . . . I believe that such standard dictionary definitions of *acedia* as "apathy," "boredom," or "torpor" do not begin to cover it, and while we may find it convenient to regard it as a more primitive word for what we now term depression, the truth is much more complex. Having experienced both conditions, I think it likely that most of the restless boredom, frantic escapism, commitment phobia, and enervating despair that plagues us today is the ancient demon of acedia in modern dress.[3]

Kathleen Norris, *Acedia & Me: A Marriage,*
Monks, and a Writer's Life

Make a joyful noise to the LORD, all the earth.
    Worship the LORD with gladness;
    come into his presence with singing.

Know that the LORD is God.
    It is he that made us, and we are his;
    we are his people, and the sheep of his pasture.

Enter his gates with thanksgiving,
    and his courts with praise.
    Give thanks to him, bless his name.

For the LORD is good;
    his steadfast love endures forever,
    and his faithfulness to all generations.

Psalm 100

Everlasting Father and Prince of Peace

Everlasting Father" (Isa. 9:6)—how can this be the name of the child? Only because in this child the everlasting fatherly love of God is revealed, and the child wants nothing other than to bring to earth the love of the Father. So the Son is one with the Father, and whoever sees the Son sees the Father. This child wants nothing for himself. He is no prodigy in the human sense, but an obedient child of his heavenly Father. Born in time, he brings eternity with him to earth; as Son of God he brings to us all the love of the Father in heaven. Go, seek, and find in the manger the heavenly Father who here has also become your dear Father.

"Prince of Peace"—where God comes in love to human beings and unites with them, there peace is made between God and humankind and among people. Are you afraid of God's wrath? Then go to the child in the manger and receive there the peace of God. Have you fallen into strife and hatred with your sister or brother? Come and see how God, out of pure love, has become our brother and wants to reconcile us with each other. In the world, power reigns. This child is the Prince of Peace. Where he is, peace reigns.

❖ ❖ ❖

In our lives we don't speak readily of victory. It is too big a word for us. We have suffered too many defeats in our lives; victory has been thwarted again and again by too many weak hours, too many gross sins. But isn't it true that the spirit within us yearns for this word, for the final victory over the sin and anxious fear of death in our lives? And now God's word also says nothing to us about our victory; it doesn't promise us that *we* will be victorious over sin and death from now own; rather, it says with all its might that someone has won this victory, and that this person, if we have him as Lord, will also win the victory over us. It is not we who are victorious, but Jesus.[4]

"Christus Victor" address, November 26, 1939

On that day, when evening had come, he said to them, "Let us go across to the other side." And leaving the crowd behind, they took him with them in the boat, just as he was. Other boats were with him. A great windstorm arose, and the waves beat into the boat, so that the boat was already being swamped. But he was in the stern, asleep on the cushion; and they woke him up and said to him, "Teacher, do you not care that we are perishing?" He woke up and rebuked the wind, and said to the sea, "Peace! Be still!" Then the wind ceased, and there was a dead calm. He said to them, "Why are you afraid? Have you still no faith?" And they were filled with great awe and said to one another, "Who then is this, that even the wind and the sea obey him?"

Mark 4:35–41

Beside Your Cradle Here I Stand

Averse is going around repeatedly in my head: "Brother, come; from all that grieves you / you are freed; / all you need / I again will bring you." What does this mean: "All you need I again will bring you"? Nothing is lost; in Christ everything is lifted up, preserved—to be sure, in a different form—transparent, clear, freed from the torment of self-seeking desire. Christ will bring all of this again, and as it was originally intended by God, without the distortion caused by our sin. The teaching of the gathering up of all things, found in Ephesians 1:10, is a wonderful and thoroughly comforting idea. "God seeks out what has gone by" (Eccl. 3:15) receives here its fulfillment. And no one has expressed that as simply and in such a childlike way as Paul Gerhardt in the words that he places in the mouth of the Christ child: "All you need I again will bring you." Moreover, for the first time in these days I have discovered for myself the song, "Beside your cradle here I stand." Until now I had not thought much about it. Apparently you have to be alone a long time and read it meditatively to be able to perceive it. . . . Beside the "we" there is also still an "I" and Christ, and what that means cannot be said better than in this song.

When God's Son took on flesh, he truly and bodily took on, out of pure grace, our being, our nature, ourselves. This was the eternal counsel of the triune God. Now we are in him. Where he is, there we are too, in the incarnation, on the cross, and in his resurrection. We belong to him because we are in him. That is why the Scriptures call us the Body of Christ.[5]

Dietrich Bonhoeffer

With all wisdom and insight he has made known to us the mystery of his will, according to his good pleasure that he set forth in Christ, as a plan for the fullness of time, to gather up all things in him, things in heaven and things on earth. In Christ we have also obtained an inheritance, having been destined according to the purpose of him who accomplishes all things according to his counsel and will, so that we, who were the first to set our hope on Christ, might live for the praise of his glory.

Ephesians 1:8b–12

The Joyous Certainty of Faith

On the basis of God's beginning with us, which has already happened, our life with God is a path that is traveled in the law of God. Is this human enslavement under the law? No, it is liberation from the murderous law of incessant beginnings. Waiting day after day for the new beginning, thinking countless times that we have found it, only in the evening to give up on it again as lost—that is the perfect destruction of faith in the God who set the beginning once and for all time. . . . God has set the beginning: this is the joyous certainty of faith. Therefore, beside the "one" beginning of God, I am not supposed to try to set countless other beginnings of my own. This is precisely what I am now liberated from. The beginning—God's beginning—lies behind me, once and for all time. . . . Together we are on the path whose beginning consists in the fact that God has found his own people, a path whose end can consist only in the fact that God is seeking us again. The path between this beginning and this end is our walk in the law of God. It is life under the word of God in all its many facets. In truth there is only one danger on this path, namely, wanting to go behind the beginning. In that moment the path stops being a way of grace and faith. It stops being God's own way.

I believe that God can and will bring good out of evil, even out of the greatest evil. For that purpose he needs men who make the best use of everything. I believe that God will give us all the strength we need to help us to resist in all times of distress. But he never gives it in advance, lest we should rely on ourselves and not on him alone. A faith such as this should allay all our fears for the future. I believe that even our mistakes and shortcomings are turned to good account, and that it is no harder for God to deal with them than with our supposedly good deeds. I believe that God is no timeless fate, but that he waits for and answers sincere prayers and responsible actions.[6]

"After Ten Years: A Reckoning Made
at New Year 1943"

We know that all things work together for good for those who love God, who are called according to his purpose. For those whom he foreknew he also predestined to be conformed to the image of his Son, in order that he might be the firstborn within a large family. And those whom he predestined he also called; and those whom he called he also justified; and those whom he justified he also glorified.

Romans 8:28–30

At the Beginning of a New Year

The road to hell is paved with good intentions."
This saying, which is found in a broad variety
of lands, does not arise from the brash worldly wisdom of an incorrigible. It instead reveals deep Christian insight. At the beginning of a new year, many
people have nothing better to do than to make a list
of bad deeds and resolve from now on—how many
such "from-now-ons" have there already been!—to
begin with better intentions, but they are still stuck
in the middle of their paganism. They believe that a
good intention already means a new beginning; they
believe that on their own they can make a new start
whenever they want. But that is an evil illusion: only
God can make a new beginning with people whenever God pleases, but not people with God. Therefore, people cannot make a new beginning at all; they
can only pray for one. Where people are on their
own and live by their own devices, there is only the
old, the past. Only where God is can there be a new
beginning. We cannot command God to grant it; we
can only pray to God for it. And we can pray only
when we realize that we cannot do anything, that we
have reached our limit, that someone else must make
that new beginning.

❖   ❖   ❖

New Year's Text:

If we survive during the coming weeks or months, we shall be able to see quite clearly that all has turned out for the best. The idea that we could have avoided many of life's difficulties if we had taken things more cautiously is too foolish to be entertained for a moment. As I look back on your past I am so convinced that what has happened hitherto has been right, that I feel that what is happening now is right too. To renounce a full life and its real joys in order to avoid pain is neither Christian nor human.[7]

Bonhoeffer to Renate and Eberhard Bethge,
written from Tegel, January 23, 1944

From now on, therefore, we regard no one from a human point of view; even though we once knew Christ from a human point of view, we know him no longer in that way. So if anyone is in Christ, there is a new creation: everything old has passed away; see, everything has become new!

2 Corinthians 5:16–17

Do Not Worry about Tomorrow

Possessions delude the human heart into believing that they provide security and a worry-free existence, but in truth they are the very cause of worry. For the heart that is fixed on possessions, they come with a suffocating burden of worry. Worries lead to treasure, and treasure leads back to worry. We want to secure our lives through possessions; through worry we want to become worry free, but the truth turns out to be the opposite. The shackles that bind us to possessions, that hold us fast to possessions, are themselves worries. The misuse of possessions consists in our using them for security for the next day. Worry is always directed toward tomorrow. In the strictest sense, however, possessions are intended only for today. It is precisely the securing of tomorrow that makes me so insecure today. "Today's trouble is enough for today" (Matt. 6:34b). Only those who place tomorrow in God's hands and receive what they need to live today are truly secure. Receiving daily liberates us from tomorrow. Thought for tomorrow delivers us up to endless worry.

my cell from you during the past year, and has made every day easier for me. I think these hard years have brought us closer together than ever we were before. My wish for you and Father and Maria and for us all is that the New Year may bring us at least an occasional glimmer of light, and that we may once more have the opportunity of being together. May God keep you both well.[10]

> Birthday letter to Bonhoeffer's mother
> from prison, December 28, 1944

❖   ❖   ❖

For everything there is a season, and a time for every matter under heaven:
> a time to be born, and a time to die;
> a time to plant, and a time to pluck up what is
> > planted;
> a time to kill, and a time to heal;
> a time to break down, and a time to build up;
> a time to weep, and a time to laugh;
> a time to mourn, and a time to dance;
> a time to throw away stones, and a time to
> > gather stones together;
> a time to embrace, and a time to refrain from
> > embracing;
> a time to seek, and a time to lose;
> a time to keep, and a time to throw away;
> a time to tear, and a time to sew;
> a time to keep silence, and a time to speak;
> a time to love, and a time to hate;
> a time for war, and a time for peace.

> *Ecclesiastes 3:1–8*

Morning by Morning He Wakens Me

Every new morning is a new beginning of our life. Every day is a completed whole. The present day should be the boundary of our care and striving (Matt. 6:34; Jas. 4:14). It is long enough for us to find God or lose God, to keep the faith or fall into sin and shame. God created day and night so that we might not wander boundlessly, but already in the morning may see the goal of the evening before us. As the old sun rises new every day, so the eternal mercies of God are new every morning (Lam. 3:22–23). To grasp the old faithfulness of God anew every morning, to be able—in the middle of life—to begin a new life with God daily, that is the gift that God gives with every new morning. . . .

Not fear of the day, not the burden of work that I have to do, but rather, the Lord wakens me. So says the servant of God: "Morning by morning he wakens—wakens my ear to listen as those who are taught" (Isa. 50:4c). God wants to open the heart before it opens itself to the world; before the ear hears the innumerable voices of the day, the early hours are the time to hear the voice of the Creator and Redeemer. God made the stillness of the early morning for himself. It ought to belong to God.

Because intercession is such an incalculably great gift of God, we should accept it joyfully. The very time we give to intercession will turn out to be a daily source of new joy in God and in the Christian community. . . . For most people the early morning will prove to be the best time. We have a right to this time, even prior to the claims of other people, and we may insist upon having it as a completely undisturbed quiet time despite all external difficulties.[11]

Bonhoeffer, Life Together

> The Lord GOD has given me
>   the tongue of a teacher,
> that I may know how to sustain
>   the weary with a word.
> Morning by morning he wakens —
>   wakens my ear
>   to listen as those who are taught.
> Isaiah 50:4

The Feast of Epiphany

The curious uncertainty that surrounds the feast of Epiphany is as old as the feast itself. We know that long before Christmas was celebrated, Epiphany was the highest holiday in the Eastern and Western churches. Its origins are obscure, but it is certain that since ancient times this day has brought to mind four different events: the birth of Christ, the baptism of Christ, the wedding at Cana, and the arrival of the Magi from the East. . . . Be that as it may, since the fourth century the church has left the birth of Christ out of the feast of Epiphany. . . . The removal of the birth of Christ from his baptismal day had great significance. In gnostic and heretical circles in the East, the idea arose that the baptismal day was actually the day of Christ's birth as the Son of God. . . . But therein lay the possibility of a dangerous error, namely, a misunderstanding of God's incarnation. . . . If God had not accepted Jesus as his Son until Jesus' baptism, we would remain unredeemed. But if Jesus is the Son of God who from his conception and birth assumed our own flesh and blood, then and then alone is he true man and true God; only then can he help us; for then the "hour of salvation" for us has really come in his birth; then the birth of Christ is the salvation of all people.

Today you will be baptized a Christian. All those great ancient words of the Christian proclamation will be spoken over you, and the command of Jesus Christ to baptize will be carried out on you, without your knowing anything about it. But we are once again being driven right back to the beginnings of our understanding. Reconciliation and redemption, regeneration and the Holy Spirit, love of our enemies, cross and resurrection, life in Christ and Christian discipleship.[12]

"Thoughts on the Baptism of
Dietrich Wilhelm Rüdiger Bethge,"
May 1944

When they had heard the king, they set out; and there, ahead of them, went the star that they had seen at its rising, until it stopped over the place where the child was. When they saw that the star had stopped, they were overwhelmed with joy. On entering the house, they saw the child with Mary his mother; and they knelt down and paid him homage. Then, opening their treasure chests, they offered him gifts of gold, frankincense, and myrrh. And having been warned in a dream not to return to Herod, they left for their own country by another road.

Matthew 2:9–12

NOTES

Editor's Preface

1. Stephen R. Haynes and Lori Brandt Hale, *Bonhoeffer for Armchair Theologians* (Louisville, Ky.: Westminster John Knox Press, 2009). See esp. 132–33 and 77–78.

2. Eberhard Bethge, *Dietrich Bonhoeffer: A Biography*, rev. ed. (Minneapolis: Fortress Press, 2000), 260.

3. Letter from Dietrich Bonhoeffer to Eberhard Bethge, November 21, 1943, in *Letters and Papers from Prison: New Greatly Enlarged Edition*, ed. Eberhard Bethge (New York: Touchstone, 1997), 135.

4. Haynes and Hale, *Bonhoeffer for Armchair Theologians*, 70–76.

Advent Week One: Waiting

1. Dietrich Bonhoeffer, *Dietrich Bonhoeffer's Christmas Sermons*, ed. and trans. Edwin Robertson (Grand Rapids: Zondervan, 2005), 171–72.

2. Ruth-Alice von Bismarck and Ulrich Kabitz, *Love Letters from Cell 92: The Correspondence between Dietrich Bonhoeffer and Maria von Wedemeyer, 1943–45* (Nashville: Abingdon Press, 1992), 133.

3. *Ibid.*, 128.

4. Dietrich Bonhoeffer, "The Coming of Jesus in Our Midst," in *Watch for the Light: Readings for Advent and Christmas* (Maryknoll, N.Y.: Orbis Books, 2001), 205.

5. Dietrich Bonhoeffer, *I Want to Live These Days with You* (Louisville, Ky.: Westminster John Knox Press, 2007), 369.

6. Bonhoeffer, *Letters and Papers from Prison*, 135.

7. Bonhoeffer, *I Want to Live These Days with You*, 366.

Advent Week Two: Mystery

1. Bonhoeffer, *I Want to Live These Days with You*, 152.

2. Bismarck and Kabitz, *Love Letters from Cell 92*, 138.

3. Bonhoeffer, *I Want to Live These Days with You*, 149.

4. Brennan Manning, *The Ragamuffin Gospel Visual Edition* (Sisters, Ore.: Multnomah Publishers, 2005), n.p.

5. Bonhoeffer, *I Want to Live These Days with You*, 377.

6. Eugene Peterson, "Introduction," in *God with Us: Rediscovering the Meaning of Christmas*, ed. Greg Pennoyer and Gregory Wolfe (Brewster, Mass.: Paraclete Press, 2007), 1.

7. Scott Cairns, in *God with Us*, 57.

Advent Week Three: Redemption

1. Dietrich Bonhoeffer, *A Testament to Freedom: The Essential Writings of Dietrich Bonhoeffer*, ed. Geffrey B. Kelly and F. Burton Nelson (San Francisco: HarperOne, 1990, 1995), 217.

2. Bonhoeffer, *Dietrich Bonhoeffer's Christmas Sermons*, 22–23.

3. Ibid., 103–4.

4. Bonhoeffer, *Testament to Freedom*, 223.

5. Bonhoeffer, *Letters and Papers from Prison*, 323.

6. Bonhoeffer, *Testament to Freedom*, 185–86.

7. Ibid., 218.

Advent Week Four: Incarnation

1. Bonhoeffer, *Dietrich Bonhoeffer's Christmas Sermons*, 151. By Christmas of 1940, the Nazis had forbidden Bonhoeffer to preach publicly. This excerpt comes from a Christmas sermon he wrote that was circulated in print.

2. Frederica Mathewes-Green, *At the Corner of East and Now: A Modern Life in Ancient Christian Orthodoxy* (New York: Penguin Putnam, 1999), posted online at http://www.frederica.com/east-now-excerpt-1/.

3. Bonhoeffer, *Dietrich Bonhoeffer's Christmas Sermons*, 38–39.

4. Ibid., 151–52.

5. Ibid., 37.

6. Luci Shaw, in *God with Us*, 77–78.

7. Bismarck and Kabitz, *Love Letters from Cell 92*, 132.

The Twelve Days of Christmas

1. Bismarck and Kabitz, *Love Letters from Cell 92*, 145.

2. Bonhoeffer, *Letters and Papers from Prison*, 166.

3. Kathleen Norris, *Acedia & Me: A Marriage, Monks, and a Writer's Life* (New York: Riverhead, 2008), 2–3.

4. In *Dietrich Bonhoeffer: Writings Selected with an Introduction by Robert Coles* (Maryknoll, N.Y.: Orbis Books, 1998), 88.

5. Dietrich Bonhoeffer, *Life Together: The Classic Exploration of Christian Community* (New York: Harper, 1954), 24.

6. In *Dietrich Bonhoeffer: Writings*, 111–12. This New Year's reflection was written by Bonhoeffer in 1943 and circulated in a small way among his friends and coconspirators against Hitler, but it was not published until after his death.

7. Bonhoeffer, *Letters and Papers from Prison*, 191.

8. Ibid., 419.

9. Bonhoeffer, *Life Together*, 82.

10. In *Dietrich Bonhoeffer: Writings*, 126–27.

11. Bonhoeffer, *Life Together*, 87.

12. Bonhoeffer, *Testament to Freedom*, 504–5.

SCRIPTURE INDEX

ST. MARY'S COLLEGE OF
MARY'S CITY

W9-ACV-456

MUSIC AND POETRY

28686

MUSIC AND POETRY

ESSAYS

UPON

SOME ASPECTS AND INTER–RELATIONS
OF THE TWO ARTS

BY

SIDNEY LANIER

GREENWOOD PRESS, PUBLISHERS
NEW YORK

Originally published in 1898
by Charles Scribners Sons

First Greenwood Reprinting, 1969

Library of Congress Catalogue Card Number 69-13966

PRINTED IN UNITED STATES OF AMERICA

Contents

Music and Poetry

I

From Bacon to Beethoven

THEMISTOCLES being "desired at a feast to touch a lute, said 'he could not fiddle, but yet he could make a small town a great city.' If a true survey be taken of councillors and statesmen, there may be found (though rarely) those that can make a small state great and yet cannot fiddle; as, on the other side, there will be found a great many that can fiddle very cunningly but yet . . . their gift lieth the other way, to bring a great and flourishing estate to ruin and decay. And certainly those degenerate arts and shifts whereby many councillors and governors gain both favor with their masters and estimation with the vulgar deserve no better name than fiddling, being things rather pleasing for the time, and graceful to themselves only, than tending to the weal and advancement of the state which they serve."

My Lord Bacon has here used the term "fiddling" — with a propriety wholly unsuspected by himself — to denote the whole *corpus* of musical art. He clearly believes that in discussing the value of musical as opposed to political affairs he has expressed the pithiest possible contempt for the former by the mere nickname he has given them in translating the *mot* of Themistocles.

It was just about the time when the wise fool Francis was writing his essay *Of Kingdoms and Estates* that the world was beginning to think earnestly upon the real significance of tones ; for it was in this period that music — what we moderns call music — was born.   The prodigious changes which the advent of this art has wrought in some of our largest conceptions could not have been foreseen even by the author of the *Instauratio Magna*.

As for Themistocles, one can even sympathize with his saying.   Harmony is little more than three centuries old, and the crude and meagre melodies which constituted the whole repertory of the " lute " players in Themistocles's time could not have been likely to charm away an ambitious man from the larger matters of statemaking.

It is, in truth, only of late years that one can announce, without being liable to a commission of lunacy, an estimate of the comparative value of music and statecraft so different from that of Themistocles and Bacon as that it affirms the approach of a time when the musician will become quite as substantial a figure in every-day life as the politician.   There are those who think it wise to declare to the young men of our age that what Lord Bacon calls " the weal and advancement of the state " may be as fairly forwarded by that citizen who shall be a good fiddler — always provided that our definition of a good fiddler be accepted — as by him that shall be versed in the making of laws and treaties.

The amiable Tyndall relates that when he was once about to perform a new experiment for Mr. Faraday in his laboratory, the latter stopped him, saying, " First tell me what I am to look for."   Following this wise precaution, let the reader look for, and carry mainly with him, in the following discussion, these principal ideas : —

That music is the characteristic art-form of the modern time, as sculpture is of the antique and painting is of the mediæval time ;

That this is necessarily so, in consequence of certain curious relations between unconventional musical tones and the human spirit, — particularly the human spirit at its present stage of growth ;

That this growth indicates a time when the control of masses of men will be more and more relegated to each unit thereof, when the law will be given from within the bosom of each individual, — not from without, — and will rely for its sanctions upon desire instead of repugnance ;

That in intimate connection with this change in man's spirit there proceeds a change in man's relations to the Unknown, whereby (among other things) that relation becomes one of love rather than of terror ;

That music appears to offer conditions most favorable to both these changes, and that it will therefore be the reigning art until they are accomplished, or at least greatly forwarded.

Perhaps the most effectual step a man can take in ridding himself of the clouds which darken most speculations upon these matters is to abandon immediately the idea that music is a species of language, — which is not true, — and to substitute for that the converse idea that language is a species of music. A language is a set of tones segregated from the great mass of musical sounds, and endowed, by agreement, with fixed meanings. The Anglo-Saxons have, for example, practically agreed that if the sound *man* is uttered, the intellects of all Anglo-Saxon hearers will act in a certain direction, and always in that direction for that sound. But in the case of music no such convention has been made. The only method of affixing a definite meaning to a musical composition is to associate with the component tones of it either conventional words, intelligible gestures, or familiar events and places. When a succession of tones is played, the intellect of the hearer may move ; but the movements are always determined by influences wholly extraneous to the purely musical tones, — such as associations with words, with events, or with any matters which place definite intellectual forms (that is, ideas) before the mind.

It is to this idiosyncrasy of music that it owes the honor of having been selected by the modern Age as a characteristic art-form. For music, freed from the stern exactions of the intellect, is also freed from the terrible responsibilities of realism.

It will be instructive to array some details of the working of this principle.

Let the general reader recall to himself three great classifications of human activity. The universe consists (say) of man, and of what is not man. These two being co-existent, it is in the nature of things that certain relations shall straightway spring up between them. Of such relations there are three possible kinds, regarding them from the standpoint of man. These kinds are the intellectual, the emotional, and the physical. Whenever a man knows a thing, the intellectual relation is set up. When he loves or desires a thing, the emotional relation is set up. When he touches or sees a thing, the physical relation is set up.

Now, whatever may be the class of relations with which music deals, it is *not* the first class above named, —the intellectual. This has sometimes been doubted. But the doubt is due mainly to a certain confusion of thought which has arisen from the circumstance that the most common and familiar musical instrument happens to be at the same time what may be called an intellectual instrument, —*i.e.*, the organ of speech. With the great majority of the human race the musical tones which are most frequently heard are those of the human voice. But these tones — which are as wholly devoid of intellectual signification in themselves as if they were enounced from a violin or flute — are usually produced along with certain vowel and consonantal combinations which go to make up words, and which consequently have conventional meanings. In this way significations belonging exclusively to the *words* of a song are often transferred by the hearer to the *tones* of the melody. In reality they are absolutely distinct. Nothing is easier than to demonstrate this. Let any vocalist, for example, execute the following passage :

La la la la la la la la la la la la la.

The question may be safely put to any auditor, when the vocalist has finished, what does this mean? As long as the vague syllable *la* is used as the vehicle of the tones, no human being can truthfully say that the passage (it is the opening phrase of the Scherzo in a lovely Symphony of Gade's) brings any report whatever to his intellect.   If, instead of the meaningless particle *la*, words should be employed, the case would not be changed as to the *tones* of the musical phrase.   The hearers might associate the import of each word with the tone upon which it happened to fall, but the tone would not be thereby impressed with the meaning of that word.   It might occur a moment after, conjoined with any number of different words.   The mixture of meaning and tone is merely mechanical, not chemical.

In other words, the intellectual relations are not affected by pure tones, — not by the tones of the human voice any more than the tones of a violin.   Whenever intellectual relations are determined by tones, it is not in virtue of their character as tones, but because of certain conventional agreements whereby it has been arranged that upon the hearing of these tones, as upon the hearing of so many signals, the intellects of the auditors will all move in certain directions.   It may strengthen the conception of this principle to recall here that other signals than tones might have been agreed upon for this purpose.   Gestures, indeed, are used with quite as much effect as tone-language in many dramatic situations, and constitute the entire speech of many persons.   The selection of tones, rather than of other sorts of signals, to convey ideas has not been made because the tones had intrinsic significations, but upon purely *à posteriori* and economic considerations, the main one being that there is no means of producing so great a variety of signals with so little expenditure of muscular force comparable to that of the human voice.

This principle cannot be justly embarrassed with any appearance of conflict between it and the doctrine of the origin of language in imitative sounds.   There is no incompatibility whatever. The imitative sound will always owe its character of word-progenitor not to any intrinsic meaning in the sound itself, but to a purely extrinsic association by which the intellect has learned to connect it with some phenomenon having a definite meaning. To a person acquainted with the phenomenon of thunder, for example, the sound of the word "thunder" might suggest the phenomenon; but this suggestion is the result of circumstances utterly apart from any intellectual influence communicable by the mere tones of the vocable itself.

Once for all, — for it is a principle of such fundamental importance as to warrant its repetition in many forms, — musical tones have in themselves no meaning appreciable by the human intellect.

Some steaming-hot quarrels among modern musicians clear away immediately before the steady application of this doctrine. For example, there are many conscientious and beautiful-souled artists who deny themselves all the glory and delight to be found in the so-called "programme-music." Their motives are unquestionably those of rigorous conscientiousness. Programme-music has been held up to them as a sort of unclean thing. It is indeed no wonder at all that the steady-going classicists should have been startled and alarmed by the tremendous explosion of Berlioz in their midst. At this distance of time, the quiet thinker who has not been brought up in the traditions of any school can easily see that in the state of music at that period a clap of good rousing thunder was exactly the best thing which could happen, and for this purpose Berlioz was sent. Unfortunately, the shock of this vivid genius has been transmitted from teacher to pupil in many instances, and there are still large numbers who are unable to examine the question of programme-music in any such tranquil spirit as to warrant the hope of a philosophic conclusion. When it *is* examined in this spirit, it does not seem to present great difficulties.

"Programme-music," at first a sarcastic term, has now come to be almost technical, as denoting a musical composition in which the otherwise vague effects of the tones have been sought to be specialized and intellectualized by the employment of conventional words. These words are conjoined with the tones in various ways. Sometimes, as in Liszt's so-called tone-poem of Immortality, the words occur in the form of an extract from a poem which is prefixed to the musical score. In this case the hearer is merely supposed to have read the words; and the effect of the whole proceeding is little more than an invitation that the hearer will please send his intellect, during the playing of the piece, in the direction marked out by the poetic preface. But again the attempt may be more completely to unite the words and tones: as in the "Lelio" of Berlioz or in the musical rendition of "Paradise and the Peri" by Sterndale Bennett, where the words are recited either along with, or between detached passages of, the instrumental music. Now, why should not this be done? It can be shown that programme-music is the very earliest, most familiar, and most spontaneous form of musical composition. For what is any song but programme-music developed to its furthest extent? A song is, as has been shown on an earlier page, a double performance: a certain instrument — the human voice — produces a number of tones, none of which have any intellectual value in themselves; but, simultaneously

with the production of the tones, words are uttered,
each in a physical association with a tone, so as to produce upon the hearer at once the effects of conventional
and of unconventional sounds.   The unconventional
sounds might be made alone by the human voice : in
this event the song would simply be deprived of the
intellectual elements imparted by the words.   Suppose,
now, that the singer shall play the air on a violin, and
pronounce the words in conjunction with their appropriate tones as he goes along.   What difference can be
detected between playing the words and singing the
words?   It is but a change of instruments : instead of
the voice, which is a reed-instrument, he now employs
the violin, a stringed instrument.   Why is not the latter
as legitimate as the former?

It is, as I have before intimated, only from a failure
to perceive the fact that the tones of the human voice
are in themselves as meaningless, intellectually, as the
tones of all other reed-instruments, that any hesitation
in answering this question could arise.   Certainly if
programme-music is absurd, all songs are nonsense.
The principle of being of every song is that intellectual
impressions can be advantageously combined with musical impressions, in addressing the spirit of man.   It is
precisely this principle that underlies programme-music.
Yet one of the most genuine music-lovers I have ever
met always comes away from Beethoven's Pastoral Symphony with a melancholy sense of sin.   He thinks he
ought not to have enjoyed it so much ; he feels that he
has done wrong in deriving pleasure from an inartistic attempt even of the great king of tones.   "It is
programme-music," he says.   This same person will
listen with the most intense delight to Beethoven's cycle

of songs, "To My Love Far Away," for example ; and
yet the latter is programme-music carried to such a
development that every single tone is supposed to bear
with it a special message to the intellect by virtue of its
amalgamation with the conventional signal of a word.
In the Pastoral Symphony the suggestions of ideas are
only made in the most evanescent way.   There is not
the least attempt at puerile imitations.   The Nightingale
is merely suggested, for example, since no mortal ear
could ever regard as an imitation the orchestral voice
which gives this particular hint.   Beethoven wishes to
suggest a definite intellectual image to his hearer along
with a certain set of tones : instead of employing a conventional word to accomplish his purpose, he chooses to
employ an imitative tone.   Nothing could be more natural, nothing more legitimate.   Why not hint a storm
with stormy tones, as well as describe a storm in stormy
words?   Why write one way for the reed in the clari-
net, another way for the reed in the throat?

In other words, if the composer choose to invite our
intellect to get up and ride, along with our emotion,
why should not we accept?   There is but one question,
— can he carry double?

Beethoven could.   So, indeed, could Berlioz.   What
good reason why we should not mount and off?

No man can say.   In truth, one would wonder at the
blindness of artists who persistently keep themselves in
leading-strings for the purpose of avoiding purely fanciful dangers, if one did not remember how music is yet
so young an art that we have not learned to make it, far
less to understand it.

What has now been said upon the matter of programme-music is not at all by way of digression.   It

has illustrated in the best possible manner the main thought so far insisted on, — to wit, how absolutely non-intellectual is the effect of pure tone, insomuch that if the composer wish to carry anything like a cognition along with music he must do so either by employing words or associations such as those suggested by imitative sounds which the mind has learned to connect with given phenomena.

A point is now reached from which an important step may be taken in the argument. This peculiarity of music completely separates it from all other arts, and places it on a plane alone. One of the results of this unique position has been already referred to. On an earlier page I spoke of the non-liability of music to the onerous exactions of realism. A somewhat more detailed statement of this idea will carry us far on our way towards an understanding of the satisfaction which music brings to our modern needs in this connection.[1]

[1] It is made necessary by some former experiences to add here that no one must imagine the ensuing comparative remarks as between music and painting (or sculpture) to be made in any spirit of silly glorification of the former, or of equally silly depreciation of the latter. There is no question of merit or demerit. The argument is merely that music is the modern art because it suits the modern need, and the attempt is to show how. At another age painting might suit the need better, in which event painting would be the art of the time; but the ensuing remarks would still hold good.

If any further profession be necessary, one joyfully embraces an occasion to declare that the rise of landscape-painting seems surely one of the most notable events in the history of art; that the Americans are, or are at least to be, the greatest in this branch, and that some of them appear to me now among the very sweetest preachers of beauty in all time. The Frenchmen certainly show more technic thus far, but never such seizure of Nature, such grasp of her unspeakable loveliness and nearness to man.

Let us compare it with painting from the point of view of realistic necessities.

A painting is an imitation, upon a flat surface, of things which are not flat; it is an imitation, upon a surface lying wholly in one plane, of things whose planes lie at all manner of angles with each other; it is an imitation of three dimensions by two, and of horizontal distance upon vertical distance. These imitations — of course " imitations " is not a precise word here — can be accomplished because human vision is not unerringly keen.

It is through the limitations of the eye that painting is possible. Perhaps this could not have been properly understood before Bishop Berkeley unfolded the true nature of vision and the dependence of the reports brought in by the sense of sight upon many other matters which are the result of judgments founded on experience. It may fairly be said to have been established by that acute speculator that we do not *see* either distance or magnitude, — that is, that these two particulars are not immediate deliverances of the sense of sight, but are the results of a comparison which the mind draws between present and certain remembered appearances gathered by touch, hearing, and other senses. This comparison is made rapidly, and the judgments founded on it are practically instantaneous; but the fact remains that distance and magnitude are mainly not given by the eye, but deduced by reason as inferences from several particulars which have been communicated by other senses in addition to sight.

It is, then, this defective organ which is practised upon (of course not in the bad sense) by the art of painting. Every one, therefore, upon approaching a painting, goes through a preliminary series of allowances and of (in a certain sense) forgivenesses. These allowances are made so habitually that they frequently become unnoticed, and many will be surprised at remembering that they are made at all. But something like this typic discussion always occurs in practice when one is before a painting for the first time. " Here," says the eye, "is an imitation of a mountain."

" Absurd," replies the judgment, which has often before tested the reports of the eye by reports of the touch, the ear, and other senses, and has learned to correct them accordingly; " the mountain is a mile high, while the canvas is not three feet. But let it pass."

" Here," continues the eye, "is a representation of trees with round trunks, standing at various distances from each other, along a wide landscape."

" Impossible, save by some trick of suggestion," replies the judgment; " for the canvas is flat; and if you look closely you will see that the trees are merely placed higher or lower than each other, the vertical being artfully made to do duty for the horizontal; and the horizontal itself is a mere make-believe; do you not see it is just as near you in reality as the foreground? But let it pass."

Nor is this all. The eye, though defective in the particulars mentioned, is equally effective in others, and in its turn it becomes the critic of the painting. For example: *Is* this really like a mountain? queries the eye, and straightway falls to examining the imitation and comparing it with realities. Is this genuine oak-foliage? Would these shadows fall in this manner, and is their value truly estimated and depicted? A thousand such preliminary questions the eye asks. If they are not satisfactorily answered by the painting, it fails at the very start, and there is no use in going further to examine what æsthetic appeal it may make.   Through such a vestibule, resisting the chill of these cold intellectual considerations of *vraisemblance,* and sobered by all these allowances and forgivenesses, must every soul pass on to the ultimate purpose and meaning of a picture.

Now, it is easy to conceive a stage of growth of the human spirit when the necessity of making these realistic comparisons would be no hindrance at all, but a refreshment and an advantage.   In the mediæval time, for example, when the subtle disquisitions of the schoolmen abandoned the real entirely and busied themselves with pure figments of human fancy, — when bigotry was piled upon bigotry, and fanaticism upon fanaticism, until all trace of the actual earth and of actual human nature was obscured, — in such a time, men's minds would experience a sense of relief and of security in contemplating works of art composed of firm and definite forms whose accuracy could be brought to satisfactory tests of actual measurement.   Accordingly, we find the artist of the mediæval time to be a painter, seeking refuge from the instabilities and vaguenesses of the prevalent thought of the time in the sharply-outlined figures which he could fix upon his canvas.

These considerations apply with still greater force to the antique time, with its peculiar art of sculpture.   In an age when men knew so little of the actual physical world that the main materials and subjects of thought were mere fancies and juggles of ingenious speculators, it must have been a real rest for the mind to fix itself upon the solid and enduring images of undeceptive stone which the artists furnished forth from their wonderful brains and chisels. The need of such rest, though not, of course, consciously recognized by the sculptors, was really the reason of their being. In such matters Nature takes care of her own. She knows the peculiar hunger of an age, and fashions the appropriate satisfactions to it.

Here, now, we are arrived at the crisis of the argument. What has been said of the relations of sculpture and painting to the times in which they flourished is but the special application of a general underlying principle which may be thus stated : The Art of any age will be complementary to the Thought of that age.

In the light of this principle, let us examine the attitude of music towards the present time. *A priori*, one will expect to find that in an age of physical science, when the intellect of man imperiously demands the exact truth of all actual things and is possessed with a holy mania for reality, the characteristic Art will be one affording an outlet from the rigorous fixedness of the actual and of the known into the freer regions of the possible and of the unknown. This reasoning becomes verified as soon as we collate the facts. With sufficient accuracy in view of the size of the terms, it may be said that the rise of modern music has been simultaneous with that of modern physical science. And what more natural? I have endeavored to show that music is of all arts that which has least to do with realism, that which departs most widely from the rigid definitions and firm outlines which the intellect (I use this term always in its strict sense as referring to the cognitive or thinking activity of man, in contradistinction to the emotional or conative activity) demands. In music there is no preliminary allowance to be made by the ear, as was alleged to be made by the eye in painting; there is no forgiveness, in consideration of the impossible; there is no question of *vraisemblance*, no chill of discussion, at the outset. Even in the case of programme-music, where a suggestion is made to the intellect by imitation of familiar sounds, the imitation is, as already shown, really no imitation, does not pretend to be or set up for a *vraisemblant* representation, but is a mere hint, with purposes wholly ulterior to and beyond the small puerility which imitation would be if sought as an end in itself. Moreover, in all cases of programme-music, even if the attempt at carrying along the intellect fails, the music as an emotional satisfaction remains. If bad as a programme, it is still good as music.

Music, then, being free from the weight and burden of realism, — its whole *modus* being different from that of imitative and plastic art, — its peculiar activity being in the same direction with that of those emotions by which man relates himself (as I hope to show further on) to the infinite, — what more natural than that the spirit of man should call upon it for relief from the pressure and grind of Fact, should cry to it, with earnest pathos, " Come, lead me away out of this labyrinth of the real, the definite, the known, into, or at least towards, the region of the ideal, the infinite, the unknown: knowledge is good, I will continue to thirst and to toil for it, but, alas! I am blind even with the blaze of the sun; take me where there is starlight and darkness, where my eyes shall rest from the duties of verification and my soul shall repose from the labor of knowing."

But this is only a rudimentary statement of the agency of music in modern civilization, intended to bring prominently forward its attitude towards science. The musician is the complement of the scientist. The latter will superintend our knowing; the former will superintend our loving.

I use this last term advisedly, intending by it to advance a step in the investigation of the nature of music. For the mission of music is not merely to be a quietus and lullaby to the soul of a time that is restless with science. This it does, but does as an incident of far higher work.

On an earlier page, the reader's attention was recalled to three classes of activities by which a man relates himself to that part of the universe which is not himself, — namely, the cognitive (or "intellectual," as I have used the term here, not to be too technical for the general reader), the emotional, and the physical. Now, man strives always to place himself in relation not only with those definite forms which go to make up the finite world about him, but also with that indefinite Something up to which every process of reasoning, every outgo of emotion, every physical activity, inevitably leads him, — God, the Infinite, the Unknown. The desire of man is that he may relate himself with the Infinite both in the cognitive and in the emotional way. Sir William Hamilton showed clearly how impossible was any full relation of the former sort, in showing that cognition itself was a conditioning (*i. e.*, a defining, a placing of boundaries appreciable by the intellect), and that therefore the knowing of the Infinite was the conditioning of the Unconditioned, — in short, impossible. This seemed to preclude the possibility of any relation from man to God of the cognitive sort; but Mr. Herbert Spencer has relieved the blankness of this situation by asserting the possibility of a partial relation still. We cannot think God, it is true; but we can think *towards* Him. This in point of fact is what men continually do. The definition in the catechism, " God is a spirit, infinite, eternal, and unchangeable in His being, wisdom," etc., is an effort of man to relate himself to God in the cognitive, or intellectual, way: it is a thinking towards God.

Now, there is a constant endeavor of man, but one to which less attention has been paid by philosophers, to relate himself with the Infinite not only in the cognitive way just described, but also in the emotional way. Just as persistently as our thought seeks the Infinite, does our emotion seek the Infinite. We not only wish to think it, we wish to love it; and as our love is not subject to the disabilities of our thought, the latter of these two wishes would seem to be capable of a more complete fulfilment than the former. It has been shown that we can only think *towards* the Infinite; it may be that our love can reach nearer its Object.

As a philosophic truth, music does carry our emotion towards the Infinite. No man will doubt this who reflects for a moment on the rise of music in the Church. The progress of this remarkable phenomenon will have probably come, in some way, under the notice of the youngest person who will read this paper.

I remember when the most flourishing church of our town regarded with intense horror a proposition to buy an organ, considering it an insidious project of the devil to undermine religion. The same church has now the largest organ in the city, with a paid organist and choir. Scarcely any person who has lived in the smaller towns of the United States but will recall similar instances. At present the organ, the song, are in all the growing churches. What would be Mr. Moody without Mr. Sankey, or Mr. Whittle without Mr. Bliss?

And not only does music win its way into the Church, but it gradually takes on more and more importance in the service of worship. How many are there in these days to whom the finest preaching comes from the organ-loft! Greater and greater every year grow the multitudes of those who declare that no sermons, no words, no forms of any sort, avail to carry them on the way towards the desired sacred goal as do the tones of Palestrina, of Bach, of Beethoven, when these are given forth by any organist of even moderate accomplishment. Everywhere one finds increasing the number of fervent souls who fare easily by this road to the Lord. From the negro swaying to and fro with the weird rhythms of "Swing Low, Sweet Chariot," from the Georgia Cracker yelling the "Old Ship of Zion" to the heavens through the logs of the piney-woods church, to the intense devotee rapt away into the Infinite upon a Mass of Palestrina, there comes but one testimony to the substantial efficacy of music in this matter of helping the emotion of man across the immensity of the known into the boundaries of the Unknown. Nay, there are those who go further than this: there are those who declare that music is to be the Church of the future, wherein all creeds will unite like the tones in a chord.

Now, it cannot be that music has taken this place in the deepest and holiest matters of man's life through mere fortuitous arrangement. It must be that there exists some sort of relation between pure tones and the spirit of man by virtue of which the latter is stimulated and forced onward towards the great End of all love and aspiration. What may be the nature of this relation, —

why it is that certain vibrations sent forward by the tym-
panum along the bones and fluids of the inner ear should
at length arrive at the spirit of man endowed with such
a prodigious and heavenly energy, — at what point of
the course they acquire this capacity of angels, being, up
to that point, mere particles trembling hither and thither,
— these are, in the present state of our knowledge, mysteries which no man can unravel.

It is through this relation of music to man that it
becomes, as I said in the principles affirmed at the
outset, a moral agent.   Let us not pester ourselves with
remembering how such and such a musician was a pro-
fligate, a beast, a trifler, and so on.   This is only submitting ourselves to what our wise Emerson calls the
tyranny of particulars.   The clear judgment in the
matter is to be formed by looking at the consummate
masters of the art.

Palestrina, Bach, Beethoven — what had these gentlemen to do with sheriffs and police, with penalties and
legal sanctions?   They were law-abiding citizens; but
their adherence to the law was the outcome of an inner
desire after the beauty of Order, not from fear of the
law's punitive power.

In short, they were artists, and they loved goodness
because goodness is beautiful.   Badness was not a temptation, because it is ugly, and the true artist recoils energetically from ugliness.

I know very well how many names there are in art
which are associated with profligacy.   But I think it
clearly demonstrable that in all these artists there was a
failure in the artistic sense precisely to the extent of the
failure in apprehending those enormous laws of nature
whose practical execution by the individual we call

morality. You can always see where the half-way good man was but the half-way artist.

One hears all about the world nowadays that art is wholly un-moral, that art is for art's sake, that art has nothing to do with good or bad in behavior. These are the cries of clever men whose cleverness can imitate genius so aptly as to persuade many that they have genius, and whose smartness can preach so incisively about art that many believe them to be artists. But such catch-words will never deceive the genius, the true artist. The true artist will never remain a bad man; he will always wonder at a wicked artist. The simplicity of this wonder renders it wholly impregnable. The argument of it is merely this: the artist loves beauty supremely; because the good is beautiful, he will clamber continuously towards it, through all possible sloughs, over all possible obstacles, in spite of all possible falls.

This is the artist's creed. Now, just as music increases in hearty acceptance among men, so will this true artistic sense of the loveliness of morality spread, so will the attractiveness of all that is pure and lovely grow in power, and so will the race progress towards that time described in the beginning of this essay as one in which the law would cease to rely upon terror for its sanction, but depend wholly upon love and desire.

If any ask whether there are signs of such a beneficial spreading of music among the general classes of men, one has but to reply, Look around. In the first place, there is the wonderful growth of music in the churches, which has already been spoken of. But that is only half the phenomenon. Turn from the churches into the homes of the United States. It is often asserted that ours is a materialistic age, and that romance is dead.

But this is marvellously untrue, and it may be counter-asserted with perfect confidence that there was never an age of the world when art was enthroned by so many hearthstones and intimate in so many common houses as now. For the pianos are almost everywhere. Where there are not pianos, there are cabinet-organs; and where not these, the guitars; not to speak of the stray violins, the flutes, the horns, the clarinets, which lie about in houses here and there and are brought out on the nights when the sister is home from boarding-school or when the village orchestra meets. These pianos have done a great work for music. No one who knows the orchestra well can admit the piano for itself as a final good, because it is an instrument of fixed tones, and therefore imperfect; but when one thinks of the incalculable service which the piano has rendered in diffusing conceptions of harmony (which is the distinguishing characteristic of modern music) among the masses, one must regard it with reverent affection.

Never was any art so completely a household art as is the music of to-day; and the piano has made this possible.

As the American is, with all his shortcomings of other sorts, at any rate most completely the man of to-day, so it is directly in the line of this argument to say that one finds more "talent for music" among the Americans, especially among American women, than among any other people. The musical sense is very widely diffused among us, and the capacity for musical execution is strikingly frequent.

When Americans shall have learned the supreme value and glory of the orchestra, — when we shall have advanced beyond the piano, which is, as matters now exist, a quite necessary stage in musical growth, — when our musical young women shall have found that, if their hands are too small for the piano, or if they have no voices, they can study the flute, the violin, the oboe, the bassoon, the viola, the violoncello, the horn, the corno Inglese, — in short, every orchestral instrument, — and that they are quite as capable as men — in some cases much better fitted by nature than any man — to play all these, then I look to see America the home of the orchestra, and to hear everywhere the profound messages of Beethoven and Bach to men.

Meantime, what shall we say of an art which thus is becoming so much the daily companion of man as to sit by every fireside and in every church, — nay, which, I might have added, thrusts itself into the crowded streets in a thousand shapes, wherever the newsboy whistles, the running clerk hums the bass he is to sing in the chorus, the hand-organ drones, the street-band blares, which presides at weddings, at feasts, at great funerals, which marches at the head of battle, and opens the triumphant ceremonials of peace?

As for Beethoven, it is only of late that his happy students have begun to conceive the true height and magnitude of his nature. The educational value of his works upon the understanding soul which has yielded itself to the rapture of their teaching is unspeakable, and is of a sort which almost compels a man to shed tears of gratitude at every mention of this master's name. For in these works are many qualities which one could not expect to find cohering in any one human spirit. Taking Beethoven's sonatas (which, by the way, no one will ever properly appreciate until he regards them really as symphonies, and mentally distributes the parts among flutes, reeds, horns, and strings as he goes through them), his songs, his symphonies, together, I know not where one will go to find in any human products such largeness, such simplicity, such robust manliness, such womanly tenderness, such variety of invention, such parsimony of means with such splendor of effects, such royal grandeur without pretence, such pomp with such modesty, such unfailing moderation and exquisite right feeling in art, such prodigious transformations and re-transformations of the same melody, — as if the blue sky should alternately shrink into a blue violet and then expand into a sky again, — such love-making to the infinite and the finite, such range of susceptibility, such many-sidedness in offering some gift to every nature and every need, such comprehension of the whole of human life.

There is but one name to which one can refer in speaking of Beethoven : it is Shakspere.

For as Shakspere is, so far, our king of conventional tones, so is Beethoven our king of unconventional tones. And as music takes up the thread which language drops, so it is where Shakspere ends that Beethoven begins.

II

The Orchestra of To-day

NOT long ago, a flute was found near Poictiers, in France, among surroundings which pointed to the age of pre-historic man as the epoch of its construction. It lay among the implements of the stone age, and was merely a piece of stag's-horn pierced with three holes, which gave it a capacity of four tones, without counting possible harmonics. The utmost discoursing of this rude instrument must have been but trifling compared with the weighty message of its silence, as it lay there among its uncouth axes and knives; for it told the strange story of instrumental melody backward to a point beyond history, and hinted that man commenced to hunger for music about the same time as for bread. But along with this antiquity of orchestral constituents, the thoughtful musician finds the seemingly incongruous fact that what we call the orchestra is the product of only the last two centuries. How is it that melody is so old, and harmony so young?

The answer to this question involves considerations extending to the very deepest springs of modern life, and leads the investigator into directions little suspected at the outset. It would require far too much space to be attempted here; but before proceeding to set forth — as the main body of this paper is intended to do — a plain and untechnical account, for non-musical readers.

of the nature of orchestral instruments and the work of their players, I wish at least to state the problem clearly and to call the reader's attention to some circumstances which look toward its solution; hoping thus to present a nucleus about which the scattered items of fact to be subsequently conveyed may group themselves into portable form.

Consider, for example, how persistently the human imagination, whenever it turned at all in the direction of music, for long ages addressed itself to gigantic speculations upon the power of it, rather than to the more satisfactory business of expressing itself immediately in terms of the musical art. Instead of making music, it made a great ado about music. Hence we have (practically) no remains of ancient music; but what a lot of fablings, often beautiful and noble, upon it! Compare for a moment a whole mythology of these with the fruits which the modern mind brings out of the same realm : the results are striking enough. From the modern musical imagination we get, not fables about melody, but melodies; not unearthly speculations upon music, but actual unearthly harmonies; not a god playing a flute, but the orchestra.

Why has this immense development of music occurred in our particular modern age, rather than in some other?

It is already commonplace to say that what we call the modern epoch is contra-distinguished from all others by the two characteristic signs of the rise of music and the rise of science. This contemporaneity of development cannot be a merely accidental coincidence. That same scientific spirit of which the modern time has witnessed such an influx that one may not irreverently term it Pentecostal, is the stimulus which, acting in one direction, has produced the body of modern music, in another direction the body of modern science. For, if the scientific spirit be but a passionate longing to put oneself in relation with the substance of things — with the truth as it actually exists outside of oneself, — then it is easily conceivable that such a longing might influence very powerfully both of those two great classes of man's spiritual activities which we are accustomed to call, the one intellectual, the other emotional; and that, driven by such a longing, intellectual activity might result in science, emotional, in music.

We all know how invariably, from of old, every attempt to draw near to the substance of things has ended in quickly bringing the investigator to the same awful term, to wit — God, though the investigator has often named it far otherwise. And — if such be the real outcome of science — can any one attend, on the other hand, to an intelligent rendition of the Fifth Symphony without finding beneath all its surface-ideas this same powerful current of Desire which sets the soul insensibly closer toward the Unknown by methods which are inarticulate and vague, as those of science are articulate and precise?

Moreover, when looked at from the standpoint of any large classification of eras, we find the musicians and the scientists about shoulder to shoulder in time; we find Copernicus, Galileo, Newton, Descartes, De Maillet, Haller, Hunter, Harvey, Swedenborg, Vesalius, Linnæus, Lamarck, Cuvier, Buffon, Franklin, Hutton, Lyell, Audubon, Faraday, Helmholtz, Agassiz, Le Conte, Huxley, Tyndall, Darwin, to be substantially contemporaries of Palestrina, Purcell, the Scarlattis, Handel, Bach, Gluck, Haydn, Mozart, Beethoven, Cherubini, Schubert,

Von Weber, Mendelssohn, Spontini, Spohr, Rossini, Berlioz, Schumann, Chopin, Glinka, Gade, Kuhlau, Boieldieu, Rubinstein, Raff, Gounod, Hamerik, Wagner.

In truth — and with this suggestion one can now come to the more immediate purpose of this writing — perhaps it will finally come to be seen that if we shred away from music and science all that manifold husk of temporary and non-intrinsic matters which envelops the nut of every important movement, we will find both presenting themselves as substantially the forms in which the devoutness of our age has expressed itself — that devoutness without which no age *is*, and which comes down from one to another in imperishable yet often scarcely recognizable shapes; insomuch that our great men are as it were but more sensible re-appearances of monks — our musicians having retired for worship into music, as into a forest, and our scientific men sending out the voice of uncontrollable devotion from a theory, as from a Thebaid cave.

The instruments of which a full orchestra is composed are of three general classes : " the wind," "the strings," and the " instruments of percussion."

To begin some account of the first-named class : perhaps nothing is more perplexing to one unfamiliar with orchestras than the goings-on and general appearance of the wind-side of it; the shapes of the instruments seem grotesque, and the arrangement of the keys on a Bœhm flute (for example) or a bassoon seems utterly lawless and bewildering. But perhaps by reducing all wind-instruments to one common type and then clearly setting forth the precise manner in which air, when set in musical vibration by the human breath or otherwise, is definitely controlled to this or that pitch, much of the embarrassment of this apparent complexity can be avoided.

Let this common type, then, be a straight tube of wood, closed at one end, say two feet in length and an inch in diameter, pierced with a hole at the distance of an inch from the closed end, after the manner of a flute embouchure. Let the lips now be applied to this embouchure, and a stream of air constantly increasing in force be sent across it. The first tone heard will be the lowest tone of which the tube is capable ; from a tube of the dimensions named, this lowest tone will not be a great way from the middle C of the pianoforte, and we will here assume it to be exactly that C. Now, most persons who have not reasoned upon the subject are found to expect that as the breath increases in force a series of tones corresponding to the ascending scale from C will be produced. But this is far from being the case ; on the contrary, the tone first produced will grow louder and louder, until suddenly its octave will sound, and no management of the breath can by any possibility bring out an intermediate tone between this normal C and its octave. If the force of the breath be still increased, presently the g above this octave will be heard ; if still increased, the c above this g; still increased, the e above this last c ; and so on, in a series which I will not here further detail. This process is typical for all tubes, of whatever size or material, and however the air may be agitated in them. Its explanation forms one of the most striking triumphs of modern science, but is too long to be given here.

It appears, then, that our tube gives us already five tones, without any appliances whatever except the simple expedient of increasing the force of the breath. Suppose, now, that we shorten it by cutting off about an inch ; on applying the breath gently at the embouchure, the first tone heard will now be D (the next tone in the scale to the C first mentioned) ; and if we continue to increase the force of the breath, as at first, a series of tones will be heard bearing the same relation to D as the first series bore to C, that is, the *d* octave of D, then the *a* above this *d*, then the *d* above this *a*, then the *f* sharp above this *d*, and so on. If we should again shorten the tube by about an inch, then the first tone heard will be E, or the second tone in the scale above the first C of the long tube ; and, again forcing the breath, another series exactly similar to the last will be produced. It would thus seem that in order to produce those interme-diate tones of the scale needed to fill up the gap between the first C and the octave of it, we are under the neces-sity of shortening the tube inch by inch. And so we are, but there is a method of shortening the tube which does not involve cutting it off. Piercing it with a hole of from an eighth to a quarter of an inch in diameter is found to have the same effect as if the tube were cut off at the point where the hole is pierced, and this discovery affords an easy method of producing on one tube all the notes belonging to the gap between the two extremes of the first octave ; for, instead of shortening the tube by cutting it off, we successively shorten it by piercing holes at the points where it ought to be shortened. If we cover all these holes with the fingers, the tube is practi-cally two feet long, and will give, on being blown, the C first mentioned ; if we then open the hole farthest from the embouchure by lifting up the finger which covers it, the tube becomes practically shortened by an inch, and gives us the next tone in the scale, D, which we can then vary with all the hitherto enumerated changes which it undergoes by merely increasing the force of the breath. If we lift up the next finger, we again practically shorten the tube by an inch and get the next tone of the scale, E, together with its upper tones, or harmonics. It will be observed that in obtaining these first seven tones from the normal C to its octave, we have really obtained an instrument capable of thirty-five tones, for each of the first seven represents not only itself but the four harmonics producible by merely forcing the breath upon it without changing the position of the fingers. In practice, some of the higher tones of these harmonic series are found not to be available — for reasons too abstruse to be mentioned here; but the lower ones are, and it is upon a combination of the principle which they involve with the principle of shortening the tube to make the first octave, that all wind instruments are constructed. In the case of the trombone, one sees the performer actually shortening and lengthening the normal tube, which is in two parts, one sliding into and out of the other like a telescope-joint. In the other brass instruments the long normal tube is bent into several crooks which can be thrown into one tube or successively shut off to diminish the aggregate length, by means of the pistons or valves which the performer works with his finger.

By remembering, therefore, these three things: that the shortening of a tube heightens the pitch of its tone; that a tube may be shortened either by holes in the side (as in the flutes, the oboes, the clarionets, the bassoons), or by shutting off some of its crooks (as in the horns, the trumpets, and the like), or by directly contracting its

length (as in the trombones) ; and that each of the
tones of the lowest (or first) octave produces from two
to five other tones by simply blowing it more strongly,
the reader will understand the principle, varying only
in details, which underlies the whole wind-side of the
orchestra.

The two largest classifications of the wind-instruments
are called among players " the wooden wind " and " the
brass." The first of these is further subdivided into the
reeds and the flutes. And first of the reeds, about which
I find the haziest ideas prevailing, even among the oldest frequenters of orchestral performances.

The reed-instruments in common use are the oboes
(or hautboys), the bassoons, and the clarionets.

The oboe is an instrument somewhat like the familiar
clarionet in appearance, but of a slenderer make, and
differing entirely at the mouth-piece. This is composed
of two delicate pieces of reed, shaven quite thin, in
shape much like the blade of an oar, and bound face to
face. These pieces are attached to a quill which is inserted in the small end of the oboe tube. The mouth-
pieces are usually kept separate from the tube ; when
the performer is about to play, he opens a small box in
which they are protected from exposure, and proceeds
to select one by sucking each through the quill. That
one which first responds with a squeak is chosen ; the
quill is inserted in the tube, and the mouth-piece is
placed between the lips, the under-lip being slightly
drawn in. Much practice is required to become accustomed to the tickling of the lips produced by the fluttering of the thin reeds as the breath is forced over them.
The tone of the oboe, though intolerably nasal and harsh
when produced by an unskilful player, becomes exqui-

sitely liquid and engaging if the performer be skillful. It is peculiarly simple, child-like and honest in quality, and orchestral composers delight to use it for expressing ideas of spring-time, of green leaves, of sweet rural life, of all those guileless associations connected with the antique oaten pipe. Those who have been so fortunate as to hear the rendition of Berlioz's "Dream of an Artist" will remember the exquisite passages in which the oboes represent the pipings and replyings of shepherds to each other from neighboring hills. In Schultz's concert-piece called "*Im Freien*" ("In the Open Air"), the two oboes lead off in a lovely candid opening which seems to infuse one's soul with the very spirit of young, green leaves, and of liberal spring airs.

The bassoon is a long wooden instrument held vertically in front of the player and running down along his right side. From the wooden portion projects a small silver tube, bent somewhat like the spout of a kettle, into which a mouth-piece similar to that of the oboe is inserted. Both the bassoon and the oboe are called double-reed instruments, in distinction from the clarionet, which has a mouth-piece constructed of a single reed. The bassoon has at least two very distinct qualities of tone ; in the upper and lower extremes of its register it is weird and ghostly, but in the middle portion warm and noble. For the production of ghostly effects, for calling up those vague apprehensions of the night, when churchyards yawn, and the like, it is much used by composers. In a singular passage of the "Artist's Dream," hereinbefore mentioned, it is made the interpreter of a colossal, grotesque, and inconsolably bitter sorrow. The beauty of its middle register seems not to have been much employed ; but no one can listen to the ravishing bassoon-solo in the slow movement of the concerto for piano and orchestra by Chopin which Madame Schiller and Thomas have made known to northern audiences, without perceiving in this portion of the bassoon's compass a very remarkable combination of gravity and sensuous richness — a combination much like that suggested when we think of a very stately young Spanish lady, high in blood and in color, and grandly costumed. This instrument usually appears on the orchestral score as *fagotto*, Italian for fagot, so called from the resemblance of its lower portion to such a fagot as might result from binding two stout pieces of wood together with a metal band.

The clarionet is, as was above remarked, a single-reed instrument. This single reed, instead of playing against another reed like itself, as in the oboe and bassoon, is simply bound alongside of the bevelled plug which closes the small end of the clarionet-tube, leaving a narrow slit between the reed and the plug. The player usually has three clarionets standing at his side : two of these are constructed of a different pitch from the other non-transposing instruments of the orchestra, so that the same written note when played by them gives a wholly different sound. The reasons for, and details of, this arrangement would lead this paper beyond its scope ; and it will suffice to add that these three clarionets are known as the C clarionet, the A clarionet, and the B-flat clarionet, being so called from the tones of the other instruments with which the C of each variety coincides. Thus, if you sound a written C on the A clarionet, the resulting tone is the same as the written A of the other instruments ; if you sound a written C on the B-flat clarionet, the resulting tone is the same as if the other instruments had played a written B-flat, and so on. It is proper to add that in modern times clarionets have been made in other keys — that is, have been made with such lengths of tubes that their C's would respectively coincide with other tones in the first octave of the other instruments; but the three above named are those almost universally used in non-military orchestras.

Of course, the proper allowance has to be made for this peculiarity of the clarionet's construction in writing for it. The player always finds the words " A clarionet," or " B-flat clarionet," at the head of his part, indicating which one of his instruments he is to use; and the composer has to vary the key accordingly, all the clarionets except the C clarionet necessarily playing in a different key from the other instruments.

I have spoken of this peculiarity of the clarionet — although unable here to explain or detail it — particularly for the purpose of making intelligible to the reader what I shall presently have to say with reference to the work of the conductor of an orchestra.

The tone of the clarionet will be easily singled out by most persons from among the mingling voices of the orchestra, by its penetrating sweetness in the highest part of its register, its liquid-amber quality in the middle part, and its reedy but pathetic mellowness in the lower part. No one will fail to be struck with the peculiarly feminine character of its higher utterances.

Besides the clarionets already named, large orchestras often employ the bass-clarionet. The name of this instrument indicates its nature; its tube is longer and larger than that of the others, and yields a tone much lower in pitch, though of similar quality.

Having thus given a most meagre outline of the reed-

division of the "wooden wind," it will not be necessary
to say much of the other division, which is much more
familiar — the flutes. It will be useful, however, to
describe the Bœhm flute — the modern form of the
old-fashioned flute — inasmuch as many persons are
unacquainted with this most happy of all the more modern improvements made in orchestral instruments. For
a long time the flute was a black beast in the orchestra;
it could not be made perfectly in tune throughout its
entire compass; insomuch that all sorts of bad stories
(such as that there was but one thing in the world worse
than a flute, to wit: two flutes — and the like) were told
of it. The reason of this inability to make the flute
wholly in tune was this. In consequence of the peculiar
formation of the hand, the fingers would be unable to
adjust themselves to the holes of a flute if those holes
were (as they ought to be) of equal size, and placed
nearly at equal distances. To remedy this, the holes
had to be placed at unequal distances, and the errors
in tune thus produced were compensated by unequally
changing the size of the holes. But this compensation
was in the first place not thorough, for the instrument
was still out of tune; it was, in the second place,
attended with the serious disadvantage of almost abolish-
ing the whole lower octave of the flute from orchestral
resources, since that octave was rendered so weak as to
be, one may say, silly in tone; and, in the third place,
the equality of power and color was destroyed, some
tones sounding veiled and some open, some rich and
some thin, and so on. The invention which relieved the
flute from all this odium and brought it to the rank of a
true solo instrument dates from about the last quarter of
a century, and has been claimed both by Captain Gor-

don and by Bœhm. The latter, at any rate, succeeded
in giving his name to it, having manufactured for several
years the instrument now universally known as the
Bœhm flute. The nature of this invention was briefly
as follows. Instead of stopping the holes directly with
the balls of the fingers, as before, all the holes were
closed with padded keys; and handles were so arranged
to these keys — by means of a very ingenious mechanism of hollow shafts which allowed other shafts to pass
through and to play inside of them — that any hole on
the flute was brought practically in reach of any finger,
the fingers pressing upon the handles instead of directly
upon the holes. It now became possible to make all
the holes much larger than the ball of the finger could
cover directly — which had long been a much-desired
object, the large holes being found to yield a much more
powerful tone — and to place the holes at the precise
distances from each other demanded by the mathematical laws of vibration.

The first form of the new instrument received additional improvements from time to time, and the result
was the present Bœhm flute — an instrument whose true
capacities, especially when used in masses, may be said
to be as yet almost unemployed by composers. The
lowest octave of the Bœhm flute, when sounded by a
player who knows how to avoid the disagreeable cornet-
tone which only vulgar ears affect, is of the most precious
character, at once soft, suggestive, rich, and passionate.
It is wholly different from any tone attainable from any
other instrument, and when sounded in unison by eight
or ten players is capable of the most delicate and yet
striking shades of expression. The failure of orchestral
composers to employ it, or, indeed, to learn of it, earlier,

is easily accounted for. Flute-soloists have rarely been able to resist the fatal facility of the instrument, and have usually addressed themselves to winning the applause of concert audiences by the execution of those brilliant but utterly trifling and inane variations which constitute the great body of existing solos for the flute. These variations are written mainly for the second and third octaves of the instrument, and the consequence has been an utter lack of cultivation of the lower octave by solo-players, and a necessarily resulting ignorance of its capacity by composers. Not only the solo-players, indeed, have been thus led away from the lower octave ; even the hack orchestral players suffered the same fate, for the reason that the old flute had practically no lower octave, and the old composers wrote entirely in the upper two. At present there are rarely more than three flutes even in the largest orchestras ; but this writer does not hesitate to record his belief — even at the risk of exciting the eyebrows of many steady-going musicians — that the time is not far distant when the twenty violins of a good orchestra will be balanced by twenty flutes.

And in view of the question which would probably be asked by these objectors, to wit : *Where would you get the players for such a number of flutes ?* — I may with propriety at this point diverge for a moment from the direct course, to make a suggestion to my countrywomen in which I feel a fervent interest. With the exception of the double-bass (violin) and the heavier brass, — indeed I am not sure that these exceptions are necessary, — there is no instrument of the orchestra which a woman cannot play successfully. The extent, depth, and variety of musical capability among the women of the United States are continual new sources of astonishment and pleasure to this writer, although his pursuits are not specially of a nature to bring them before his attention. It may be asserted without extravagance that there is no limit to the possible achievements of our countrywomen in this behalf, if their efforts be once turned in the right direction. This direction is, unquestionably, the orchestra. All the world has learned to play the piano. Let our young ladies — always saving, of course, those who have the gift for the special instrument — leave that and address themselves to the violin, the flute, the oboe, the harp, the clarionet, the bassoon, the kettledrum. It is more than possible that upon some of these instruments the superior daintiness of the female tissue might finally make the woman a more successful player than the man. On the flute, for instance, a certain combination of delicacy with flexibility in the lips is absolutely necessary to bring fully out that passionate yet velvety tone hereinbefore alluded to ; and many male players, of all requisite qualifications so far as manual execution is concerned, will be forever debarred from attaining it by reason of their intractable, rough lips, which will give nothing but a correspondingly intractable, rough tone. The same, in less degree, may be said of the oboe and bassoon. Besides, the qualities required to make a perfect orchestral player are far more often found in women than in men ; for these qualities are patience, fervor, and fidelity, combined with deftness of hand and quick intuitiveness of soul.

To put the matter in another view: no one at all acquainted with this subject will undervalue the benefits to female health to be brought about by the systematic use of wind-instruments. Out of personal knowledge, the writer pleases himself often with picturing how many consumptive chests, dismal shoulders, and melancholy spines would disappear, how many rosy cheeks would blossom, how many erect forms delight the eyes which mourn over their drooping, — under the stimulus of those long, equable, and generous inspirations and expirations which the execution of every moderately difficult piece on a wind-instrument requires.

But, returning to the main course : it is proper now to speak of the other great division of wind-instruments known as "the brass." This usually consists of the trombones, the trumpets, and the horns, with perhaps a cornet-à-pistons, though this last is not thought by musicians to be worthy of much rank in other than brass bands and military orchestras. The trombone in its older form is probably familiar to most persons as the long brass instrument which the performer elongates and shortens alternately by sliding it out and in. Its tone is gigantic, jubilant, and vigorous. The trumpet tone is also familiar for its bold and manly character, or for the startling and crashing breaks which it sometimes makes upon the softer harmonies. The horn is the instrument which curls upon itself in a circular coil, the performer often thrusting his unemployed hand into its large bell to assist in controlling the great difficulties of pure intonation upon this instrument. Its tone is indescribably broad, mellow, and noble, and is capable of very great variation in degrees of loudness. Most persons who have heard Thomas's orchestra will remember the lovely long-drawn *pianissimo* notes of this instrument which introduce the overture to " Oberon," or the far-off ravishment with which it steals upon the enormous chord of violin-tones in Asger Hamerik's " First Norse Suite."

Leaving now the wind-side of the orchestra, let us

pass over to "the strings." This term, in the ordinary parlance of musicians, is understood to mean the four classes of the viol-tribe, namely, the violins, the violas, the violoncellos, and the contra-basses or double-basses. In its largest application it would of course include the harps, and such rarely used instruments as the guitar and the *viol d'amour.* The violin is too familiar to need comment in so cursory a paper as this. The viola is an instrument almost exactly like the violin, but somewhat larger, and four tones lower in pitch. It has not the brittleness, the crispness, nor the brilliance of the violin; but is distinguished by a melancholy and pathetic tone quite peculiar to itself. Those who have heard the "Italy" of Berlioz will easily recall the viola, which is the hero of the whole piece. It is matter of regret that this noble instrument has now so few cultivators.

The violoncello is a more familiar instrument to most persons than the viola. It is tuned just an octave lower than that instrument. Since the time of Beethoven it has been much cultivated, and passages are now freely written for it which would have made the older players stare and stop for another pinch of snuff. Its powers are quite varied; it is competent for a serenade or a prayer; for suggesting mere lazy tropical sensuousness or manly protests against wrong. Perhaps the most remarkable deliverance intrusted to it by a modern composer occurs in the "Jewish Trilogy" of Hamerik. Here, after a lovely harmonic conception, the whole orchestra ceases, and one violoncello begins a strange monody, which is continued for a long time: a monody as of a prophet standing between the people and the altar and recounting with intense passion the captivities, the escapes, the sins, the covenants, the blessings, in truth, the whole romantic past, of the Jews — the entire effect deriving extraordinary power from the sense of tenacity due to the peculiar sustaining power of this instrument, and from the sense of isolation excited by the lonesomeness of its voice when thus lifted up in the suddenly silent orchestra.

The double-basses are well known to all as the largest of the violin-tribe ; and the harps are also familiar ; so that, although both are of great interest to the musician, the points that make them so are too technical for mention in this place, and we may pass on now to a word about the instruments of percussion.   Those in common use are the commonly called bass-drum, the snare-drum (employed by ordinary military companies), the cymbals, and the kettledrum.   This latter, of which there are always at least two in an orchestra, is like a large, round-bottomed brass pot, the mouth of which is covered with a membrane stretched across.   Its pitch is varied by screws which tighten the membrane ; the two tones to which the two drums are tuned being usually the tonic and the dominant of the key in which the orchestra is playing.   Those who remember the lovely little " Scandinavian Wedding March " by Söderman will recall the adroit employment of the kettledrum in the opening to intensify the mood of expectation upon which the soft harmonies are presently to fall.

In closing this rapid account of the orchestral constituents, it is proper to mention that several instruments whose employment is more or less unusual have been omitted ; such as the bass-flute (sometimes called the alto-flute), which is of quite recent invention, and bears much the same relation to the ordinary flute as that of the viola to the violin; the piccolo, which is a very short small flute, set an octave higher than the concert-flute, and which is in nearly every orchestra; the harmonicon, the small harmonium, the corno Inglese (a large cousin of the oboe), the castanets, various sized cymbals, the zither, and others. The zither has been made known to many persons by the pretty tinkling air it plays in a dream-piece by Lumbye, which one used to find often recurring in Theodore Thomas's programmes.

As soon as the members of the orchestra have assembled, say for a rehearsal, the first business is to bring all the instruments to the same pitch. For this purpose the oboe, considered to be the least variable instrument, sounds a long and insistent A, with which each player proceeds to make his A (or the corresponding tone if he has a transposing instrument) coincide. The conductor mounts his platform and raps with his baton, holding the latter poised aloft for a moment. Each player must now have his eyes at once upon the conductor and upon the written part before himself, — a dual attention which must be maintained steadily throughout the composition, and which requires more concentration than one is at first inclined to appreciate. With the first down-stroke of the conductor's baton the first bar of the piece commences. Fancy, for example, that you are first flute-player, and that the figures thirty-seven occur over a blank space of the staff on your part. This means that you are not to come in until thirty-seven bars are played by the other instruments; and you are now to carry on a double set of countings in your mind, the one recording the beats of each bar, the other recording the number of bars. You therefore commence, with the conductor's first down beat, to count mentally, keeping a tally of each set of four beats ; supposing the piece is in four-four time, that is, that there are four of the conductor's beats to each . bar, you say, *one* (two-three-four), *two* (two-three-four), *three* (two-three-four), *four* (two-three-four), *five* (two-three-four), and so on. About the time you have reached *thirty-one* (two-three-four), you will infallibly — if an inexperienced player — fall to wondering whether you did not omit to say *thirty* (two-three-four), and while this inward debate is going on, you have, of course, neglected the *thirty-two* (two-three-four), to remedy which you jump to the thirty-three, but in so doing reflect that you were probably discussing long enough to occupy *two* bars, and ought to have jumped to thirty-four, or, even perhaps thirty-five — by which time your heart is thumping with anticipation of the conductor's scowl, when you shall presently come in wrong and compel him to stop the whole orchestra in order to commence over — until finally you are in a state of hopeless, inane confusion, and the chances are a thousand to one that you do come in wrong, with all manner of vile discord and resultant trouble. Of course there are many passages which are easier, by reason of one's familiarity with the composition. A certain automatic precision of count comes with long experience.

But if the player's part is by no means the trifling work which many imagine, the conductor's will certainly impress one who becomes acquainted with it for the first time as requiring an amount of mental strain little suspected by those who only see the graceful curves of the baton and the silent figure that moves it. The conductor must read simultaneously all the bars written for each class of the instruments in his orchestra, the notes being written under each other, those for the piccolo and flutes at the top, those for the double-basses at the bottom, the rest between. But this large collection of notes, which have thus to be instantaneously read, is written not only in different keys, but with different clefs; the horns and clarionets may each be playing in different keys from the other instruments; the tenor trombones will be playing notes written upon a still different system; the violoncellos, notes written upon a still different system; the double-basses and bassoons and bass-trombones and drums, notes written upon yet another system. And this is not half; for while the conductor's eye is reading these notes his ear has to watch over each one of his sixty to a hundred and fifty instruments, and instantly report the least failure of one to play exactly what is written; and this is not nearly all; for besides, the conductor's arm must keep up the unceasing beats of time, and must make the different expression-signs, *i. e.*, the signals for loud or soft, or slower or faster, and the like. Fancy, in other words, that you had a class in elocution of sixty pupils, all of whom simultaneously read aloud to you — some in Greek, some in Hebrew, some in French, some in Latin, some in English — and that the least fault in pronouncing any word of any of these languages, or the least error even in inflection or intonation, must be detected. This is a fair analogy to the labor of the orchestral conductor.

In the judgment of the writer, although the improvements of the orchestra have been very great in modern times, it is yet in its infancy as an adequate exponent of those inward desires of man which find their best solace in music. No prudent person acquainted with the facts will now dare to set limits to the future expressive powers of this new and manifold voice which man has found. The physics of music have made such enormous advances under the scientific labors of Helmholtz, Alfred M. Mayer, and others, that the art cannot but receive additional aid through the facts thus discovered, and one cannot help looking to see new instruments before long which will indefinitely increase the resources of the orchestra of the future. Many reasons seem to justify the belief that the home of the orchestra is to be in this country: meantime, one can frame no fairer wish for one's countrymen than that they may quickly come to know the wise expansions and large tolerances and heavenly satisfactions which stream into the soul of him that hath ears to hear, out of the orchestra of the present.

III

The Physics of Music[1]

TAKE if you please the lowest work of genius and the highest work of talent : the former is always Art, the latter always mere cleverness. The one is always in some sense true : the other is often in all senses false. In truth, there is that in the very nature of Cleverness which renders it particularly liable to mislead either itself or other people. Confront it with something new that is to be taken account of : it has not that indescribable insight of fervent love which lies at the bottom of genius ; it cannot burn away the husk of things with that instinct towards the kernel which genius possesses ; it is busied, like a newspaper reporter, more with thinking how much can be said than with observing the facts that should be said ; it can evolve a paragraph easier than record a circumstance. Its facile dexterity is often its ruin — as if a hasty spider should mesh his own legs.

Now the doctrine of *falsus in uno* is not true except with very careful limitations ; but — to descend to particulars — if a man can be shown to have written a paper every important proposition of which contains inaccuracies, and several important propositions of which are preposterous, then it would seem to be fair at least to regard with suspicion all his utterances in other papers upon the same general subject.

[1] Written in 1875.

The object of this present writing is, downright, to discredit Mr. Richard Grant White as authority in any matter whatever pertaining to music : and there are grave reasons why this subject is a praiseworthy one, — one, indeed, so far removed from a mere flippant discussion that it is thoroughly in the nature of a religious purpose. For every fervent and pious lover of art must look with displeasure upon the quarrel into which Mr. White has been urging musicians through the columns of the *Galaxy* for some months, actually entrapping many of the unwary. The descriptive part of what is called " descriptive music " has no arms, nor sheriff, nor other physical sanction of law : not the least atom of obligation rests upon any human being to go by the programme of what is called " programme music " : any soul may hear the music and draw just what glories of delight or of sadness from it that his own whimsiest mood may suggest. The only view of art is that of " liberal applications," as Wordsworth happily called them : that which, allowing a man to smile, or to shed tears, over a violet (*i. e.*, Nature) just according as it breeds in him a happy or a regretful mood, in the same way allows him to interpret at his own will a picture, a tone-poem, a word-poem, or any other artistic form. It is all free trade in Art : there are no duties.

The heart of man is big enough and hungry enough for all the good music that can ever be written, descriptive or otherwise. If descriptive music is a mistake, let it be : the mistake usually lies in the description only, not in the music, for much of it is wonderfully lovely ; shall a Protestant reject all the Madonna pictures because he rejects the theology of their painters? The solitary question to ask of a new composition is — not, is it descriptive, but is it beautiful in any, the largest, sense of that term? If it is, why then in God's name — spoken with reverence — let us hear it, and hear it often.

Mr. White has recently printed in the *Galaxy* magazine a paper entitled *The Science and the Philosophy of Music :* the "Science" in this title meaning the physical science of acoustics as far as it relates to musical sounds, and not the science of music, proper, whose existence the author has often denied. Of this paper about the first four and a half pages concern themselves with the "science," the remainder with the "philosophy," of music. The former is the part to be herein spoken of.

It is subdivided into twelve paragraphs, containing more or less distinct propositions. Now, speaking with scientific accuracy, there is not one of these paragraphs but falls within the following categories, to wit: the demonstrably absurd, the wrong in statement, the wrong in substance : and some belong to all three at once. It is so curiously wrong that there are scarce a half dozen sentences which do not contain inaccuracies : and these are sentences of connection rather than of matter. The whole no better constitutes a view of the Science of Music than a wrongly-wired skeleton constitutes a view of the science of anatomy. It is the very climacteric and crooked top-piece of error.

Of course such assertions as these are both trifling and arrogant unless immediately followed up by detailed proofs. In the course of what is hereinafter said, I shall have occasion to quote nearly the whole of Mr. White's paper as printed, so far as it refers to the science of music.

He begins: "In a recent article I had occasion to

show that the commonly-used phrase ' scientific music '
is incorrect and misleading, because music is not a
science, but an art involving neither in its composition
nor its performance any knowledge whatever of any
science, either musical or other."

Each of the three clauses of this sentence is absurdly
erroneous.   A science is a body of facts, classified upon
system, and generalized into laws.   These laws are simply
expressions in short of the numbers of individual and similar facts.   The law of gravity, for instance, is only a short
summing up of all those multitudinous occasions when
men have observed that small bodies fall towards large
ones.   There *is* a science of music, embodying a great
number of classified facts, and presenting a great number of scientific laws which are as thoroughly recognized
among musicians as are the laws of any other sciences
among their professors.   There is a science of harmony,
a science of composition, a science of orchestration, a
science of performance upon stringed instruments, a science of performance upon wind instruments, a science
of vocalization ; not a branch of the art of music but has
its own analogous body of classified facts and general
laws.   Music is so much a science that a man may be
a thorough musician who has never written a tune and
who cannot play a note upon any instrument.   One
asks with astonishment if it be possible that a writer in an
intelligently-conducted magazine could undertake a paper
on The Science and The Philosophy of Music, who was
ignorant of that great body of literature in which the
science of thorough-bass, the science of orchestration,
the science of execution, and the like, are formally set
forth ?   But the case is worse : for Mr. White himself, a
little further on, employs some of the terms and recog-

nizes some of the laws of the Science of Thorough-bass. We find him talking of the tonic, the third, the fifth, and incidentally recognizing the law that, with any tone of a scale as tonic, these three form a chord, of idiosyncratic properties and relations : and we find him giving quotations from Mr. Rice which bristle thickly with the terminology of music.

The truth is, that the concluding clause of Mr. White's first sentence calls for flat contradiction, term for term : and that music is an art which *does* involve both in its composition and its performance a precise knowledge of musical science.

"It is nevertheless true, as was then intimated, that there is a science of music, a very exact and absolute science, the laws of which control the vibration of every string in a grand orchestra, and to which every chord struck or uttered must conform.   But of this science there were probably never four persons more ignorant than Handel, Haydn, Mozart, and Beethoven. This I do not mean to assert positively, for I do not know it to be true : but I know of no fact in the life of either that points to a knowledge of this science, which would not have been of any service to them whether as composers or performers. This science is not that of acoustics, although it is an acoustic science. The science of acoustics includes the science of music.

"A little book has lately been published which may be made the occasion of giving an idea of what this science of music is, upon which depends the construction of every musical phrase, the performance of every musical artist, and which yet is of no more service to a composer or to a singer than an acquaintance with chemistry or with optics would be to a painter."

Now without stopping to chide the petty artifice of language by which Mr. White endeavors to make the unsuspecting reader glow with wonder at the fact that Handel, Haydn, Mozart, Beethoven, with all their four-fold force, could not break through the physical laws of nature, *i.e.*, that although these men were ignorant of the physical laws of vibration, yet nevertheless every fiddle-string upon which their compositions were played did verily and in the strangest manner vibrate always according to the natural laws of vibration; and without doing more than barely pointing out how, so far from its being true, as Mr. White declares, that the construction of every musical phrase depends on the physical science of music, the fact is that the construction of *no* musical phrase depends in the least degree on the physics of music and would not be in the remotest way affected if every law of vibration were reversed or if all of them were abolished : let us confine our attention to the last clause of this last extract, and inquire if Mr. White can really conceive a painter unacquainted with optics? What kind of pictures would that artist paint who did not have literally at his fingers'-ends the laws of perspective, the laws of the radiation of light in right lines, the laws of shadows, the laws of apparent projection upon plane surfaces? Or, — to go further into the mere curiosities of error — will Mr. White undertake to say, in view of the aniline dyes and the like, that a painter acquainted with chemistry might not discover new pigments more brilliant, more various, more powerful, than any now known, and that it would not be " of service " to him? Nay, — leaving these merely childish *cui bono* views — what can a gentleman of Mr. White's culture mean by this strenuous limitation of the artist to ignorant work, and by these persevering asseverations that the artist, be he painter, musician, or other, would be no whit the better for an intelligent understanding of those wonderful and beautiful phenomena which occur when his dreams take physical form? Why, but to know them is a new and illimitable inspiration in itself; and he is a bold man who will attempt, at this particular stage of progressive physics, to prescribe the boundaries of that flight which music will compass when musicians shall have learned to feather the arrow of their art with the guidances of their whole science.

"The author of this work," (proceeds Mr. White) "Sedley Taylor (who, however, confesses his obligations to Professor Helmholtz, a very profound investigator into the laws of acoustics), tells us that he aims at placing before persons unacquainted with mathematics an intelligible and succinct account of that part of the theory of sound which constitutes the physical basis of the art of music."

Than the last seventeen words of which, nothing could more clearly illustrate that employment of inexact language which results in absurdity. How can a theory (of sound, or of anything else) constitute a physical basis of the art of music, or of any other art or thing? The physical basis of the art of music is, roughly speaking, 1st, vibrations; 2d, air; and 3d, man's auditory apparatus. Can a theory — nay, a part of a theory — "constitute" these?

"He assumes no preliminary knowledge save of arithmetic, and of the musical notation in common use. No lover of music need therefore be deterred, by fear of incompetence from the perusal of his very interesting little volume, of which, however, we shall concern ourselves only with the elementary parts. For they are not only the most generally interesting, but they present all that is necessary to the understanding of those relations of sounds without which the thing that modern and civilized people call music would be impossible. Passing over therefore what is said by the author upon sound in general, which all who read this article probably know is always the product of vibration — the vibration, for example, of a string, of a column of air (as in a wind instrument), of a piece of parchment, as in a drum, which vibration communicates itself to the surrounding air and is thus conveyed to the ear — we come to the consideration of musical sound proper. Mr. Taylor defines ' a musical sound as a steady sound, and a non-musical sound as an unsteady sound.' Without professing to be able to give a more descriptive and exact definition of a musical sound, I cannot accept this one as either exact or descriptive."

In which last sentence one finds Mr. White attacking, as neither exact nor descriptive, the very fundamental definition of a book which he has just declared, in the third sentence back, to " present all that is necessary to the understanding those relations of sounds " which render music possible. It may be said, indeed, that Mr. Taylor, in the effort to render his book easily understood, has made his definition perhaps needlessly meagre. Every person of average intelligence can understand the principle upon which musical scientists differentiate a musical sound from sound in general or mere noise, to wit, that a musical sound is one produced by vibrations recurring in equal times. Further than this no man can go. Musicalness — in the sense in which Mr. White attempts to " define " it — is a quality perceived by the ear, just as sweetness is a quality perceived by the tongue. Will any man "define" the taste of sugar?

"There are many sounds which are steady and which are not musical, except in a very loose and unscientific as well as inartistic use of that term. Such are the humming of a bee, the roar of a waterfall, the rumbling of a ninepin ball, and the filing of a saw. Perhaps a musical sound might be safely defined to be a sound produced by regular vibrations, giving pleasure to the human ear, and capable of being used as a means of expression. It might be said that regularity of vibration always produces steadiness of sound. This is true: and steadiness of sound is one, and an essential element of musical tone. But it is not the only one. The capability of exciting pleasure and that of being used as a means of expression seem to be no less essential qualities of any sound properly called musical."

This "definition" of Mr. White's cannot stand a moment. A single illustration will demolish it: the quarter tones, for example, and all tones less than half tones, are certainly musical sounds: yet they fail in two out of Mr. White's three particulars; for they do not give pleasure, and there is no known method by which they can be used as a means of expression.

"The possibility of music as an art depends not only upon regularity of vibration, but on certain relations of the vibrations by which sounds are produced. These have been discovered by experiment, and are found to have certain laws which are of mathematical nature and precision. Upon these relations harmony depends; and without harmony there is no music; for every melody supposes a harmony upon which it is said to be based."

But no : the possibility of music does *not* so depend, nor does that of harmony : and without harmony there verily *can* be music. There has been music without harmony pretty much ever since we knew of anything that has been : and Melody was an old man when Harmony was born. The Greeks had a great deal of music : but Mr. Donkin, who is authority, does not think they had any harmony.

" A vibrating string affords the simplest and perhaps the most trustworthy means of testing and analyzing these relations. A string made to vibrate with sufficient rapidity produces sound which will be of a certain pitch. Now if that string be lightly touched exactly in the middle," — (but why " lightly touched "? It will do the same thing if heavily touched, or if in any way made half as long. Mr. White is thinking of harmonic tones, or overtones.) — "and the vibration kept up, the pitch of the sound produced rises exactly an octave ; that is, the sound maintains the same relations to the musical scale which it had before, but it is higher. To define an octave in this sense is exceedingly difficult, simple as the conception of it is to every musically endowed person. For a note and its octave are the same and yet not the same. A melodic phrase repeated in various octaves has precisely the same melodic and harmonic relations ; it is the same phrase, the same melody ; and yet the actual sounds produced may be as unlike and as remote as the highest and shrillest tone of a violin and those of the lowest grumblings of a double-bass viol."

The sweeping assertion cannot be made that an octave has the same harmonic relations as its fundamental tone : and any person can demonstrate for himself that

it often has not.   Let any one, for example, strike the
following tones together on a piano,

and he will produce a jangle entirely hideous; but let
him strike the following:

and although the latter chord is wholly composed of octaves of the notes composing the former one, the exper-
imenter will hear a sound so beautiful that, for one, I
can never get upon it without lingering and lingering,
for the pure sensuous beauty of it, — and that in spite of
the fact that it is a chord of progress imperatively calling
for speedy relief from the tonic.   " This rising of an
octave in the sound of the vibrating string is found to be
caused by the doubling of the rapidity of the vibrations.
The string on being touched in the middle divides itself
into two parts, and each of these parts vibrate just twice
as fast as the whole string does.   An increase of the rapidity of the vibration does not produce any difference in
the intensity or the volume of sound, only in its pitch.
On the other hand, increased loudness of sound is
produced by an increase of the distance of vibration.
The violin player when he wishes to increase the volume
and the intensity of his tone, presses his bow upon the
string more firmly and moves it more rapidly.   The

string vibrates further — that is, through a greater space than before — but it makes no more vibrations in a second than it does when he produces the same note as lightly and as softly as possible."

This last proposition is true only within limits : beyond which the rapidity of vibration *does* vary with the force with which the vibrating body is agitated.   Inexperienced violin players are often astonished, upon striking an open string with the bow, to hear the octave come out instead of the fundamental tone : by being struck too hard, the string has been caused to form a node in the middle, and thus divide itself into two vibrating sections, giving its octave.   Many of the high notes on wind instruments are made simply by increasing the force of the breath.

" A vibrating string may be infinitesimally divided ; the finger may be run up and down the whole length of it, and the pitch of the sound thus produced will rise and fall accordingly.   But of the sound thus produced only that which is heard at certain degrees is at all available for the purpose of musical art.   These degrees are those which produce what is called the diatonic scale."

In these last two sentences Mr. White sweeps out of existence, at one blow, the chromatic scale, and all the vast fabric of loveliness which has been built on it : for he declares that only the sounds heard at such degrees as produce the *diatonic* scale are at all available for the purposes of musical art ; and inasmuch as the chromatic sounds (what the general reader calls *flats and sharps*) are not and cannot be heard at the diatonic degrees, — *ergo*, the chromatic sounds are not available, etc.

One may safely venture to say that such an assertion

was never made in the columns of the *Galaxy* or any
other magazine before.

"It is found that the string will divide itself into the
vibrating sections which produce these notes, on being
lightly touched (not shortened by being pressed down)
at certain places. This diatonic scale is therefore not
arbitrary, but the result of a law of acoustics. It exists
in nature."

But the fact is not so: the string will *not* make the
diatonic scale, when thus treated : the diatonic scale is
not the result of any known law of acoustics : and it does
not exist in nature. Of which any reader, musical or
otherwise, can judge, after the following short explanation.

If you will take a tube in the shape of any horn, without keys or other ventages than just the mouth and bell,
and of such a length as to make (say) the tone C upon
blowing into it with a certain force : then, upon increasing the force of blowing, it will presently make the C an
octave above ; it cannot be caused to make any intermediate note, by force of breath solely. Blow, now, with
more force, and you will get the G above the last C ;
with more force still, you will get the C above that ;
with more, the E above ; more, G above ; more, A
above ; more, a note something like B flat above, but
not B flat nor B natural ; more, C ; and so on ; or, to
present the result at a glance, you will get the following,
in order from the bottom :

Octave below.

A string will divide itself in the same way, when, lightly touching, the finger is run down it. The phenomenon is invariable, and is caused by the singular property which vibrating bodies have of dividing themselves into sections, separated by nodes.

The above series of notes represents then what Mr. White would get from his string; but the diatonic scale is this series of notes :

Let any one compare the two, and say whether Mr. White has enounced as a fundamental scientific principle what is really only the fanciful hypothesis of a theorizer.

" The melody and harmony which are possible only by means of this scale are therefore dependent upon certain ratios of rapidity in vibration. For example, as we have seen that the octave or unison is the product of vibrations which are as 2 to 1, we find that the fifth, the most perfect concord, is the product of vibrations which are as 3 to 2. In other words, when two sounds differ by a fifth, the higher sound is the product of three vibrations and the lower of two vibrations during the same time. So when two sounds differ by a fourth, the higher sound is the product of four vibrations and the lower of three vibrations during the same time. To follow these proportions throughout the scale is needless, and would be uninteresting : for our purpose here is only to consider the nature of this science, not to examine its details."

The first division of this last sentence belongs also among the curiosities of error. The following of the proportions referred to, throughout the scale, is not only *not* " needless," but it is necessary, in any meagre examination of the nature of musical physics ; and if the reader should think this hyper-criticism, I have only to refer him to a point a little farther on in Mr. White's article where this very need has forced itself on him, and where he has actually done the very thing he here declares needless,— to wit, given these very proportions throughout the whole diatonic scale.

And again : the following of these proportions throughout the scale is not only *not* " uninteresting," but it is precisely in this connection that some of the most brilliant triumphs of modern science, — certainly the most striking ones, to general readers — have been achieved. The wonderful methods of reducing these proportions of vibration to curves visible to the eye, carried to such an extent that among musical scientists tones are known by their curves ; and curious applications of them to other departments of science, are always sure to bring down a lecture-audience ; and when the lecturer proceeds to cast these proportions upon a screen, in bands of brilliant light, and to bring out the most graceful and beautiful figures, ever increasing in complexity as he superimposes curve upon curve of note after note, the enthusiasm of the dullest person is sure of being aroused. The very culminating fascination of a science which is surely the least dry of all physics, — this is what Mr. White has selected to pronounce " needless and uninteresting."

But the limits of this paper are being rapidly reached, and the smaller errors in what follows must be passed over without mention, in order to give room for the exposure of one or two more of great importance.

After explaining the phenomenon of resonance in a

very objectionable way, Mr. White reiterates in the next paragraph the doctrine that the knowledge of the physics of music is " needless to the artist-musician " : which has already been discussed.

He then proceeds : "Musical sounds heard together are concordant or discordant. Discord is produced by what is called 'beats' : that is, the vibrations of the two sounding bodies are so close to each other in their rapidity that they clash, and produce a roughness of sound which is painful to the sensitive ear."

Leaving aside the thorough insufficiency of Mr. White's explanation of " beats," and regretting, particularly on account of the prominence of this phenomenon in modern musical physics, that the deficiency cannot be remedied here, it must be said that the theory of " beats " as the physical origin of discord has been so qualified and eviscerated even by those who were most committed to it, that it has been practically abandoned. It was first announced by Professor Helmholtz ; but, in spite of the magnificent authority which that great philosopher exercises in all departments of physical science, the theory was found to fail utterly, by practical musicians : it had to be modified, limited ; and so, what with modification and limitation, it may now be said to be pretty much no theory. The very book which Mr. White is reviewing in this article is careful to protect itself on this point ; yet Mr. White announces it as if it were an unquestioned principle. In truth, — without at all wishing to be dogmatic, — it can be mathematically shown, and experimentally shown, that beats have nothing whatever to do with discord, in the generally received sense of the word " discord " : and it is only by making the word " discord " have the same meaning as the word "concord" that its most desperate advocates have been able to maintain any ground: which is much as if one should assert that a horse is a cow, and then protect his assertion by the proviso that in using the term "horse" he meant — not the animal commonly so named — but an animal with horns and a milk-bag.

After instancing some discordant intervals, the paper proceeds:

"Concords consist at most of but three notes. From the largest orchestra, as from a mere stringed quartette or a pianoforte, if we hear a concord, we hear but three notes — doubled, trebled, or quadrupled through the octaves included within the range of the instruments. And the following triads include all the concords that can be heard:

These triads contain the tonic in combination with the minor third and fifth, with the major third and fifth, with the minor third and minor sixth, with the major third and major sixth, with the fourth and the minor sixth, with the fourth and the major sixth. Their character is determined by the third, in whatever part of the triad it appears. There are three major triads and three minor. These chords, or their inversions, are all the concords that we hear."

To this there are five serious objections. First, upon any reader not already thoroughly familiar with the subject it makes an impression just as wrong as wrong can be: and this impression will linger until the reader is told that the words "concord" and "discord," "con-

cordant " and " discordant," as here used, have no reference to the common signification of those words as
denoting chords agreeable or disagreeable to the ear.
The chord which was given just now by me as one of
the most beautiful chords in all music, contains one of
those sevenths which Mr. White declares to be the most
" discordant " interval of the scale : and the whole
chord is a discord, in the terminology here used by Mr.
White. How this anomalous terminology has grown up
in Thorough-bass cannot here be explained. Bearing
this anomaly in mind, any reader will perceive that the
wonder intended to be excited by the second sentence
of this last extract will necessarily be wholly based on a
misunderstanding by the reader of the word " concord "
therein used.

But this is scarcely the beginning of transgressions,
with this unlucky last extract. It contains at least two
errors of statement, and three of substance. I have
already spoken of one of the errors of statement. The
other is contained in the last sentence of the extract,
when taken in connection with the rest. Mr. White
says : " These chords, or their inversions, are all the
concords that we hear." If Mr. A. T. Stewart should
cause a clipping as big as a pin-head to be made from
off each different sort of goods in his retail-store, and
holding them all in his hands should declare that what
he there held, was all he had in that store, we would
either understand him to mean that what he held was *a
sample* of all in the store, or we would understand him
to be crazy. Mr. White's well-demonstrated force of intellect will not admit such a supposition as this last ;
therefore every musician must believe that in this statement he merely means that the chords he enumerates

are samples as it were of all the *technical* concords we hear. But I submit if any untechnical reader would gather aught but error from the statement as made.

To go on, however, to errors of substance : the statement, as made, is absurdly erroneous in point of fact. The chords numbered 1 and 2 (they have been numbered by me for convenient reference) are the only generic chords (in the technical sense which Mr. White is here himself employing) in the enumeration ; the other four are only inversions of chords identical in formation with the first two. No. 3 is only an inversion of a triad which is formed on A flat in precisely the same way as number 2 is formed on C. So, also, 4 and 5 are only inversions of a minor chord formed precisely as 1 is formed. When, therefore, Mr. White speaks, in the last sentence of this extract, of " these chords or their inversions " (" these chords " being, as detailed in the previous sentence, the " three major triads and three minor triads "), he speaks an absurdity as to four out of the six chords : for those four are themselves inversions, and are not capable of inversion, which is a process performed only upon such triads as 1 and 2.

The second error of substance is : that Mr. White's enumeration of triads entirely omits the well-known diminished triad formed on the seventh degree of the scale, which *is* generically different from both 1 and 2.

A third error of substance consists in Mr. White's failure to mention the method of varying the typical chords by dispersion, — a method co-extensive with that vast range of notes found between the double-bass and the piccolo, and quite as effectual as inversion.

The next paragraph of Mr. White's paper is devoted to temperament ; it is the one which contains the detailed enumeration of the proportions of vibration between all the notes in the scale, which has been herein before referred to. This paragraph is also in error. "But even they" (*i. e.*, stringed instruments) "are not absolutely perfect, because they must have four notes of a fixed pitch, whereas absolutely perfect intonation admits of but one note the pitch of which is fixed, — the tonic."

Now the violin (for example: the same remark applies to all the strings), so far from having four notes fixed, has but one; and that one is only fixed, *quoad* flattening; it can be made as much sharper as the performer desires. The D, A, and E of the violin's open strings can be varied at will.

I will not pursue the next paragraph, in which Mr. White discusses with Mr. Taylor whether a basso would be able to take an E flat true, after an F sharp with thirteen bars rest. Mr. Taylor thinks the basso could not, and wishes to recommend a system of notation which would help him to do it better than the system now in use. Mr. White thinks the basso would do it without difficulty; he is sure he would after the first trial, "because he would feel intuitively the position of E flat in the chord on which he was to come in." But if he came in *no* chord, in solo: or if, coming in on a chord, he had no intermediate cue from the other voices, how then? In fact — by way of reply to Mr. White's airy dismissal of Mr. Taylor's point — I have seen the oldest strings in the orchestra boggle over much easier intervals than that from F sharp to E flat after thirteen bars' rest.

And now, inasmuch as here ends the scientific portion of Mr. White's article, one would think he *could* not commit any more errors on that subject. Yet he has; and they are worse than any that have been specified. They consist in what he has *not* said.

What would be thought of any presentation, however meagre, of the science of optics which did not even so much as mention the fact that white light is composite, and which contained not a solitary reference to the prism or the spectroscope?

The fault of omission in the paper we have been discussing is precisely similar. *It* does not so much as mention that the musical tones ordinarily heard are highly composite in their nature, — a fact from which flow many of the most interesting portions of the physical science of music; nor does it contain a solitary reference to the Siren — that beautiful instrument, the *vade mecum* of the musical physicist, with which he has accomplished so many wonders.

In truth, when one reads in the concluding paragraph of this presentation of musical physics, that " from what has been said the musical reader will gather something of what the Science of Music really is," may not one ask, without incurring any accusation of flippantly taking words out of one's opponent's mouth, if " from what has been said " the musical reader will not gather a great deal of what the Science of Music really is *not?*

IV

Two Descriptive Orchestral Works

Rubinstein's " Ocean Symphony " and Hartmann's " Raid of the Vikings "

[The following is a fragment of Mr. Lanier's interpretation of these two musical works upon the occasion of their production at the first Peabody concert of 1880. Much of the original article, indeed most of the discussion from the standpoint of a musical critic, was omitted by the daily paper in which it appeared. The " Maryland Musical Festival," in the next chapter, is also very fragmentary, from the same reason.]

THE opening movement (of Emil Hartmann's overture " The Raid of the Vikings ") seems to show us the Vikings taking a tender leave of wives and sweethearts, and solemnly committing themselves to the Higher Powers as they embark on their expedition. A sudden change in the music presents the great sea ships bounding off before a keen and whistling wind, impatient warriors striding about the deck, eager preludes of the battle-tune. Other changes bring forward in succession the fierce descent on the coast, the march into battle, the fight, the victorious return. As this is an overture, these changes take place without such pauses between them as separate the longer movements of a symphony. In Rubinstein's Symphony we have still the sea, but a wholly different sea of associations. The first movement opens up to us the expanse of the ocean; we exult in a free and melodious swing of waves; we "hear old Triton blow his wreathed horn," the waters laugh in the sunlight, yet withal a certain mystery creeps about, especially where, while the violins are sending out a clear and fluent melody, we distinguish the clarionet, in a strange, broken, and wholly different tune, singing like a siren under the sea of sound. In the second movement nothing could be more suggestive of the interminable wallow and welter of waves than the singular violoncello accompaniment to the lovely melody of violins and clarionet, immediately following the first two chords of this movement. The terror of the great deep, the perils of them that go down to the sea in ships, the helplessness of man before this prodigious power, the inexorable riddle of sudden death, the despair of the drowning man, tempests turned into melodious lamentation, prayer, the endless protest and longing of bereaved love, — all these are typified in this movement. The third movement pictures the uncouth and awkward jollity of sailors on ship-board, and the fourth, after many monstrous ideas, alternating with solemn chorales, ends in a mighty sea-hymn.

V

The Maryland Musical Festival [1]

.   .   .   .   .   .

THE whole of the music during the evening was
Beethoven's, and it was so selected as to present an
admirable opportunity for studying the genius of this
Shakspere of tone in its two greatest aspects, to wit:
with regard to his love for physical nature and his love
for human nature.

The Seventh Symphony, with which the concert
opened, cannot be properly criticised without reference
to the curious relation which Beethoven bears to the distinctive culture of our day. That culture is rooted in
physical science. The thirst after exact knowledge of
the secrets of the physical universe is the characteristic
mark by which the modern epoch differentiates itself from
the mediæval and the antique. Now it is a circumstance
probably not yet sufficiently appreciated that the same
age which has developed physical science to an extent
undreamed of by ancient philosophers has also developed
music to an extent undreamed of by ancient artists.

The hearer of the Seventh Symphony last night — and,
it may be added, of the descriptive piece called " The
Calm of the Sea " — will find himself at the verge of a
whole new field of appreciation for those pieces if he

[1] A Musical Festival held in Baltimore in May, 1878, and extending over several days.

will remember that the same era which produces Maillet, Darwin, Spencer, Huxley, and Tyndall has produced also Beethoven in music and the landscape school in painting. For these three phenomena — the modern scientist, the musician, and the landscape painter — are merely three developments, in different directions, of one mighty impulse which under-runs them all. This impulse is that direct sympathy with physical nature which the man of to-day possesses, and which the man of old did not possess. The Greek had an intermediate set of beings between him and his mother earth; he invented the Faun, the Oread, and the Nymph to stand between man on the one side, and the forest, the mountain, the stream on the other.

We are under no such necessity. Our Darwin boldly takes hold of Nature as if it were a rose, pulls it to pieces, puts it under the microscope, and reports to us what he saw without fear or favor. Beethoven, on the other hand, approaching the same good Nature — from a different direction, with different motives — and looking upon it with the artist's — not the scientist's — eye, finds it a beautiful whole; he does not analyze, but, pursuing the synthetic process, shows it to us as a perfect rose, reporting his observations to us in terms of harmony.

Now those who reverently listened to the performance of the Seventh Symphony of last night, as if Beethoven had come back from a journey under bases of mountains and roots of flowers, and was telling us what he saw, were in the way towards a proper reception of the majesty and delicacy of this wonderful music. As the first movement opened with a full chord the hautboys emerged from the mass of tone like the slender fairy emerging from the petals of the great lily in the Pantomime. The introduction then proceeded with continuous majesty to the curious dialogue of the flute and reeds, which seems as if two voices were calling to each other from the opposite ends of creation, and then these two voices fused and begun the vivacious melody which continues to the end of the movement. As the orchestra began the strange sigh which initiates the second movement, there was a perceptible settling of the audience, and a quietude or attention that gave admirable scope to the low throbbing which the strings set up, as if one were in that silence which Lord Houghton has so well described in his famous

> " The beating of our own hearts
> Was all the sound we heard."

The strings beat like a heart. This second movement is in fact a wonderful march, in which the rhythm of the step is also the rhythm of the human heart-beat. We all remember where our own poet uses this same association of rhythms in the sentiment that our hearts, like muffled drums, are beating funeral marches to the tomb. I make no doubt Beethoven was thinking of this typical organ of man's life beating its way through the dangers of physical nature from birth to death.

It is interesting to compare the final utterance of great souls in the presence of this death, the most enormous phenomenon which confronts him who looks into Nature. Life, cries an old Greek poet, is but a passage from the tomb to the tomb. Our little life, says Shakspere, is rounded with a sleep. What Beethoven says in this second movement is essentially the same. No one could have failed to notice the profound sigh which the wind instruments so admirably rendered last night at the beginning and again at the close of this movement. In thus inclosing the beating of the human heart between two sighs, the great musician has but echoed Shakspere and the Greek poet. From a sigh to a sigh —that is the musical exclamation of Beethoven when confronting the awful physical facts of birth and death.

The third movement of the symphony changed the theme to the wild, lonesome, and secret powers of Nature. Some weeks ago a suggestion in regard to this movement was made in a public print, which was so striking and beautiful that it should not be allowed to pass away. It was that this third movement was like the flight of bats and swallows from a ruin.

Every one who heard the movement played last night must remember how perfectly this idea of the rallying forth of birds, and their constant return, from and to a ruin, at twilight or in darkness, was embodied by the flutterings out and in of the wind-tones, which constantly skimmed out, sailed around, and then returned to hide themselves in the crevices of silence.

In the fourth movement, again, we saw the gigantic figure of jovial animality in nature careering about the world of tone in unrestrained jubilation. It was the play of that impulse under which the colts caper in meadows and students yell *burschen* songs over their beer. One could but remember, as the orchestra crashed and thundered through this movement, the words of Mozart when he heard the young Beethoven play : " This youth," he said, "will one day make a noise in the world." The fourth movement of the symphony certainly fulfilled the prediction in both senses.

The " Calm of the Sea " was admirably rendered, both

by orchestra and chorus. It is not necessary here to interpret Beethoven's nature-worship in this remarkable composition, for the words of the song are like stage directions to the mighty sea drama which was enacted in his mind during its composition. Every one could understand the broad, blue, transparent phrases of the calm, and the riotous exultation of bounding wave and favorable breeze, with the jovial *yo-heave* of the sailors in the succeeding strain. The performance of the chorus brought great and deserved applause from the house. The body of tone was certainly glorious.

I have taken these two pieces together because they belong to the nature-loving side of Beethoven's genius. When we came to the other pieces on the programme we find them all flowing out of his other side, the humanly affectionate passions in which he was so mighty. As representing these emotions Mr. Remmertz sang " In Questa Tomba " and " Adelaïde." His rendition of these works was, for the first, exceedingly noble and mournful, and for the last, full of the ecstasy of passionate tenderness. If " Adelaïde " is the most tender love song, " In Questa Tomba " is the most majestic death song in the world. Mr. Remmertz's beautiful voice interpreted those compositions well; and one can say little more than that.

The piano concerto (in G — played by Madame Falk-Auerbach) refers also to the human side òf Beethoven. The second movement particularly impresses all as a great discussion between justice on the one hand and mercy on the other, the stern strings in unison representing the former, and the serene piano tones the latter. Madame Auerbach's conception and execution of this piece is beyond all praise. Her greatness and simplicity seem to be genuine emanations from Beethoven's genius.

The Leonora Overture has been often heard and criticised here, and it is only necessary to say now that it was, as a whole, the best orchestral performance of the evening as to technical merit.

The well-known Hallelujah chorus from the " Mount of Olives " terminated in fine style the most notable concert ever given in Baltimore.

. . . . . .

With last night's concert closed the first Maryland musical festival, at the Academy of Music. An audience larger and, if possible, more brilliant than that of the opening, attended and enthusiastically applauded it to the end. As on Tuesday evening too, it was upon the conjunction of chorus, orchestra, piano, and soli that expectancy mainly rested, and that stood the severest test of merit. The soli in the Choral Fantasy from Beethoven, which united the whole force of the festival, were Misses Baraldi, Kate Benner, Jennie Myers, Chisholm, Seeger, Herman, Gillett, Emma Dressel, and Mrs. Neilson; Messrs. John Schomann, Schmidt, Kaiser, Wahman, Bitter, Steinmuller, and Mr. Brown, of Wilmington, Del. The receipts of the festival, although not yet officially ascertained, will be in the neighborhood of $3,000.

Coming now to the set programme, there is a point of view from which it becomes exceedingly interesting to compare the Gade Symphony (opus 5, C minor), which opened the first part of the programme, with the beautiful " Jewish Trilogy " of Hamerik, which opened the second part, and for this purpose the latter will have to be considered out of its order. It must have forcibly struck every one who heard the Jewish Trilogy last night that from beginning to end it breathes forth the vital spirit of that wonderful race in a veritable orchestral song. That a young composer, the pupil and friend of Gade (that most Norse of modern Norsemen), and saturated from early life with those striking idiosyncrasies which so thoroughly differentiate Norse compositions in general from all others, should thus successfully project himself beyond himself and into the very heart of a culture so complex and unique as that of the Jews, argues a dramatic power which should be welcomed with pride and delight. It was for the purpose of calling special attention to this display of dramatic power in the Trilogy that a comparison of it with the Gade Symphony was invited in the beginning of this article. The latter is, perhaps, the loveliest and most conclusive type of the whole genius of Norse music ever written. The waves of the wild seas, the depths of great forests in which hunters roam and elves dance by night, the passionate love-making of men at once fierce and tender, and, finally, the marches and jubilations of heroes with blonde beards and massive sinews,— in fine, all those representative ideas which pass through our minds at the mention of the Norseman's name, are set forth in this symphony with a clearness and gracious splendor of instrumental effects beyond description. When, therefore, those who heard the Symphony and the Trilogy in such close contact last night remember how captivating are the strongly marked harmonic progressions of the former, and how firmly they must have fixed themselves in the nature of one who comes, as does Mr. Hamerik, from the very home of such music, they will readily perceive that the Trilogy, which differs from the Symphony as widely as a Jew differs from a Dane, is a real exploit of genius.

Madame Auerbach's performance of the piano part in the Choral Fantasy displayed all those qualities which have given her an easy place among the first artists of the world. Without notes, as usual, and with a simplicity of behavior as truly admirable as it is unusual, she sat at the piano, and throughout the whole long part given to that instrument sustained the solo singers, the chorus, and the orchestra with her surprising airy disposal of technical difficulties and her bright precision of attack.

Those who heard Mr. Remmertz's powerful rendition of the air from Handel's " Samson " will not hesitate at sympathizing with the utterance of Moscheles upon his great work : " Handel's ' Samson,' which always strengthens and elevates my soul. The first time I heard it I was in ecstasies of delight ; since then I have heard every rehearsal and performance of this masterpiece, and always found myself refreshed anew." Handel's mother had herself become blind, and he must have known personally that passion of tenderness which cries in the aria, " Whilst I have eyes, he wants no light." This oratorio was brought out, too, after Handel's triumphant re-entry into London, which he had quitted in debt and disfavor. One easily fancies that a certain strain of triumph, born out of these memories, is also to be detected in these broad and manly phrases which Mr. Remmertz rendered with such noble conception.

The last three numbers of the programme were devoted to Richard Wagner. Of the " Siegfried Idyl "— the first of these three — an analysis is not possible in the limited space at command, but there is one view of it so curious as to merit special mention. We have all seen a certain cyclic tendency of modern things to return to old forms. We have seen modern science reverting to and reaffirming the atomic theories of an ancient Greek speculator. We have seen medicine re-confirming itself with the maxims of old Hippocrates, and Hahnemann erecting into a practical system the *similia similibus* of Paracelsus. In the same way one finds Wagner in the "Siegfried Idyl" using, with a freer development, the old form of music known as the Discant. From the thirteenth century to the sixteenth the Discant was the typic form of concerted music. It consisted of several melodies, which were sung inde-pendently by different voices, but which were so con-structed as not to jar with each other save in merely passing discords. Wagner appears to revive this form of polyphonic music in the Idyl — and, indeed, in much of his other orchestral work — and to support it with the wholly modern art of harmony.

This is the explanation of much of the difficulty which most persons feel in perceiving the drift of Wagner's pieces. Probably it will be long before the ears of average audiences will be practised to such keenness that they can detect the multitudinous melodies which arise, sing together, vanish, and re-appear, all through the Idyl. First the violins give out a beautiful tune: presently from another side of the orchestra a different tune strikes in, then another from another side, and so on until every instrument is engaged simultaneously in playing independent tunes. To follow these through their sinuous windings and interweavings is possible only to a practised ear and concentrated attention. An idea of the continual motion of these strange tunes will be

gained by any one who has ever stood near the pool
in Druid Hill Park and watched the fish in the depths
of the water. First one sees the gleam of an upturned
silvery side far down, as one hears some bright momen-
tary phrase in the Idyl; then a subdued flash here and
there below the surface of the water calls our attention
to dimly outlined forms swimming underneath; then
the whole brilliant shoal rises to the top and shines
in the sunlight, as in those glorious *crescendos* and
sudden outbursts when Wagner puts the whole orchestra to bowing and beating for dear life; then the shoal
again sinks, the dark forms of the fish move hither and
thither under the water, and finally all disappear.

In the Scene and Romance from "Tannhäuser," Mr.
Remmertz merited all that praise which becomes monotonous when we have to speak of his performance.

The concert closed with the March and Chorus from
"Tannhäuser," and it is enough praise for this special
performance to say that it was a fitting termination to
the two concerts. The chorus which has gone through
these trying rehearsals deserve every mark of recognition
for its constancy and its musical grasp of the conductor's
ideas. The brilliant outburst of tone in the sharp key
of the Tannhäuser Chorus revealed the capabilities of
the choral members perhaps more clearly than anything
they have sung, and bred the universal wish that the
organization thus begun might become permanent in
the form of a choral association. Taken as a whole,
the concert was probably a more enjoyable one to an
average audience than that of the previous night, and
the heartiness and spontaneity of the applause crowned
with unmistakable approval this first effort towards a
Maryland musical festival.

VI

The Centennial Cantata

[A letter printed in the NEW YORK TRIBUNE, in May 1876: when the premature publication of the Cantata — in advance of its musical presentation — had subjected it to widespread misconception.]

I ASK space in your columns for calling the attention of my brother artists in America to a field of inquiry whose results, though as yet partial, are so curious that I cannot but believe some account of them will be at once of genuine service to American art and of interest to your readers.

Probably there are not five English-speaking persons who have ever given an hour's systematic thought to the following question: What changes have been made in the relations of Poetry to Music by the prodigious modern development of the orchestra?

It is probably known to most even of non-musical readers that the orchestra of to-day compares with the early orchestra much as a railway train with a stage-coach. Many of the old instruments have been vastly improved; new ones have been invented; improved schools of *technique* have brought about that passages which once would have been entrusted only to solo artists are now written without hesitation for the ordinary orchestral player. This extension of orchestral constituents has been accompanied by a corresponding extension of the province of orchestral effects. To the modern musical composer the human voice is simply an orchestral instrument; while on the other hand each orchestral instrument has become a genuine voice with its own peculiar *rôle* of expression. A composer, therefore, of the modern school in setting words to music will no longer, as of old, write a solo for the human voice with an accompaniment for the orchestra; but he will write for the orchestra proper, bringing prominently forward in his harmonization only those voices (whether human or merely instrumental) whose peculiar expressive powers appear to be required in order to interpret the conceptions of the poetic text.

Now, what purely intellectual conceptions (for clearly not all) are capable of such orchestral interpretation. This question is intended to leave wholly untouched the great province of emotional expression, in which this author believes the power of music to be supreme and unlimited. The inquiry, strictly stated, is now: What common ground exists to conventionally significant words and the unconventionally significant tones of the modern orchestra?

Before advancing to state some very unexpected principles which will result from this inquiry, it is here necessary to observe that the attitude of American criticism toward a recent poem of the author's, known as the Centennial Cantata — an attitude varying between the extremes of enthusiastic admiration and brutal abuse — has clearly revealed the circumstance that the fundamental question herein mooted has not even occurred to more than one or two either of those who blamed or those who praised, though it would seem that not only a discussion but some definite solution of that question must necessarily precede anything like an intelligent judgment of the poem.

It is necessary, also, to state one final consideration which makes it the plain duty of this author to begin that discussion in person. Much of this praise has come from the section in which he was born, and there is reason to suspect that it was based often on sectional pride rather than on any genuine recognition of those artistic theories of which his poem is — so far as he now knows — the first embodiment. Any triumph of this sort is cheap because wrongly based, and to an earnest artist is intolerably painful. Here is a situation which leaves me no resource except to make some systematic declaration of the principles underlying this matter, so that whatever praise or blame they deserve may be meted out to them rather than to the wholly immaterial matter of the locality of the author's birth.

I desire, therefore, first to propound three principles which appear to result from that new attitude of poetry toward music brought about by the modern extension of the orchestra; secondly, to verify these *a priori* deductions by facts *a posteriori*, that is to say, by examples of the precise sort of ideas which have been actually selected by the greatest masters of modern music for representation in tone; and thirdly, having thus supported theory by fact, to call attention in the briefest manner to the minute particularity with which these principles are followed out in the poem alluded to.

In any poem offered by a poet to a modern musical composer, the central idea, as well as every important subordinate idea, should be drawn only from that class of intellectual conceptions which is capable of being adequately expressed by orchestral instruments. The possibility of such expression, emerging from the beautiful soul of Gluck, has come down to the modern artist strengthened by occasional holy sanctions from Schubert and Beethoven, by startling confirmations from Berlioz and Liszt and Saint Saëns, and even by occasional recognitions from Meyerbeer (notably in his interpretation of a ghost with the bassoons), and from Rossini (as in the William Tell overture). Finally, the gigantic illustrations of Richard Wagner, while they refer more particularly to the interpretation of ideas by tones with the additional assistance of the stage properties — *i. e.*, the musical drama — have nevertheless widened the province of orchestral effects to such a magnificent horizon that every modern musical composer, whether consciously Wagnerite or not, is necessarily surrounded with a new atmosphere, which compels him to write for the whole orchestra, and not for the human voice as a solo instrument and for the orchestra as a subsidiary one. This principle (*a*) would therefore seem to be self-evident, inasmuch as every part of the text which does not conform to it is manifestly not available for the musical composer, and is so much waste matter *quoad* music.

(*b*) Inasmuch as only general conceptions are capable of such interpretation, a poem for (say) a cantata should consist of one general idea, animating the whole; besides this, it should be composed of subordinate related ideas; each of these subordinate ideas should be the central idea of a separate stanza, or movement; each stanza should be boldly contrasted in sentiment with its neighbor stanzas, in order to permit those broad outlines of tone-color which constitute the only means known to music for differentiating ideas and movements from each other; and, finally, the separate central ideas of these subordinate stanzas, or movements, should not run into each other, but begin and end abruptly.

An attentive consideration of this principle (*b*) will go far toward effecting a complete reversal of the generally-received opinion that a poem for musical representation ought necessarily to be perfectly clear, smooth, and natural. For consider: without now having the space to detail an exhaustive list of such conceptions as can be reproduced in music, it is sufficient to say that those conceptions are necessarily always large, always general, always abruptly outlined when in juxtaposition. An illustration drawn from the art of painting will at once make this plain. The illuminating power of music (if one may so express it) is, when compared with that of the non-musical inflections of the human voice in pronouncing words, about as moonlight when compared with sunlight. Now fancy that a capricious sovereign should order his court-painter to execute a picture which was to be looked at only by moonlight; what would be the artist's procedure? In the first place he would choose a mystical subject: for moonlight, with its vague and dreamy suggestions, would be favorable to its treatment. He would next select gigantic figures, for the same reason; and while these figures would have to be even harshly outlined in order to make them distinct, the painter would permit himself indefinite liberty as to the background and as to the space between separate figures, in order to fill these as far as possible with the same vague and dreamy subtleties appropriate to moonlight.

The poet, called on to write a cantata-text for music,

is precisely in the position of a painter called on to paint a picture for moonlight; and the author desires that this illustration should be kept in mind when he comes to show presently how this parallel course has been followed.

(c) When a poetic text is to be furnished for an orchestra in which the human voices greatly outnumber the instrumental voices, the words of the poem ought to be selected carefully with reference to such quality of tone as they will elicit when sung. For example, when a language consists, as ours, mainly of the two classes of Saxon and Latin derivations, and when the nature of the orchestral effect desired is that of a big, manly, yet restrained jubilation, I think the poem ought to be mainly of Saxon words rather than the smoother-sounding Latin forms of our language. At any rate, I tried this experiment in the poem alluded to; and I shall presently have occasion to refer to the satisfactory result of it.

Having thus announced — let it here be said, with all disclaimer of dogma and with all the timidity which every pioneer should preserve — these meagre outlines of principles, I come to the second part of my task, which is to verify them by inquiring which kind of ideas or poems have been selected by the greatest musical masters of modern times for orchestral representation.

The noblest work of Berlioz immediately occurs, in support of the position that a text for music should present gigantic figures, broadly outlined and even abruptly so sometimes, but giving backgrounds and spaces of vagueness which the artist leaves to the hearer's imagination to fill up; I mean the well-known "Opium Dream of an Artist," where the first movement presents gigantic horrors surrounding the vision of the loved one, the second contrasts this with a ballroom scene, the third this with a pastoral scene, the fourth this with the march of a doomed man to the scaffold, and so on. Passing from Berlioz to Liszt, I instance the latter's nobler translation into music of Lamartine's *Meditation upon Death*.

This immediately suggests the very striking tone-picture which Saint-Saëns has made of a French verse describing a dance of skeletons; indeed, the first line of the verse itself is pure gibberish, being only "Zig, zig, zig."

As a final example the author may mention that a short time ago, the Peabody orchestra, a band of forty-six musicians at Baltimore, directed by Asger Hamerik, was requested by Dr. Hans von Bülow to play for him, as a personal favor, his own composition called *Des Sänger's Fluch* (The Minstrel's Curse), being a tone-translation of Uhland's poem of the same name. Late in an afternoon we accordingly met (the author was a member of that orchestra) in the hall of the Peabody Academy, no one being present besides Dr. von Bülow, Mr. Hamerik, and the orchestra. Dr. von Bülow mounted the stand and conducted his own piece with electric fire, and of course with intelligent comprehension. During this highly advantageous rendition nothing could have been clearer than the justice of the principles which have been herein before announced; for although Uhland's poem of the *Minstrel's Curse* is a connected narrative, yet in the tone-rendering all such parts of the poem as were (what I may call) connective tissue, were simply skipped over and there emerged from the magnificent mass of tones only the large conception of the two minstrels, the King, the Queen, the farewell, the curse, and so on; and these were the points which the director accentuated in his leading of the band, practically leaving all else to his hearers' imaginations.

Without the space to multiply these examples, the author now proceeds to the third and last part of this paper, which is an illustration from the Centennial Cantata itself of the manner in which the foregoing principles were carried out in that poem.

When the author received his very unexpected appointment from the Centennial Commission to write the text for a cantata which was to be interpreted by an orchestra of one hundred and fifty instruments and a chorus of eight hundred voices, it immediately suggested itself to him that the principal matter upon which the citizens of the United States could legitimately felicitate themselves at this time was the fact that after a hundred years of the largest liberty ever enjoyed by mortals they had still a republic unimpaired. The idea, then, of the Triumph of the Republic over the opposing powers of nature and of man immediately suggested itself as logically proper to be the central idea of the poem; and inasmuch as the general idea of triumph over opposition is considered reproducible by well-known orchestral effects, it was made at once the logical and musical Refrain of the work, nature and man shouting several times, "No! thou shalt not be!" and the Land finally exclaiming in triumph, "I was, I am, and I shall be." Thus was satisfied the principle above marked (*a*). In accordance with principle (*b*) the poem was constructed in eight different metred stanzas, each of which was informed by its own sentiment, and was differentiated from its neighbor by making that sentiment such as required strong musical contrasts as compared with the sentiment preceding or following it. For example, the first stanza of ten lines was to be interpreted by sober, firm, and measured progressions of chords, representing a colossal figure in meditation. The next (Mayflower) stanza contrasted this with an *agitato* sea movement, rising gradually to a climax with the shouted Refrain, "No! it shall not be." The next (Jamestown) movement contrasted this with a cold and ghostly tone-color, the author having filled the stanza with long *e* vocables in order to bring out a certain bassoon quality of tone from the human voices on the "thee, thee," "ye," and the like, and having made the stanza itself a gaunt and bony one in metre and form, to type the trials of the early colonists as they rose before the meditative eye of Columbia out of the weltering sea of the Past. The next (Tyranny) stanza contrasted this with a renewed, but different, fury of *agitato* movement, presenting to the musical composer a lot of ideas — religious and political oppression, war, error, terror, rage, crime, a windy night, voices of land and sea, and finally a climacteric shout of the Refrain, "No! thou shalt not be," — all of which were easily reproducible in tone by the resources of the modern orchestra; the next (Huguenot) stanza contrasted this with a rapid and somewhat stealthy movement of alternating hope and fear; the next brought its contrast of the outburst of Triumph in, "I was, I am," etc.; the next offered an entire contrast in the Angel's Song, which I wrote with the understanding that Mr. Whitney of Boston was to sing it; and finally this basso solo was contrasted by the unrestrained outburst of all the voices into the jubilation and welcome of the last stanza.

These separate characterizations were indicated upon the original copy of the form sent the musical composer by marginal notes affixed to each stanza ; and the author cannot think it improper for him to avail himself of this occasion to acknowledge the intelligent comprehension with which Mr. Buck seized these ideas and the dramatic fire with which he embodied them in tone. Finally, to conclude these illustrations drawn from the Cantata —the author desiring to experiment upon the quality of tone given out by choral voices when enunciating Saxon words, as compared with that from smoother Latin derivatives, wrote his poem almost entirely in the former. Disregarding their hardness in reading — the poem was to be sung, not read — he unhesitatingly discarded smooth Latin derivatives for the sake of Saxon ones, being all the more decided in this course by the logical propriety of it. The result was a complete vindication. The manner in which the short, sharp, vigorous Saxon words broke, rather than fell, from the lips of the chorus, and a certain suggestion of big manliness produced by the voices themselves in enunciating these abrupt vocables, will probably never be forgotten by any unprejudiced person who was in hearing of the chorus on the opening day of the International Exhibition.

In closing this paper, the author begs to remind the reader that all herein said of his cantata-text has reference solely to its technical adaptability to musical interpretation, and that when he had thought out the principles herein announced his task had but begun ; for it still remained to evolve out of these materials anything possessing such unity as might entitle it to the name of poem. In point of fact, the course pursued was simply to saturate his mind with these ideas and then wait for the poem to come.

Nor does the author desire it to be considered that he indorses all the claims of modern music so far as they profess to include the genuine reproduction of pure intellectual conceptions by orchestral tones. In the present stage of his thought, without daring to have a decided opinion either way, he simply awaits further evidence. But for the purposes of this cantata-text, inasmuch as it was to be put forth as representative — to the limits of its province — of American art, the author considered that the doctrines of what is unquestionably the predominant school of music ought to be recognized in all their fulness.

Which latter remark enables the author to close his paper by putting the following question:

Since, taking the meanest possible view of his cantata-text, it was at all events a faithful attempt to embody the status of poetry with regard to the most advanced musical thought of the time, made upon carefully evolved laws and with clear artistic purposes, which is more worthy of his countrymen's acceptance, that, or the far other endeavor of certain newspapers to belittle the largest anniversary's celebration of our country by the treatment of one of its constituent features in a manner which evinced not only a profound unconsciousness of principles, even preliminary to the possibility of any right judgment in the matter, but also a more inexcusable disregard for the proprieties of a dignified occasion and for the laws of respectable behavior?

NEW YORK, May 19, 1876.

VII

The Legend of St. Leonor

[A fragment from an unfinished lecture on "The Relations of Poetry and Science."]

THE scientific man is merely the minister of poetry. He is cutting down the Western Woods of Time; presently poetry will come there and make a city and gardens. This is always so. The man of affairs works for the behoof and use of poetry. Scientific facts have never reached their proper function until they merge into new poetic relations established between man and man, between man and God, or between man and Nature.

I think I can show you that this has been precisely recognized by the hard practical sense of the common people in other times. I have called the man of science a pioneer who cuts down the Western Woods of the Universe, in order that presently Poetry may come to that spot and build habitations and pleasances good for man. Now I never think of the man of science without comparing him to one of those wonderful monks of the sixth, seventh, and eighth centuries who came over into the stern forests of Armorica, bearing religion with them, but depending, mark you, on the felling of the forest and the cultivation of the ground as initial steps in the conversion of the people. And hereby hangs the legend which I wish to relate.

Once upon a time St. Leonor, with sixty disciples, came to an inhospitable region at the mouth of the Rance in Armorica, and settled. Their food was of the rudest description, being only what they could obtain from the woods and waters. One day the good Bishop Leonor, while praying, happened to see a small bird carrying a grain of wheat in its beak. He immediately set a monk to watching the bird, with instructions to follow it when it flew away. The monk followed the bird, and was led to a place in the forest where he found several stalks of wheat growing. This was probably the last relic of some ancient Gallo-Roman farm. St. Leonor, on learning the news, was overjoyed. " We must clear the forest and cultivate the ground," he exclaimed, and immediately put the sixty at work. Now the work was hard, and the sixty disciples groaned with tribulation as they toiled and sweated over the stubborn oaks and the briary underbrush. But when they came to plough, the labor seemed beyond all human endurance. I do not know how they ploughed; but it is fair to suspect that they had nothing better than forked branches of the gnarly oaks with sharpened points for ploughs, and as there is no mention of cattle in the legend, the presumption is fair that these good brothers hitched themselves to the plough and pulled. This presumption is strengthened by the circumstance that, in a short time, the sixty rebelled outright. They begged the Bishop to abandon agriculture and go away from that place. " Pater " (naïvely says the Bollandist recounter of the legend), — " Pater," cried the monks, "oramus te ut de loco isto recedas."

But the stout old father would not recede. No; we must get into beneficial relations with this soil. Then the monks assembled together by night, and, having compared opinions, found it the sense of the meeting that they should leave the very next day, even at pain of the abandonment of the Bishop. So, next morning, when they were about to go, behold! a miracle stopped them: twelve magnificent stags marched proudly out of the forest and stood by the ploughs, as if inviting the yoke. The monks seized the opportunity. They harnessed the stags, and these diligently drew the ploughs all that day. When the day's work was done, and the stags were loosed from harness, they retired into the forest. But next morning the faithful wild creatures again made their appearance and submitted their royal necks to the yoke. Five weeks and three days did these animals labor for the brethren.

When the ground was thoroughly prepared, the Bishop pronounced his blessing upon the stags, and they passed quietly back into the recesses of the forest. Then the Bishop sowed his wheat, and that field was the father of a thousand other wheat-fields, and of a thousand other homes, with all the amenities and sweetnesses which are implied in that ravishing word.

Now, here is the point of this legend in this place. Of course, the twelve stags did not appear from the forest and plough; and yet the story is true. The thing which actually happened was that the Bishop Leonor, by his intelligence, foresight, practical wisdom, and faithful perseverance, reclaimed a piece of stubborn and impracticable ground, and made it good, arable soil. (It is also probable that the story was immediately suggested by the re-taming of cattle which the ancient Gallo-Roman people had allowed to run wild. The bishops did this sometimes.) This was a practical enough thing; it is

being done every day ; it was just as prosaic as any com-
mercial transaction.   But, mark you, the people — for
this legend is a pure product of the popular imagination
of Brittany — the people who came after saw how the
prosaic wheat-field of the Bishop had flowered into the
poetical happiness of the rude and wild inhabitants who
began to gather about his wheat patch, and to plant fields
and build homes of their own ; and, seeing that the prose
had actually become thus poetic, the people (who love
to tell things as they really are, and in their deeper relations) the people have related it in terms of poetry.
The bird and the stags are terms of poetry.   But, notice
again, that these are not silly, poetic licenses ; they are
not merely a child's embellishments of a story ; the bird
and the stags are *not* real ; but they *are* true.   For what
do they mean ?   They mean the powers of Nature.
They mean, as here inserted, that if a man go forth, sure
of his mission, fervently loving his fellow-men, working
for their benefit ; if he adhere to his mission through
good and evil report ; if he resist all endeavor to turn him
from it, and faithfully stand to his purpose, — presently
he will succeed ; for the powers of Nature will come
forth out of the recesses of the universe and offer themselves as draught-animals to his plough.   The popular
legend is merely an affirmation in concrete forms of this
principle ; the people, who are all poets, know this truth.
We moderns, indeed, — we whose practical experiences
beggar the wildest dreams of antiquity, — have seen a
wilder (beast) creature than a stag come out of the
woods for a faithful man.   We have seen steam come
and plough the seas for Fulton ; we have seen lightning
come and plough the wastes of space for Franklin and
Morse.

VIII

Nature-Metaphors

METAPHORS come of love rather than of thought. They arise in the heart as vapors; they gather themselves together in the brain as shapes; they then emerge from lip, from pen, from brush, from chisel, from violin, as full works, as creations, as Art.

Love — a term here used to signify the general underlying principle of all emotion, the τὸ ὑποκείμενον of all passion — originates metaphors by reason of its essential duality. Like Novalis' "Pupil," love "can see nothing alone." It exists upon a necessary hypothesis of two parties, one loving and one beloved. As between these two parties, the overwhelming desire of love is always union. Marriage, indeed, is a large term. For all loves, human, divine, friendly, social, political, ethnical, and certain other loves for which we have yet no name, since man has but recently come into the full possession and exercise of them, — all these primarily and immediately demand some sort of union, some sort of marriage, between the two parties.

It is the last-named kind of these loves — the kind for which we have yet no name — that specially concerns us in this writing, for the unions or marriages produced by this kind of love are what I have called nature-metaphors.

I speak of the love of man for physical nature, and of that strange and manifold transfusing of human nature into physical nature which has developed the most interesting phasis of modern culture and which constitutes the most striking characteristic of modern art.

In a certain sense — which will appear in what follows — this humanization of physical nature is not only a striking but also a distinctive characteristic of modern as opposed to ancient art. To transfer actions, thoughts, and feelings to natural objects and phenomena; to represent these as existing and occurring, if not consciously, at least by the will and pleasure of inhabiting divinities; nay, to completely transform these so that they were recognized and alluded to as beings, loving, fighting, working, planning: it is true that even in the ancient times this was a quite common procedure of that old instinct in man which draws him into blind love and reverence for the sun-risings, the star-gatherings, the seas, the storms, the trees, the mountains; and these old metaphors of the first poets reappear to us sometimes in the strangest guises. We find them becoming, after the lapse of years, fair religions which govern the hearts and control the souls of great peoples for long ages. Recent comparative philology, examining the mythologies of Greece, of Persia, of Egypt, of India, of Scandinavia, assures us with much show of truth that these systems which once, while in their primary purity, commanded the loving respect of men, derive their origin in great measure from stocks of metaphorical names applied by the old poets to natural objects and occurrences, especially to the sun and his doings.

But nature-metaphors, after having in the ancient days played so important a part, — of giving a faith to the otherwise untutored and uncontrollable soul of the young world, — continue in far other fashion to exert their fine influences upon men in these later days. Yet even now the nature-metaphor finds among us a recognition which, though universal and unequivocal, is still inexplicit and undefined to such a degree that by a large class of very intelligent critics the reproach of metaphor-mongering has been cast upon poets whose hold on the popular heart is impregnable. Nor is this all. Of the many people whose lives are daily refreshed by those good streams of subjective and domestic poetry which flow so freely of late days, few enjoy the pure and serene delight of metaphors without feeling a certain sense of shame in deriving pleasure from what is explicitly regarded as not the highest in art, or without endeavoring to find underneath the mere beauty some didactic truth or wholesome aphorism to chaperone their young delight, to protect it from light company, and to shed dignity upon it. These persons cannot free themselves from the haunting recollection that the ascendant criticism of the day regards nature-metaphors rather in the light of " fancies," and calls vociferously for something solid to underlie all beautiful expressions of that sort.

This inconsistency between our instinctive taste — which undoubtedly loves nature-metaphors — and our critical education — which undoubtedly is a little afraid of them — leads one to go behind it, and to inquire what after all *is* precisely the nature-metaphor, how does it as a poetic form consist with the modern *modus* of thought, and what is its importance to the interests of modern culture.

It has been before remarked that the metaphor is always a union of two objects. The nature-metaphor is

a union of human nature with physical nature.   Clay
informed with a soul, this is a type of the nature-metaphor.   Man himself precisely answers these conditions.
Man is clay informed with a soul.   It is therefore only a
seeming stretch of language to say that man is the first
metaphor.   In this union of the physical and the spiritual, such as man himself presents, there is a most taking
sweetness, since the parties to it are the two most widely
differing forms in the universe.   Matter is in itself dead.
Traditions prove it to have been so regarded by all nations in all times.   Even the heathen find themselves
under the necessity of inventing deities to preside over
all its movements, over the thunder, over the growing of
the grass, over the moving of the winds and seas, over
the flowing of the rivers.   In all the mythologies these
things go on by virtue of divinities within, never by virtue
of themselves.

Spirit, on the other hand, lives, and by some name or
another is recognized everywhere and at all times as the
converse of matter in this respect.

When, therefore, these two come together and a beautiful One is formed ; when, that is, a nature-metaphor is
made, in which soul gives life to matter and matter gives
Antæan solidity to soul, each complementing the other's
significance, each *meaning* the other in such will-o'-wisp
transfigurations as the mind cannot easily analyse — one
must confess that here is something more than a mere
" frothy fancy," however light may be the apparent
weight of the ideas employed.   One must see that each
metaphor of this kind is noble by divine lineage, since
God has decreed the correlative intersignificance of man
and man's earth : noble by long pedigree, since the
youngest nations of known time found their delight and

their faith in the wildest of metaphors, and since all the highest love-songs, the *Song of Solomon,* the *Gita-Govinda,* the *Æneid,* all, down to our most loving poetry of to-day, are burdened with metaphoric sweetness; and lastly, noble by virtue of innate greatness and goodness and captivating loveliness, for all men respond to metaphor, all hearts open to give it place, and all souls in their inmost confessions acknowledge its power. One must believe that the poet who has uttered a beautiful metaphor is conscious of having beautifully re-created himself *in petto.* Fair Protean Nature, fair Protean Soul, I have married you again, I have given you another honeymoon! — must be the happy cry of the artist.

Essentially, then, the first of the questions proposed is now answered. Our nature-metaphor is a beautiful eternal bridal of spirit and matter, in which the immortality of the former gains the *form* of the latter, and the form of the latter gains the immortality of the former; each being transfused with the other like the souls of true man and wife, and both having given without losing, and acquired without taking away.

How, then, does this so intrinsically noble form of expression consist with the modern mode of thought? And what, first, *is* the modern mode of thought?

This last question cannot be better answered than by observing the difference between the genius of modern language and the genius of ancient language; for these physical forms of thought exhibit a very rigid parallelism with, and indeed mould themselves by, thought itself. To illustrate more moderate differences by an extreme one, let us compare, in only a few prominent particulars, the English tongue with the Greek.

One notices at first view that the English performs the

work — or more than the work — of the Greek with far less cumbersome machinery. In the Greek, for instance, one finds, as regards the nouns, three methods of declension, each with its five forms of inflection, terminating differently in singular, dual, and plural numbers. Three of these forms, the genitive, dative, and accusative, sustain complicated relations to the verbs and the prepositions. The adjectives, in all their degrees, which are themselves of complex form, have also their quintuple inflections, which again vary among *themselves* according to the gender. Still more cumbrous complexities present themselves in the numerous tense-forms, voice-form, and mood-forms of the verbs.

Opposed to this, one finds in English nouns but a single inflection; while English prepositions and verbs are as precise and as plastic as Greek prepositions and verbs aided by manifold changes of termination.

So to the Greek adjective, varied by five cases differing as the adjective is masculine, feminine, or neuter, differing further as the adjective is singular, dual, or plural, and still further as positive, comparative, or superlative, the English adjective opposes its form uninflected as to case, unchanged for gender or number, and varying mostly by simple laws only for degrees of comparison.

In the same way one finds that the English verb (excluding irregular verbs common to both languages) with a few simple changes of form expresses, by the not complex machinery of the auxiliary verbs, all the shades of meaning possible to the Greek verb.

No less is the prosodial machinery of the Greek language embarrassed by intricacies which do not appear in the English. One can scarcely imagine a circumstance, aside from fundamental structural harshness, more unfavorable to melody of poetic expression than those very rules of rigid "quantity" which have been supposed by modern insane Grecians to conduce to music. An English poem written in the metre, or rather the metres, of the *Prometheus Bound*, would be far less rhythmical and far less melodious than many pages selected at random from the prose-writings of English authors who could be named.

When to all these complexities of the Greek tongue one adds the varying position and number of the accents, and the changes in the sound of the same word produced by the occurrence of long or short vowels in the oblique cases, together with the lawless superposition of the accent in the nominative case, one cannot fail to conclude that the English has in a wonderful degree at once simplified the machinery and extended the possible range of language as a working instrument in prose and as a singing instrument in poetry.

Now these characteristic differences between the English and Greek languages will be found to be at bottom the characteristic differences also between modern and ancient thought. The change from ancient to modern modes of thought and language is quite parallel with and is well illustrated by that which has occurred in military tactics and organizations. The heavy infantry of only a few years ago, with its straight lines, its angular movements, and its prescribed slow gait, is gone : in its place we have the light-armed troops who move either in right lines, curved lines, or oblique lines, who walk, trot, run, kneel, lie down, who load and fire at will or command, who separate at five paces and rally by fours or by regiment, as occasion requires.

Ancient thought was strong: modern thought has retained this strength and added to it a wonderful agility. Ancient thought was a huge Genie: modern thought is a Genie or a lightsome Ariel at will.

These then being the peculiarities of modern thought, how does the nature-metaphor fulfil the requirements of this modern intellectual *modus*, which is so simple and so wide-spanning, so domestic and so daring?

Truly, the two seem made for each other. The metaphor by its very constitution demands of the artist the utmost simplicity of construction, and rewards the artist with the widest range of application and significance. For instance, the most meagre description of Napoleon and Washington will have instantly acquired, so far as the poetic impression upon the mind of the reader is concerned, a force and a beauty unattainable by any amount of detail, when the writer finishes it with: "Napoleon was lightning, Washington was sunlight." Here in a simple sextiole of words are bound up the most prominent characteristics of the men, to be unfolded at the reader's leisure. But now the idea of lightning, though so conjoined with the name of the great soldier, is by no means limited to this association; for in the next moment the poet may sing, without fear of confusion, of the lightning in a lady's eye, and so on to eternity.

True, however, as is this consonance of the nature-metaphor with modern intellectual processes, this truth is yet not the gravest one in this connection, and does not lie at the root of the matter. For — if one did not fear to write too much about love lest one (alas, the times!) be suspected of lightness — the question might have been asked, how does the nature-metaphor suit the

tendency of modern *love*, rather than of modern *thought?*
This indeed would have been the appropriate inquiry;
for wherever society locates its love (that is, its want,
its desire), there she sends intellect to work in its service; and if one wish to discover whither the thought of
a time is flying, one must discover first whither the love
(or want, or desire) of the time has flown.

Now, nothing strikes the thoughtful observer of modern literature more quickly or more forcibly than the
great yearning therein displayed for intimate companion-
ship with nature. And this yearning, mark, justifies
itself upon far other authority than that which one finds
in, for example, the Greek nature-seeking. Granted
the instinctive reverence for nature common to both
parties: the Greek believed the stream to be inhabited
by a nymph, and the stream was wonderful to him because of this nymph; but the modern man believes no
such thing. One has appeared who continually cried
love, love, love — love God, love *neighbors;* and these
"neighbors" have come to be not only men-neighbors,
but tree-neighbors, river-neighbors, star-neighbors. The
stream — to carry on the Greek parallel — has acquired
so much individuality independent of any inhabiting
nymph, that men may love it, may be neighbors to it
and neighbored by it, and may live life with it in the
finest harmony.

Here, then, it is seen how nature, which before
depended on mere blind reverence and on imagined
indwelling deities for its hold on man's soul, has now
become so far able to dispense with these as to claim a
genuine love from man on its own individual account.
How infinite is the field so added to the range of man's
love! How beautiful and how numerous the unions of

human emotion and physical phenomena made possible in virtue of this wholly new and sweet relation between humanity and nature !

This way, then, society has now sent its love — towards nature ; and the manifold relation between society and nature, demanding expression, finds it in the nature-metaphor, and revels in this with the finest and completest of satisfactions.

It must be remarked that one finds in the Hindu character a far nearer approach to this modern view of nature than in the Greek and Roman. Let us see by actual experiment how differently the hearts of the Hindu, of the Roman, and of the Englishman framed their nature-metaphors. Hear the poet Jayadeva, in the *Gita-Govinda* : —

The gale that has wantoned around the beautiful clove-plant breathes from the hill of Malaya. . . .

The Tamála, with leaves dark and fragrant, claims a tribute from the Musk, which it vanquishes. . . .

The tender blossom of the Caruna smiles to see the whole world laying sham aside. . . .

The fresh Malica seduces with rich perfume even the hearts of hermits, while the Amra-tree with blooming tresses is embraced by the gay creeper Atimucta. . . .

Another stands meditating on the Lotus of his face. . . .

Whose mantle gleams like a dark-blue cloud illumined with rainbows. . . .

Lips brilliant and soft as a dewy leaf. . . .

Her face, with eyebrows contracting themselves through a just resentment, resembles a fresh Lotus over which two black bees are fluttering. . . .

Her face is like a water-lily veiled in the dew of tears. . . .

Her sighs are flames of fire kindled in a thicket; herself is a timid roe, and love is the tiger who springs on her like Yama, the genius of death. . . .

Her eyes, like blue water-lilies, with broken stalks dropping lucid streams. . . .

Long has she been heated with sandal-wood, moonlight and water-lilies, with which others are cooled. . . .

Many a flower points his extended petals to pierce the bosoms of separated lovers. . . .

The breeze which has kissed thy cheek. . . .

A mind languid as a drooping wing, feeble as a trembling leaf. . . .

O thou who sparklest like lightning! . . .

He is a blue gem on the forehead of the three worlds. . . .

Drowned in a sea of rapturous imaginations. . . .

The moon spread a net of beams over the groves of Vrindavan, and looked like a drop of liquid sandal on the face of the sky, which smiled like a beautiful damsel.

Flowers are indeed the arrows of love, and he plays with them cruelly. . . .

Her face, like the moon, is graced with clouds of dark hair. . . .

She floats on the waves of desire. . . .

He fixes white blossoms on her dark locks, where they gleam like flashes of lightning among the curled clouds. . . .

Her arms graceful as the stalks of the water-lily, and adorned with hands glowing like the petals of that flower. . . .

Whose wanton eyes resemble blue water-lilies, agitated by the breeze. . . .

His azure breast glittered with pearls of unblemished lustre, like the full bed of the cerulean Yamuna interspersed with curls of white foam. . . .

Liquid bliss. . . .

The fire of separation. . . .

These are nearly all the metaphorical expressions in the *Gita-Govinda*.

Hear now the Hindu's opposite, Virgil. One will notice in passing how the multitudinous imagery of the Hindu, devoted to some phase of love, is contrasted with the monotonous figures of the Roman used for the same purpose. These are mostly variations of some idea connected with fire: it is always *urit* ("she burns"), *amore incensus* ("inflamed with love"); this, too, in spite of the fact that Virgil approaches nearer the passion-unfolding poets of later days than most ancient writers.   The following are nearly all the metaphorical expressions in the first two hundred lines of the Fourth Book of the *Æneid*, in which book it might be supposed that the climax of Dido's hot indecision would be revealed in the strongest forms of expression known to the poet.   These strongest forms are almost always nature-metaphors.   The translation is, of course, for such a purpose, literal :

She fosters the wound in her veins, and is consumed with hidden fire.

The following Aurora was lighting the lands with Phœbean lamp, and had removed the humid shadow from the sky.

Tossed [*jactatus*] by the fates [*sc.* as by the waves of the sea].

I recognize the marks of the old flame [of love].

But would that the earth might gape for me to the bottom, would that the omnipotent father might hurl me with lightning to the shades, the pallid shades, of Erebus and to profound night.

O dearer to thy sister than life [*luce*, light] shalt thou alone, sad, through thy whole youth be wasted [*carpêre:* be plucked, as a flower which therefore dies].

With these words she inflamed a soul already burning with love.

Winter and watery Orion grew fierce upon the sea.

Meanwhile the soft flame eats her marrow.

Unhappy Dido burns. . . . . As an arrow-pierced doe among the woods of Crete, whom incautious some pursuing shepherd has shot and ignorantly left wounded, wanders in flight through woods and groves Dictæan.

The obscure moon by turns conceals her light and the setting stars invite sleep.

When to-morrow's sun [Titan] shall have netted the earth with his beams.

Meantime, the Morning, arising, left the ocean.

First Tellus and Juno, the marriage-goddess, give sign: lightnings glittered, and the air conscious of the nuptials, and from the summit of the peak chanted the nymphs.

Inflames his mind with words.

And now the master.   How he makes all nature alive
in *The Tempest!* —

> Blow [addressing the storm] till thou burst thy wind,
if room enough!
> *Boats.* — You do assist the storm.
> *Gon.* — Nay, good, be patient.
> *Boats.* — When the sea is.   Hence!   What care these roarers
for the name of King?
> He'll be hanged yet, though every drop of water swear against
it, and gape at wid'st to glut him.

> The sky, it seems, would pour down stinking pitch,
> But that the sea, mounting to the welkin's cheek,
> Dashes the fire out.

> The very minute bids thee ope thine ear.

>   He was
> The ivy which had hid my princely trunk
> And sucked the verdure out on't.

> I' the dead of darkness.

> To cry to the sea that roared to us: to sigh
> To the winds, whose pity, sighing back again,
> Did us but loving wrong.

> Our sea-sorrow.

> In the veins o' the earth.

> His bold waves.

> It was mine art
> That made gape
> The pine, and let thee out.

> I will rend an oak
> And peg thee in his knotty entrails.

> Wicked dew.

> *Come unto these yellow sands,*
> *And there take hands.*
> *Curtsied when you have, and kissed*
> *(The wild waves whist),*

Foot it featly here and there,
And, sweet sprites, the burden bear.
Hark, hark!

[Burden]　　Bowgh, wowgh,
The watch-dogs bark.
[Burden]　　Bowgh, wowgh.
Hark! hark! I hear
The strain of strutting Chanticlere
Cry Cock-a-doodle-doo.

Most sure, the goddess
On whom these airs attend.

Mine eyes, ne'er since at ebb.

I saw him beat the surges under him
And ride upon their backs: he trod the water
Whose enmity he flung aside:
　　　　　. . . his bold head
'Bove the contentious waves, and oared
Himself with his good arms in lusty stroke
To the shore that o'er his wave-worn basis bow'd,
As stooping to relieve him.

It is foul weather in us all, good sir,
When you are cloudy.

That from Naples
Can have no note unless the sun were post
(The man in the moon's too slow).

'T is fresh morning with me
When you are by at night.

Whom destiny . . .
The never surfeited sea,
Hath cause to belch up.

Exposed unto the sea, which hath requit it,
Him and his innocent child.

For which foul deed
The powers . . . have
Incensed the seas and shores.

The billows spoke and told me of it:
The winds did sing it to me.

Night, kept chained below.

Virgin snow.

Thy banks with peonied and lilied brims,
Which spungy April at thy hest betrims.

Spring come to you at farthest
In the very hand of harvest.

They smote the air
For breathing in their faces; beat the ground
For kissing of their feet.

His tears ran down his beard like winter's drops
From eaves of reeds.

Called forth the mutinous winds,
And 'twixt the green sea and the azure vault
Set roaring war.

And as the morning steals upon the night,
Melting the darkness, so their rising senses
Begin to chase the ignorant fumes that mantle
Their clearer reason.

Though the seas threaten, they are merciful.

These specimens of nature-metaphors exhibit very
clearly the differing relations of the ancient and of the
modern poet to nature. The ancient is rigorously restricted in his use of those rich materials which nature
affords for the expression of beauty and passion. He is not
only restricted in the use, but in the material itself: nature
does not furnish so much to him as to his later brother.
At best, nature comes to him in the person of the deities
and half-deities which inhabit it; these divinities have
each an appointed office and a conventional significance,
and to these pre-appointments and conventionalities he
is limited in his employment of nature for poetic purposes. Thus, when Virgil has brought Dido and Æneas
to the same cave on the mountain-side, with the instinct

of a poet he makes resort to nature for the purpose of strengthening and heightening the climacteric situation. He cites *Tellus*, and *pronuba Juno*, and *ignes* and *conscius Æther*, and the ululating nymphs. But how limited his use of these! What an intense climax of human passion, long fought against, now conquering, brought to reach of its burning satisfaction amid rain-rivers rushing from the mountains (*ruunt amnes de montibus*), cloud with hail intermingled (*commixta grandine nimbus*), and all those fearful accessories of the storm which beat out the outer world and for the time annihilate the whole universe except these two passionate hearts that now come together for the first time! How gloriously might this have been told by a modern poet, to whom nature, instead of being a few rigidly-defined personalities, means all things, and helps him to say all things, according only as his soul has power to grasp and wield what is offered him.

In the Hindu poet one finds nature a little more freed from constraint, yet still limited. The principal parts she plays are mostly drawn either from love or from war, and only the most prominent characteristics of natural objects — such as the foam of the water, the color and shape of the leaf and the flower, and the like — are employed. Here are none of those inexhaustible resources which lie in such *details* of natural appearances as, although less prominent, are yet quickly recalled to the recollection of the most cursory observer of nature. In George Eliot's *Spanish Gypsy*, for instance, the successive gradations of light in a Spanish sunset are made to do noble work; each changing tint, from the glitter of the first glories to the gray twilight, comes thronged with marvellous-sweet images and meanings to which the ancient poet was a stranger. The ancient poet would have dismissed the sunset as a single scene, — a glory which subsided and was not.

And this brings us to the *Tempest* images, in which one sees nature still personal, it is true, but so far from being definitely personified, nature is here one person, or all persons, or any person, or any passionate phase of any person. And herein lies the gist of the matter. Nature is like music. The meanings of the tones are not — as in language — preconcerted among men ; each tone is free to mean all things, depending on its situation ; nay, further, each hearing soul may translate the same tone differently for itself, may bend the music to its own particular need, as the humor strikes. And so with nature. Its objects and its phenomena are at the will and pleasure of the poet, to be informed with whatever spiritual phasis he may choose to perpetuate. No caprice of the poet's but he may find some nature-form to put it in.

And this, of caprice, introduces another peculiarity of the modern nature-metaphor as opposed to the ancient. In regarding these peculiarities, especially as exhibited by our greatest poets, one cannot help being struck with such forms of expression as occur in the song above quoted from *The Tempest.* Ariel is singing to the sprites, while he hovers over Ferdinand's head :

> "Come unto these yellow sands,
> And then take hands.
> Curtsied when you have, and kissed
> (The wild waves whist),
> Foot it featly here and there,
> And, sweet sprites, the burden bear.
>   Hark, hark!"

— and suddenly, by an apparently immeasurable and unaccountable transition of thought, occurs —

> " Bowgh, wowgh,
> The watch-dogs bark,
> Bowgh, wowgh,
> Hark! hark ! I hear
> The strain of strutting Chanticlere
> Cry, Cock-a-doodle-doo."

Now — and this is far from being Shakspere-worship, since many similar instances are adducible out of other writers — surely no delicately-tuned poetic soul but must find in this *bizarre* introduction of watch-dog and chanticlere a rare exquisite pleasure. The secret of this pleasure, however, and the principle upon which the apparently so irrelevant idea of watch-dogs and crowing cocks is thrust into a song of sprites, are not so easy to discover. It is under the impression that these are genuine metaphorical expressions, in which the link between the primary and the conferred significations is referable to intangible and quickly-vanishing trains of thought, that they are cited in this place. For this impression strong grounds are not wanting. Who that has gazed upon a barking dog has not had come over him somewhat of that evanescent out-world sensation which arises when one (for instance) repeats a familiar word many times until it grows unfamiliar and wholly mysterious? Who has not begun to dream of the weird powers of nature that float, rather in suggestion than in person, in the strange eye of the animal? Who has not shivered at the evil secrets which seem to dwell in the red-rimmed eye of the crowing cock, secrets which somehow seem to link themselves on the one hand with that wild moment in which a cock announced to the unseen ears of the thronged night the treachery of Peter, and on the other hand with those fascinating tales which among all nations reveal a suspicion of inner meanings in animal-cries, — such, for instance, as the tale of the female magicians in the Arabian Nights, who learn the language of animals and gather strange news and prophecies from them? This — if indeed my words convey any trace of those ideas which are so intangible that they cannot be directly imparted but only chance-awakened by some happy suggestion — is the *conferred* meaning which, in the song alluded to, gives to the ideas of dog and cock their metaphorical character.

Such instances are not found in the ancient poets. They require a delicacy of organization both in writer and reader not likely to be found in earlier ages than this. In old poets one finds rather strength than delicacy, rather power than beauty. And this is the order of nature. In art, as in all things, Jupiter conquers Saturn, beauty supplants strength; or — a better fable — strength dies and is born again as beauty.

If we come now, in accordance with the procedure suggested, to inquire lastly what is the importance of the nature-metaphor to the interests of modern culture, we are, it is hoped, already prepared to declare that it is great, almost transcendant. In spite of the cries of distressed theologians who dream that their large cities constitute the world, and who proclaim with much lamentation that the said world is given over to materialism, the open-eyed observer of our era must decide that all those important institutions of society which depend for their well-being on spiritual strength and knowledge and loving sympathy, are now far in advance of the best olden times. Any one who will compare the idea of marriage, for instance, as developed in Plato's *Republic*, with the idea of marriage as developed in Tennyson's *Princess*, will sat-

isfy himself on this point. The age which proceeded
on Plato's idea must have been at bottom a barbarous age,
no matter what products of intellectual culture may have
sprung from it.   The age, on the other hand, in which
Tennyson's idea is so universally diffused that no penny-a-
liner in the country newspapers but turns it daily into intolerable verse, must be a hopeful age, no matter what
vices flaunt in its avenues.   Indeed, the cries of theologians in favor of idealism are based upon a mistaken notion, and are full of a harm which it will be the province
of our nature-metaphors in some measure to counteract.
For idealism, as a sole theory of life, is no better than
materialism, and each is bad if dissociated from the other.
Why shall men sunder the spirit of man from nature,
which God hath joined together? The soul and the
body work, in harmony well, in enmity ill.   The metaphoric "flesh" of Scripture, which is to be mortified, has
not stronger reference to the body than to the soul; for as
many of the sins comprehended under that term are spiritual as are physical, and are so enumerated in the Bible.

This harmonious union of soul and body, of spirit and
nature, of essence and form, is promoted by the nature-
metaphor, which reveals with wonderful force how these
two, united from of old, still have new points of sweet
and thrilling contact, and still adorn and complement
each other.   Spirit needs form, and finds it in nature,
which is formal; nature needs life, and finds it in spirit,
which is life-giving.   Never be these two sundered ! Forever may the nature-metaphor stand a mild priest, and
marry them, and marry them, and marry them again, and
loose them to the free air as mated doves that nestle and
build and bring forth mildnesses and meeknesses and
Christ-loves in men's hearts !

IX

A Forgotten English Poet

IT is not only from our environment in space that our thoughts and tastes take on that illogical bent called provincialism. There is a parallel process whereby our minds become unreasonably prejudiced against things which are foreign, not to our country, but to our era, and from which we estimate our distance in years rather than in miles. Every wise traveller knows how, upon reaching a new country, he is compelled to make a thorough readjustment of himself in order to arrive at sound conclusions with regard to many matters which are apt to seem outrageous simply because they are unfamiliar. In the same way he who journeys back through time to read a poem written long ago, must make quite sure that he seems no more grotesque to the poem than the poem seems to him. There is a provincialism of the period as well as of the parish; and it is interesting to observe that those who have thoroughly emancipated themselves from the latter are often found to betray unmistakable symptoms of the former. It is curious to note how different is the influence which the civilization of steam has exerted upon the provincialism of the parish from the influence which it has excited on the provincialism of the period. It may be said of the civilized world in general that the " outlandish " is a much less potent

factor in opinion since we have learned to be shy of pronouncing all things absolutely grotesque which are only
relatively unfamiliar.   But this very enlargement from
the restraint of the parish boundary which has come to
us along with an increased facility of travel has plumped
us into the middle of the new with such suddenness that
we seem immeasurably removed from the pre-locomotive
past.   Thus, while we have ceased to find amusement or
offence in that which is foreign, many of us are still in the
bonds of a very rigid provincialism as to that which is
old.   Steam has carried us nearer to our brethren, but
farther from our ancestors.

The necessity of struggling against this state of mind,
and of resolutely chasing from our door that stupid Cer-
berus of prepossession which scares so many pleasures
away from narrow souls, is particularly strong when the
reader of to-day is first appealed to by the English sonnet of the sixteenth century.   The sonnet itself, at the
outset, simply as a form of verse, comes at a disadvantage : it seems too rigidly specialized to a mind which
rejoices in a general sense of possession of the whole
universe and is constitutionally averse to precise patterns
and methods.   Further, as to the substance of these old
English sonnets, most readers have a vague preconcep-
tion that they are a sort of thing really hardly worth the
attention of an earnest person, a mass of strained device
and a string of toys, altogether too idle for this realistic
generation.   It cannot be denied that such a precon-
ception legitimately arises from the perusal of many
of the current slim octavo manuals of English literature
which so many of us dutifully study at our schools, and
thereafter pass through life with a certain comfortable
sense of being well acquainted with the movement of the

English mind since Cædmon.   The work of the English
sonnet-makers of the sixteenth century — a work which
is the glory of our tongue and the endless delight of
those who really know it — is too often perfunctorily
dismissed in these ill-assorted collections and imperfect
treatises as little more than a bundle of conceits, or at
best as a kind of formal old garden of ideas clipped into
shapes of impossible griffins and absurd lovers.

"Conceits," of course, abound; but they must be
handled very carefully.   All poetry is made up of "conceits," in the good sense of the phrase; and the bound-
ary-line between the good sense and the bad sense must
be pushed energetically and liberally outward by the
reader in bringing the artistic work of a period three
hundred years past into a fair relation with our own
time.   What would be intolerably fantastic now was not
so then, and will not be so to him who largely makes his
now a *then*, in order to get at the heart of all this beauty.
Shakspere in trunk hose and slashed doublet would
cut a very preposterous figure sauntering down Broadway
these frosty mornings, yet not more so than one of our
merchants in surtout and overshoes walking soberly along
the Fleet in the days of Elizabeth.

It behoves us to remember and to appreciate that
these sonnet-makers belong to, and many of them are
important characters in, a time of superlatively energetic
and daring men; a time of good honest flesh and of
very red blood; a time that ventured forth over the unknown seas, dared the cannibal, searched the four corners
of the earth, colonized, conquered, thought profoundly,
fought gallantly, and in many ways furnished the world
with strong fibre.   These were not the men to create a
dandy time nor to pet a dandy poetry.   Sonnets which

pleased Raleigh and Essex, Burleigh and Bacon, cannot be despised as a trifling collection of "conceits."

The sonnets may be clipped shrubs and of grotesque shapes, if so please the provincialism of the nineteenth century; but would you only stay a minute you will hear a bird in every bush.

No figure could better describe that particular sonneteer whom the present paper will occupy itself with bringing before the reader. Bartholomew Griffin is, in fact, only a name which we connect with a certain sweet song that comes to us, like that of a hidden bird, out of the very thickest clump of obscurity. A single copy of his original work exists in the Bodleian Library. The title-page is inscribed to

" FIDESSA, MORE
CHASTE THEN
KINDE
··
————
··
By B. GRIFFIN, GENT.
Printed by the
widdow Orwin for
Matthew Lownes
1596."

and the dedication

" To the Most Kinde and Vertuous gentleman, Mr. William Essex of Lamebourne in the countie of Barke Esquire "— consists of a few modest and simple sentences, deprecating its liberty, and finally saying:

" Daign (Sweete Sir) to pardon the matter, judge favorably of the manner, and accept both: so shall I ever rest yours in all dewtifull affection.

" Yours ever,   B. GRIFFIN."

Several years ago, Dr. Phillip Bliss — a man held in loving remembrance by all students of English poetry — laid the world under obligation by printing a hundred copies of this Bodleian volume; and recently the Rev. A. J. Grosart has given forth an edition of fifty copies, to subscribers only, in which some errors of the former edition are corrected and several critical notes are added. But in spite of many assiduous inquiries set on foot by Bliss and Grosart, absolutely nothing can be learned of our poet's personal history. Who he was, and who Fidessa was, except that the latter is referred to in one of the sonnets as

"Sweet modell of thy far-renownéd Sire,"

is all blank. From an old local chronicle there does emerge the meagre circumstance that on the 3d of April, 1582, a certain Bartholomew Griffin obtained a license from John, Bishop of Worcester, to eat meat in Lent; but this cannot be considered satisfactory to the loving searcher, even if we had any assurance that the luxury of this dispensation was enjoyed by our sonneteer. After all this research, therefore, it must be acknowledged that the one hundred and fifty-one copies just specified, each containing its sixty-two sonnets to Fidessa, constitute at present the entire acquaintance existing between the world and Bartholomew Griffin.

Yet if it be indeed worth while to be remembered in one's personal history by future generations, a different fate from that which has befallen him was deserved by young Griffin — since young he evidently was when he wrote. For in him there certainly were many qualities precious even when single, much more so in combination, and which abundantly entitle his pathetic praises

of Fidessa to take their place in our regard beside the
Amoretti of Spenser, the *Ideas* of Drayton, the Sonnets
of Daniel to Delia, of Sidney to Stella, of William Drummond to his short-lived lady, of Raleigh and of Con-
stable, not to speak of Nicholas Breton, the Vauxs, the
Fletchers, Warner, Peele, Greene, Watson, Lodge, Barn-
field, Nicholson, and that ilk, all of whom may be found
duly named, at least, in many of the current histories of
English literature which yet omit all mention of Griffin.

It is now proper to give the reader some taste of the
qualities thus generally referred to.   In the first place, no
unbiassed reader can fail to be struck, at first view of
Griffin's handiwork, by the remarkable ease with which
our English idioms run into the mould of the sonnet.[1]
A very general but also very vague impression is abroad
that our language is somehow incompatible with the sonnet, which is regarded as at best a form of poetry
imported and alien, a sort of *tour de force* or exercise of
technical skill.   Such an impression is certainly a naïve
proof of our singular lack of acquaintance, at first hand,
with the work of our poets.   Every one is familiar with
the process by which, when we hear day after day the
name of some one whom we have never seen, we uncon-
sciously construct a physiognomy and general shape in
our minds with which we associate the name ; and every
one knows how it always happens that when the individual thus bodied forth by our fancy comes to be actually
beheld, the first exclamation is, How different you are
from what I had pictured !   It is much in this way that

---

[1] The " English " sonnet — as distinguished from the stricter
form now generally called the Italian, or Legitimate, sonnet — is
here meant; though the remark may be sustained as to both forms
without difficulty.

many of us believe ourselves to be familiar with English literature, because our manuals have made us familiar with certain well-known names. But if, at any time, good fortune leads us actually to read the works of these writers, we are at once amazed at the completeness of our previous ignorance and enchanted by the depth of our new delight. To our astonishment, we may then discover that the sonnet, instead of being a verbal toy, is the very primitive art-form of the modern Englishman; and if we pursue the subject we presently know that, for the last three hundred years, whenever an English poet has had any peculiarly holy, private, and personal emotion to give forth in the poetic way, he has usually chosen the sonnet form for this purpose. After Cædmon wrote Saxon English, and Chaucer, Norman English, when we come to Wyat and Surrey and the stricter Elizabethans, we see modern English poetry springing into being in the form of the sonnet. It is of no great moment that the form had existed before in Italy. The notion that sonnets are foreign and merely *dilettante* forms of English poetry is a mere argument of the neglect with which many of the most artistic users of our tongue have been treated. We can understand and forgive Ben Jonson, when he declared in his big, frank, blundering way to William Drummond that the sonnet was a Procrustean bed for ideas. Jonson spoke from small experience, not then being able to look — as we can — from the vanishing standpoint which commands these last wonderful three hundred years. Had he even fully known the very man to whom he was talking, he could not have said what he did. Some of Drummond's sonnets are — one *must* use the word — simply adorable; and if this sounds extravagant there are " Be as thou wast, my Lute," and

" Dear Quirister who from these shadows sends," and twenty more, to speak for themselves in such wise as no man may gainsay.   We can only forgive Jonson because he knew them not ; but the ignorance, which was a good plea in his mouth, will not avail in face of the sweet irresistible multitude of English sonnets which have been printed since 1590.   What, for example — before proceeding to specify other qualities peculiar to Griffin's work — could be more simple, more direct, more like thoughts uttering themselves without the aid of culture and without the sense of criticism, than the following sonnet to Fidessa?   The poor young lover, fearful of being consumed in an unrewarded passion, speaks his fear with as little circumlocution as a child asking for water or a ploughman calling to his horse.   In every word, collocation, turn of phrase, sentence, and idiom, the English ear will recognize its own ; it is so straightforward as to form a communication, unobjectionable from the scriptural point of view, being but *yea, yea,* and *nay, nay,* yet it is, though by no means Griffin's best, very good music, and makes one think of a blue-eyed child singing about death : —

> " The sillie bird that hasts unto the net
>   And flutters to and fro till she be taken
> Doth looke some foode or succour there to get,
>   But looseth life, so much is she mistaken ;
> The foolish flie that flieth to the flame
>   With ceaseless hovering, and with restless flight,
> Is burnèd straight to ashes in the same
>   And finds her death where was her most delight;
> The proud aspiring boye that needs would prie
>   Into the secrets of the highest seate
> And some conceite to gain contente thereby,
>   Or else his follie sure was wondrous great,
> There did through follie perish all and die,
> And (though I know it) even so doe I."

No experienced craftsman in words will fail to perceive that the limpid transparency of these sentences is not a happy accident, but an achievement of deliberate art; for it is supported by too many other beauties which would also have to be considered results of accident, namely, by the exquisite variations in the sequences of vowel sounds, the perfect anastomosis of terminal letter with initial letter, the light and delicate use of alliteration, not only to mottle the prevalent rhythm, but to intensify a logical antithesis, and other technical particulars.

Again, in Griffin's sonnets, the beginning has always an eye to the end. Each intermediate circumstance, too, has a convergent direction by which, at last, all meet, substantially, in a keen and effective point, like the incidents which form the plot of every well-conducted story or drama. Indeed, every good sonnet *is* a drama; and the critical reader need desire no more perfect test for the hidden art of a sonnet than the completeness with which it answers to the requirements of dramatic unity. True, the whole sonnet is but a short soliloquy; nevertheless it must have its due beginning, its convergent plot, and its crisis in the last lines. In the following sonnet, for instance, the general dramatic type is artfully varied by keeping in suspense the nature of the crisis through a number of incidental particulars bearing on it only in the one point of time :

"So soone as peeping Lucifer, Aurora's starre,[1]
    The skie with golden percings doth spangle,

[1] It is difficult to tell whether the redundancy of syllables in this line is an oversight, or intended to be made up by such a rapid utterance of the word "Lucifer" as to give all three of its syllables the value of one short in the iambus with "Au." It is most probably the oversight of an evidently young writer.

So soone as Phœbus gives us light from farre,
    So soone as fowler doth the bird untangle,
Soone as the watchfull birde (clocke of the morne)
    Gives intimation of the dayes appearing,
Soone as the jollie Hunter windes his horne,
    His speech and voyce with customs Eccho clearing,
Soone as the hungrie Lion seekes his praie,
    In solitary range of pathles mountaines,
Soone as the passenger sets on his waie,
    So soone as beastes resort unto the fountaines ;
So soone mine eyes their office are discharging,
And I my griefes with greater griefes inlarging."

Or, note the same suspension carried on through thirteen lines, with the quaint intensification of pathetic hopelessness wrought by the " and I not be," of the thirteenth, to the last line, which, by a perfect feeling for art, is made, together with the thirteenth, a foot shorter than the others.

" When never-speaking silence proves a wonder,
    When ever-flying fame at home remaineth,
When all-concealing night keepes darknes under,
    When men-devouring wrong true glorie gaineth,
When soule-tormenting griefe agrees with joy,
    When Lucifer forerunneth baleful night,
When Venus doth forsake her little boye,
    When her untoward boye attaineth sight,
When Sysiphus doth cease to roule his stone,
    When Othes shaketh off his heavie chaines,
When Beautie Queene of pleasure is alone,
    When Love and Vertue quiet peace disdaines,
When these shall be, and I not be,
Then will Fidessa pitie me."

Again, besides this faculty of rounding the sonnet into a dramatic whole, Griffin has a certain bright vivacity which is constantly presenting the reader with charming surprises by suddenly changing the statuesque *dramatis personæ* of a demure tableau into actual and active people. For example, in this sonnet on Sleep — to which the reader's attention is asked on other accounts which will be specified presently — the sudden and vivid introduction of the figures of Fidessa and of Sleep, in active underplay, cuts delightfully in upon the drowsy sonnet, and gives real character to the last line, which is as artless as the earnest quest of the child asking its mother when will Santa Claus come again.

> " Care-charmer sleepe, Sweete ease in restless miserie,[1]
>   The captive's libertie and his freedome's song ;
> Balm of the bruised heart, man's chief felicitie ;
>   Brother of quiet death, when life is too, too long ;
> A Comedie it is, and now an Historie.
>   What is not sleepe unto the feeble minde ?
> It easeth him that toyles and him that 's sorrie ;
>   It makes the deafe to hear, to see the blinde.
> Ungentle sleepe, thou helpest all but me,
>   For when I sleepe my soule is vexèd most.
> It is Fidessa that doth master thee ;
>   If she approach (alas) thy power is lost.
> But here she is : see how he runnnes amaine ;
> I fear at night he will not come againe."

The treatment of the same subject by several authors always affords an interesting method of bringing their individual characteristics into clear relief. This is particularly the case when they have not only treated the same subject, but treated it in the same special form. It so happens that three of Griffin's contemporaries — Daniel, Drummond, and Sir Philip Sidney — also wrote

---

[1] It is impossible not to believe that this line, and the three immediately succeeding the next were purposely made Alexandrines for the sake of length and drowsiness ; as the two last lines of the sonnet just previously quoted were shortened in order to gain a certain abrupt strength and point.

sonnets on sleep, and it will therefore help the reader toward a distinct idea of our poet's mental personality to repeat here the sonnets of these three for the sake of comparison.

Consider first Sir Philip Sidney's, which, take it for all in all, is much the best specimen of his poetic handiwork now in existence. Note — and truly who that has ever spent a sleepless night can fail to note ? — the keeping and harmonious collocation of the smooth pillows, the sweetest bed, the chamber deaf to noise and blind to light, the rosy garland, and the weary head. Then the turn of thought in which he attempts to bribe Sleep, other inducements failing, by promising him, if he will come, to show him the best picture of Stella that ever was taken, to wit, the picture graven in his own lover's heart — with the necessarily inferred compliment that no god can hold out against that heavenly prospect — is altogether cunning and graceful. In these respects, and in the pith and point of the introductory items, it is finer than Griffin's ; while the latter, on the other hand, greatly excels in musical flow and in dramatic vivacity.

> " Come sleep, O sleep, the certain knot of peace,
>   The baiting-place of wit, the balm of woe,
> The poor man's wealth, the prisoner's release,
>   The indifferent judge between the high and low,
> With shield of proof shield me from out the prease [1]
>   Of those fierce darts Despair at me doth throw :
> Oh make in me those civil wars to cease :
>   I will good tribute pay, if thou do so.
> Take thou of me smooth pillows, sweetest bed,
>   A chamber deaf to noise and blind to light,
> A rosy garland and a weary head :
>   And if these things, as being thine by right,
> Move not thy heavy grace, thou shalt in me
> Livelier than elsewhere Stella's image see."

[1] *i. e.,* press, throng.

Sidney appears to have written under the disadvantage of a notable lack of the musical sense. Many of his sonnets, filled with exquisite conceptions, nevertheless come as gratingly upon the ear — to use a favorite simile among musicians — as broken crockery falling downstairs. Thus, as was said, his sonnet is inferior to Griffin's in all that makes music. But compare the two with the following, also on Sleep, by Samuel Daniel. In a certain tender swing of movement, attained by great art in the selection of words presenting sounds upon which the tongue and ear can linger, and which at the same time suavely melt into each other with the true liquid flow of genuine poetic sequences, Daniel must be esteemed the greatest English artist. While the following sonnet does not show him at his best in this respect, — not so well, for example, as " Let others sing of Knights and Palladines," which is well-nigh the best music ever made with English words, — it is yet sufficiently beautiful, and serves well to individualize him in the reader's mind, as distinguished from Griffin and Sidney.

> " Care-charmer Sleepe, Sonne of the sable night,
>   Brother to death, in silent darkness born,
> Relieve my languish and restore the light ;
>   With dark forgetting of my care, returne,
> And let the day be time enough to mourne
>   The shipwracke of my ill-adventred youth :
> Let waking eyes suffice to waile their scorn
>   Without the torment of the night's untruth.
> Cease dreames, the Images of day desires
>   To modell forth the famous of to-morrow :
> Never let rising sunne approve you liers,
>   To add more griefe to aggravate my sorrow.
> Still let me sleepe, imbracing clouds in vaine,
> And never wake to feel the day's disdain."

Here one immediately perceives a cast of thought still beautiful but strikingly different from that of either Sidney or Griffin. The absolute agreement between the conception and its embodiment — between idea and word — is finer than in either of the two latter. No man ever more completely identified spiritual cadences with physical than does Daniel; the soul of his music presides with absolute control over its body, and the result is a poem in which the logical arrangement is the precise analogue of the prosodial, so that to criticise the thought is to scan the verse. The tone of tender pleading which is Daniel's favorite *genre* — and which is so loyal and manly withal that we wonder continually how Delia could have held out so long against it — forms a well-marked characteristic for his sonnets as opposed to the more strongly-colored and more vigorous scenes of Griffin.

The epithet " care-charmer," with which both Griffin and Daniel begin their sonnets, is probably not a plagiarism; and the same may be said of the other similar thoughts which occur in this quartet of poems, all treating of the same subject. There is nothing suspicious in such likenesses; the thought is natural, and suggests itself too readily to appear to be stolen. Plagiarism was not much thought of in those simpler days. The frequent occurrence of the same ideas and the same expressions in poets of the period is evidence of nothing else than the free use of materials regarded on all sides as common stock. Shakspere takes a play bodily, without hesitation, and uses its plot for a new drama. Ben Jonson paraphrases " Drink to me only with thine eyes," from the Greek. Wyat, and the anonymous writers in the early collections freely appropriate from the Italian.

Nay, long before them, Chaucer had made translations upon all sides, and had never dreamed of crime in stamping his name upon the wares which he had thus fused and moulded over again. That men are more scrupulous in these days may be a sign of the general clarification of conscience. It is, at least, a development of men's conceptions of truthfulness which has been in great part occasioned by the growing spirit of exactness in all things which increases with each new generation.

It is not so much that the literary men of our earlier period borrowed from each other, as that they were not so careful either to acknowledge obligations or to eliminate real or apparent foreign matter from their work. This the modern writer is certainly more solicitous in doing than has ever been the case before; it does not, however, prove that he is honest and the Elizabethan a thief, but only that the general conception of honesty has advanced in point of definiteness and of delicacy.

Upon these considerations, as was said, the charges of plagiarism, as against men like Daniel and his fellows, are merely fitted to waste the time of pottering antiquarians in whom all sense of pure beauty has long ago decayed, only to be replaced by a heartless desire to find what some one else has not found, without reference to any intrinsic value in the fact discovered.

Without therefore lingering to ascertain whether Griffin was debtor to Daniel in the item of this epithet "care-charmer," or whether any of these poets borrowed from the other the notion of Sleep as the brother of Death — a common legacy indeed out of the classic times — let us now compare with the three sonnets already given a fourth one on Sleep by William Drummond, of

Hawthornden. The different treatment is readily observed. The whole tone here is grayer and soberer;
and in the previous three there is nothing like

" . . . With that face
To inward light which thou art wont to show "

of the ninth and tenth lines, which contains a wonderful
and subtle summing up of the strange introversion by
which in dreams our senses change their whole direction
of activity, making themselves dead to that world which
lies without the body, and alive to that which is within
it; while the terminal line rises to a point of profound
sublimity.

" Sleep, Silence' Child, sweet father of soft rest,
    Prince whose approach peace to all mortals brings,
    Indifferent host to shepherds and to kings,
    Sole comforter of minds which are opprest;
    Lo, by thy charming-rod all breathing things
    Lie slumbering with forgetfulness possest,
    And yet o'er me to spread thy drowsy wings
    Thou spar'st (alas) who cannot be thy guest.
    Since I am thine, oh come, but with that face
    To inward light which thou art wont to show;
    With fainèd solace ease a true-felt woe ;
    Or if, deaf god, thou do deny that grace,
    Come as thou wilt, and, what thou wilt, bequeath,
    I long to kiss the image of my death."

In contrast with this measured and sombre march, the
liveliness of Griffin's pace becomes very clearly marked,
while at the same time his child-like naïvety and simplicity are in strong contrast with the sedate maturity of
Drummond's thought.

It remains to notice a very engaging characteristic of
Griffin's work, which gives him a special claim to attention. This displays itself in certain of his sonnets,

wherein, mingled with the extravagance of the despairing
lover's cries, is a roguish consciousness of that extravagance plainly to be seen peeping forth at intervals so as
to make a sort of interplay between the real pathos and
the real absurdity of the situation. Sometimes a deli-
cately-shaded variation of this interplay occurs, most
easily perhaps to be described by the comparison of a
bright young girl in amateur tableaux playing Hagar in
the Wilderness, counterfeiting intelligently enough the
desolate woman, save that a certain arch-twinkle in the
eye will break out from an underlying sense of the ridic-
ulous in the whole situation.

For example, take the forty-eighth sonnet, wherein,
apparently, after some quite intolerable cruelty on the
part of coy Fidessa, the lover rushes off and relieves
himself in lines which play hide-and-seek betwixt jest
and earnest until the last two lines are reached, when
suddenly we come upon a sentiment at once Roman in
scope and thoroughly Elizabethan in pith and epigram-
matic keenness. Fancy Fidessa frowning on him;
" Murder ! " he cries :

> " Murder, oh, murder ! I can crie no longer:
>   Murder, oh, murder ! is there none to ayde me ?
> Life feeble is in force, death is much stronger:
>   Then let me dye, that shame may not upbrayde me,
> Nothing is left me now but shame or death.
>   I feare she feareth not foul murther's guilt,
> Nor doe I feare to loose a servile breath ;
>   I know my blood was given to be spilt.
> What is this life but maze of countless strayes,
>   The enemie of true felicitie :
> Fitly compared to dreames, to flowers, to playes?
>   O life, no life to me but miserie !
> Of shame or death, if thou must one,
>   Make choice of death, and both are gone."

Again, he makes a comical kind of refrain for a sonnet out of the word " more " — after a fashion in vogue
at that time for constructing a poem which should turn
upon some verbal pivot — and pours forth a sort of jolly
lamentation as follows :

LX.

> " Oh let me sigh, weepe, waile, and crye no more ;
> Or let me sigh, weepe, waile, cry more and more ;
> Yea, let me sigh, weepe, waile, crie evermore ;
> For she doth pitie my complaints no more
> Than cruell Pagan, or the savadge Moore :
> But still doth add unto my torments more,
> Which grievous are to me by so much more
> As she inflicts them and doth wish them more.
> Oh let thy mercie (mercilesse) be never more !
> So shall sweet death to me be welcome more
> Than is to hungrie beastes the grassie moore.
> Ah, she that to affliction adds yet more
> Becomes more cruell by still adding more,
> Wearie am I to speak of this word (more),
> Yet never wearie she to plaugue me more."

He throws in a preposterous touch, to increase the
damnable iteration of his torments, by tacking on a
supernumerary line and making the sonnet consist of
fifteen instead of the regulation number of fourteen
lines.

He can write, however, in good earnest, and can find
expression for true and profound passion.   Instance the
following, where the observant reader will note also that
there is absolutely no sprinkling of random adjectives,
but that every least word materially increases the weight
of thought and tends straight towards the mark set up in
the last two lines :

XLIX.

" My cruell fortunes clowded with a frowne,
 Lurke in the bosom of eternall night :
My climing thoughts are basely halèd down,
 My best devices prove but after-sight.
Poore outcast of the world's exilèd roome,
 I live in wildernesse of deep lament :
No hope reserv'd me but a hopeless tombe,
 When fruitles life and fruitfull woes are spent.
Shall Phœbus hinder little starres to shine,
 Or loftie Cedar Mushroome leave to grow ?
Sure mightie men at little ones repine,
 The riche is to the poore a common foe.
Fidessa, seing how the world doth goe,
Joyeth with fortune in my overthrow."

In the following sonnet Griffin shows a meditative sympathy with the lower forms of nature which brings to us very delightfully the fresh scent of the sixteenth century. Every one will be reminded, by the first line, of the "Wee timorous cowerin' beastie," which Robert Burns stirred up in the field. The last two lines also exhibit a happy application of the belief that death brings us an opening of the eyes whereby we shall see all things, very different in its quiet resignation from the frantic and half absurd cries of some of the other sonnets.

XXVII.

" Poore worme, poore sillie worme, (alas, poor beast)
 Feare makes thee hide thy head within the ground,
Because of creeping things thou art the least,
 Yet every foot gives thee thy mortall wound.
But I, thy fellow-worme, am in worse state,
 For thou thy Sunne enjoyest, but I want mine :
I live in irksome night : O cruel fate !
 My sunne will never rise, nor ever shine.

Thus blind of light, mine eyes misguide my feete,
    And balefull darknes makes me still afraide :
Men mocke me when I stumble in the streete,
    And wonder how my yong sight so decaied.
Yet doe I joy in this (even when I fall)
That I shall see againe, and then see all."

It will, too, probably be inferred, from the dismal hue
of the sonnets so far given, that Fidessa was a relentless
coquette, a man-devourer without mercy ; wherefore we
feel in honesty bound to redeem this young person's
character from such a stigma, by showing unmistakable hints, occurring here and there, and indicating that
when occasion served she could come out sweetly
enough as a true woman and helpful soul in time of
trouble.   There is a very grateful sonnet, written after
an illness during which, to his heavenly delight, she had
been good enough ! — alas that Fidessas of the nineteenth century eschew so lovely a custom ! — to nurse
him ; and there is other evidence that the "cruelty"
which occasions most of the sonnets is little more than
that uprising of maidenhood which appears to be a sort
of prudential arrangement of nature whereby the weaker
sex instinctively holds off the stronger for a time, at
least long enough for reflecting upon the attractive
slavery before irrevocably submitting to it.   In fact, one
finds in Fidessa not only a young maiden of great
discretion, but detects occasional manifestations of a
prudence which may sometimes have passed into priggishness, if we may be allowed to use so unpoetical a
phrase concerning the heroine of a whole volume of
sonnets.   What is more interesting, the priggishness
seems very modern in type.   For example, the writer
knew some while ago a maiden — and one of the bright-

est of the time in heart and mind — who for some
months was quite seriously possessed with the following
idea: *It was impossible,* she would declare, with a very
pretty fervor and modesty, and with some show of despair, *that she could ever love a man who loved her,
because* forsooth *she knew her own worth to be so small
that she could not admire a man with a soul little enough
to prize it!*

Quite a distinct trace of similar young woman's logic
displays itself in sonnet number XX.   Here we find that
Fidessa has acknowledged herself captive, and sings:

> "Delightful tunes of love, of true love,"

and so on; but presently declares, with much of the
involved self-depreciation of the lady just described,
that

> "Her love is counsaile that I should not love,
> But upon virtues fixe a staièd mind,"

all of which new-fangled doctrine of Fidessa's very
rightly and justly astonishes her downright lover, and
he exclaims:

> "But what? this new-coyn'd love, love doth reprove.
> If this be love of which you make such store,
> Sweet, love me lesse, that you may love me more."

X

The Death of Byrhtnoth

A Study in Anglo-Saxon Poetry

SURELY it is time our popular culture were cited into the presence of the Fathers. That we have forgotten their works is in itself matter of mere impiety which many practical persons would consider themselves entitled to dismiss as a purely sentimental crime; but ignorance of their ways goes to the very root of growth.

I count it a circumstance so wonderful as to merit some preliminary setting forth here, that with regard to the first seven hundred years of our poetry we English-speaking people appear never to have confirmed ourselves unto ourselves. While we often please our vanity with remarking the outcrop of Anglo-Saxon blood in our modern physical achievements, there is certainly little in our present art of words to show a literary lineage running back to the same ancestry. Of course it is always admitted that there *was* an English poetry as old to Chaucer as Chaucer is to us; but it is admitted with a certain inconclusive and amateur vagueness removing it out of the rank of facts which involve grave and important duties. We can neither deny the fact nor the strangeness of it, that the English poetry written between the time of Aldhelm and Cædmon in the seventh century and that of Chaucer in the fourteenth century has never yet taken its place by the hearths and in the hearts of the people whose strongest prayers are couched in its idioms. It is not found in the tatters of use, on the floors of our children's playrooms; there are no illuminated boy's editions of it; it is not on the booksellers' counters at Christmas; it is not studied in our common schools; it is not printed by our publishers; it does not lie even in the dusty corners of our bookcases; nay, the pious English scholar must actually send to Germany for Grein's Bibliothek in order to get a compact reproduction of the body of Old English poetry.

Nor is this due to any artistic insensibility on our part. Perhaps it will sharpen the outlines of our strange attitude toward the works of our own tongue if we contrast it with our reverence for similar works in other tongues, — say the Greek and Latin. In citing some brief details of such a contrast, let it be said by way of abundant caution that nothing is further from the present intention than to make a silly question as between the value of the ancient classic and the English classic. Terms of value do not apply here : once for all, the prodigious thoughts of Greek poetry are simply invaluable, they permeate all our houses like indirect sunlight; we could not read our life without them. In point of fact, our genuine affection for these beautiful foreign works is here adduced because, in establishing our love for great poetry in general, it necessarily also establishes some special cause for our neglect of native works in particular.

For example : we are all ready to smile with a lofty good humor when we find Puttenham in 1589 devoting a grave chapter to prove " that there may be an Arte of our English Poesie as well as there is of the Latine and Greeke; " we remember the crushing domination of the old culture in his time and before it, we wonder complacently at all that icy business of "elegant" Latin verses and "polite" literature, and we feel quite comfortable in thinking how completely we have changed these matters.

Have we? One will go into few moderately appointed houses in this country without finding a Homer in some form or other; but it is probably far within the truth to say that there are not fifty copies of Beowulf in the United States.[1] Or again, every boy, though far less learned than that erudite young person of Macaulay's, can give some account of the death of Hector; but how many boys — or, not to mince matters, how many men — in America could do more than stare if asked to relate the death of Byrhtnoth? Yet Byrhtnoth was a hero of our own England in the tenth century, whose manful fall is recorded in English words that ring on the soul like arrows on armor. Why do we not draw in this poem — and its like — with our mother's milk? Why have we no nursery songs of Beowulf and the Grendel? Why does not the serious education of every English-speaking boy commence, as a matter of course, with the Anglo-Saxon grammar?

These are more serious questions than any one will be prepared to believe who has not followed them out to their logical results.

For the absence of this primal Anglicism from our modern system goes — as was said — to the very root of culture. The eternal and immeasurable significance of that individuality in thought which flows into idiom in speech becomes notably less recognized among us. We

[1] Since this was written (in the winter of 1878–9), two editions of the work have been published here.

do not bring with us out of our childhood the fibre of idiomatic English which our fathers bequeathed to us. A boy's English is diluted before it has become strong enough for him to make up his mind clearly as to the true taste of it. Our literature needs Anglo-Saxon iron; there is no ruddiness in its cheeks, and everywhere a clear lack of the red corpuscles. Current English prose, on both sides of the water, reveals an ideal of prose-writing most like the leaden sky of a November day that overspreads the earth with dreariness, — no rift in its tissue nor fleck in its tint. Upon any soul with the least feeling for color the model "editorial" of the day leaves a profound dejection. The sentences are all of a height, like regulars on parade; and the words are immaculately prim, smug, and clean-shaven. Out of all this regularity comes a certain prudery in our literature. It ought not to be that our sensibilities are shocked with strong individualities of style like Carlyle's or even Ruskin's. One even finds a certain curious reaction of this sensibility upon these men, manful as they are; they grow nervous with the fine sense of a suspicion of charlatanry in using a ruddy-cheeked style when the general world writes sallow-skinned; and hence sometimes too much color in their style, — a blush, as it were. We are guilty of a gross wrong in our behavior toward these authors and their like. A man should have his swing in his writing. That is the main value of it: not to sweep me off my legs with eloquent propagandism, but simply to put me in position where I may place the frank and honest-spoken view of another man alongside my own and so make myself as large as two men, *quoad rem.*

But we lack a primal idiomatic bone and substance; we have not the stalwart Anglicism of style which can tolerate departures, breaks, and innovations; we are as uncomfortable over our robustious Carlyle as an invalid, all nerves, with a great rollicking boy in the room, — we do not know what he may do next.

How wonderful this seems, if we take time to think what a strong, bright, picture-making tongue we had in the beginning of the sixteenth century when the powerful old Anglo-Saxon had fairly conquered all the foreign elements into its own idiom! For it is about with the beginning of that century that we may say we had a fully developed English literary instrument. Chaucer was not, and could not be, the well of English undefiled which Spencer's somewhat forgetful antiquarianism would have him. He was fed with two streams of language which were still essentially distinct in many particulars. It was a long while before the primal English conquered the alien elements into its own idioms, longer, indeed, in Chaucer's world than in Langland's.

Almost every house will furnish the means of placing in sharp contrast the vivacity and robust manfulness of the English language early in the sixteenth century, and the more flaccid tongue which had begun to exist even as early as the eighteenth. Warton's *History of English Poetry*, for example, collates a couple of stanzas from *The Nut-Brown Maid* — which must belong to the end of the fifteenth or the beginning of the sixteenth century — with the corresponding stanzas of a paraphrase made by Prior in 1718. It may not be amiss to make sure by inserting one of these examples here. In the original ballad, the wild lover, testing the girl's affection, cries:

> "Yet take good hede, for ever I drede
> That ye could nat sustayne
> The thornie wayes, the depe valeis,

The snowe, the frost, the rayne,
The colde, the hete; for, dry or wete,
We must lodge on the playne;
And us abofe none other rofe
But a brake bush or twayne;
Which sone sholde greve you, I believe,
And ye wolde gladly than
That I had to the grene wode go
Alone, a banyshed man."

I cannot see how language could well have put it featlier than that; but, two hundred years afterward, this is Prior's idea of the way it should have been said:

" Those limbs, in lawn and softest silk array'd,
From sunbeams guarded and of winds afraid,
Can they bear angry Jove ? Can they resist
The parching dog-star and the bleak northeast ?
When, chill'd by adverse snows and beating rain,
We tread with weary steps the longsome plain ;
When with hard toil we seek our evening food,
Berries and acorns from the neighbouring wood;
And find among the cliffs no other house
But the thin covert of some gather'd boughs ;
Wilt thou not then reluctant send thine eye
Around the dreary waste, and, weeping, try
(Though then, alas ! that trial be too late)
To find thy father's hospitable gate,
And seats where ease and plenty brooding sate ?
Those seats, whence long excluded thou must mourn ;
That gate, for ever barr'd to thy return ;
Wilt thou not then bewail ill-fated love,
And hate a banish'd man, condemn'd in woods to rove ? "

Or, if it be objected that this may be an exaggerated single example which proves little, almost every book-case contains Thomas Johnes's translation of Froissart, in the notes to which occur here and there extracts of parallel passages from Lord Berners's translation, made in the time of Henry VIII. ; and the least comparison of

Berners with Johnes shows how immeasurably more bright, many-colored, and powerful is the speech of the former.

And this brightness, color, and power make for the doctrine of this present writing, because they are simply exuberant manifestations of pure Anglicism put forth in the moment of its triumph. We are all prone to forget the odds against which this triumph was achieved. For four hundred years — that is, in round numbers, from 670 to 1070 — the *Englisc* language was desperately striving to get into literature, against the sacred wishes of Latin; and now, when the Normans come, the tongue of Aldhelm and Cædmon, of Alfred and Ælfric and Cynewulf, must begin and fight again for another four hundred years against French, — fight, too, in such depths of disadvantage as may be gathered from many a story of the relentless Norman efforts to exterminate the native tongue. Witness, for example, Matthew Paris's account of the deposition of the Bishop of Worcester in 1095 by the Normans because he " was a superannuated English idiot who could not speak French ; " or Ralph Higden's complaint, as John Trevisa translates it from the *Polychronicon:* " Children in scole, ayenst the usage and manir of all other nations, beeth compelled for to leve hire owne langage and for to construe hire lessons and hire thinges in French ; and so they haveth sethe Normans came first into Engelond ; " moreover, " Gentilmen children beeth taught to speke Frensche from the tyme that they bith rokked in hire cradle and kumeth speke and play with a child's broche."

Eight hundred years the tough old tongue has been grimly wrestling and writhing, life and death on the issue, now under this enemy, now under that, when Lord Berners and Sir Thomas More begin to speak.

It is therefore with all the sacred sanction of this long conflict that a man can drive home upon our time these following charges : first, that it is doing its best, in most of its purely literary work, to convert the large, manful, and simple idioms of Alfred and Cynewulf into the small, finical, and knowing clevernesses of a smart half-culture, which knows neither whence it came nor whither it is going; and secondly, that as a people we are utterly ignorant of even the names of the products of English genius during the first four hundred of the eight hundred years just mentioned, insomuch that if a fervent English-lover desire to open his heart to some one about *Beowulf,* or *The Battle of Maldon,* or *The Wanderer,* or *Deor's Lament,* or *The Phœnix,* or *The Sea-farer,* or *The Address of the Departed Soul to its Body,* or *Elene,* or the like, he must do it by letter, for there are scarcely anywhere two in a town who have read, or can read, these poems.

In short, our literary language [1] has suffered a dilution much like that which music has undergone at the hands of the weaker devotees since the free use of the semi-tone began. Soon after the chromatic tone has attained its place a wonderful flexibility shows itself in music, the art expands in many directions, the province of harmony becomes indefinitely large ; but this very freedom proves the ruin of the weaker brethren : the facilities of modulation afforded by the minor chords and the diminished sevenths tempt into unmeaning and cloying impertinences of composition, and these have to be relieved, again, by setting over-harsh and crabbed chords in the midst of a too gracious flow of tone.

[1] As distinguished from the modern scientific English, which is certainly an admirable instrument in the hands of Tyndall, of Huxley, and of many more.

Now, as music has reached a point where it must pause, and re-establish the dominancy of the whole tone, fortifying it with whatever new tones may be found possible in developing the scale according to primal — or what we may call musically idiomatic — principles, so must our tongue recur to the robust forms, and from these to the underlying and determining genius, of its Anglo-Saxon[1] period.

In other words, — for what has so far been said has been in defence and explication of the sentence which stands at the beginning of this paper, — culture must be cited into the presence of the Fathers.

In the humblest hope of contributing to that end, I eagerly embrace the opportunity of calling the general reader's attention to the rhythmical movement — and afterward to the spiritual movement — of an Anglo-Saxon poem dating from about A. D. 993, known as *The Death of Byrhtnoth,* or otherwise as *The Battle of Maldon,* which, in the judgment of my ear, sets the grace of loyalty and the grimness of battle to noble music. I think no man could hear this poem read aloud without feeling his heart beat faster and his blood stir.

The rhythm of this poem — let it be observed as the reader goes through the scheme — is strikingly varied in time-distribution from bar to bar. The poem, in fact, counts with perfect confidence upon the sense of rhythm, which is well-nigh universal in our race, often boldly opposing a single syllable in one bar to three or four in the next. I should not call this "bold" except for the timidity of English poetry during the last two

---

[1] A term for which it is now pretty generally agreed to substitute " Old English." I shall use the two interchangeably in this paper.

hundred years, when it has scarcely ever dared to venture out of the round of its strictly defined iambics, forgetting how freely our. folk songs and nursery rhymes employ rhythms and rhythmic breaks, — as "Pease porridge hot," for example, or almost any verse out of Mother Goose, — which, though "complex" from the standpoint of our customary rhythmic limitations, are instantly seized and co-ordinated by children and child-minded nurses.[1]

[Apart from its literary merit, this poem has other features of interest. It is an example, perhaps singular, of an epic contemporary with the events it recites, and probably written by one who had a share in the battle. The poet's point of view never moves from the English side; he does not know what is done or said among the Danes; he knows none of their names, not even that of their leader, though he was the redoubted Anlaf, or Olaf Tryggvason, king of Norway. We may therefore rely on its being a faithful picture of what was done, said, and even thought during this last resolute stand of England against the Wikings.

The incident itself is memorable. In A. D. 979, Æthelred Lack-Counsel (generally called "the Unready") was crowned at Kingston, and the "bloody cloud in the likeness of fire, seen at midnight," which followed that event, may well have seemed to the old chronicler, in the light of later experience, a foretokening of the years to come, when the heavens, night after night, were red with the glare of burning towns and

---

[1] The historical paragraphs following (in brackets) have been supplied by Dr. William Hand Browne, to fill a gap in the original manuscript, where sixteen pages are lacking.

homesteads, and the ground was crimson with the blood of the slaughtered English.   For the Danes had begun their terrible invasions, and met with but little resistance.   In the next year, Leicester, Thanet, and Southampton were plundered, and the inhabitants "mostly slain," says the chronicle; in the next, Padstow in Cornwall was plundered, and Devonshire harried with fire and sword; in the next, London was burnt.   We come at last to the year 991, and we are told: —

"In this year came Anlaf with ninety-three ships to Staines and harried all roundabout that; and then fared thence to Sandwich, and thence on to Ipswich, and overran all that, and so to Maldon [Essex].   And there against them came the ealdorman Byrhtnoth with his army, and fought with them, and they slew the ealdorman and held the battlefield.   And in this year for the first time men counselled that they should rather pay tribute to the Danish men for the mickle terror that they wrought at the sea-coasts.   And the tribute was at first a thousand pounds.   The giver of the counsel was Sigeric the archbishop."

It is plain from this that the fall of Byrhtnoth snapped the sinews of English resistance; and from this time forth we read of nothing but feeble and futile musterings of men, without plan or concert of action, and all to no purpose: half-battles lost because the support did not arrive in time; fleets ordered to help the land force, and coming after all was over; "and ever," says the chronicler, "when they should have been forwarder, then were they later, ain ever the foes waxed more and more."   And the tribute grew heavier and heavier, and there was less to pay it with, and leaders like Ælfric turned traitors in sheer despair, until the doomed king, crowning a life of imbecility by a deed of bloody madness, slaughtered the peaceful colonists of the Danelagh, and Swegen came in a storm of fire and blood, hurling the wretched descendant of Cerdic from the throne, and England bent her neck to the Danish rule. After half a century, two phantoms of a monk and a warrior, Edward and Harold, seemed to wear the Saxon crown; but the monarchy of Alfred received its death-blow at Maldon, not because the East Saxon militia was broken, but because Byrhtnoth fell.

And now who was Byrhtnoth? The chronicler, overmuch given to recording investitures and deaths of bishops and abbots, tells us but little; but from the Book of Ely, an abbey founded by Byrhtnoth himself, we get glimpses of him, probably from the hand of one who had seen him face to face. He was Ealdorman — that is, lord or general — of the East Saxons, and one of the greatest nobles in England. " He was," says the monkish historian, " eloquent of speech, great of stature, exceeding strong, most skilful in war, and of courage that knew no fear. He spent his whole life in defending the liberty of his country, being altogether absorbed in this one desire, and preferring to die rather than to leave one of its injuries unavenged. And all the leaders of the shires put their trust altogether in him."

After telling of several of his victories, the historian comes to his last fight. His force was far inferior to that of the invaders, but he hastened to meet them without waiting for reinforcements, — a piece of rashness like that recorded in the poem, where, from mere excess of haughty courage, he disdains to defend the ford of Panta, and lets the Wikings cross unmolested, a fatal hardihood which cost him the battle and his life.

On his march thither he stopped at Ramsey Abbey, and asked for provisions for his men. The abbot said that it was not possible for him to feed so great a number, but, not to seem churlish, he would receive as his guests the ealdorman himself and seven others. Byrhtnoth rejected the mean offer with scorn : " I cannot fight without them," he said, " and I will not eat without them," and so marched on to Ely, where Abbot Ælfsig bounteously entertained him and his force. " But the ealdorman, thinking that he had been burdensome to the abbey, would not leave it unrewarded ; and on the following morning bestowed upon it six rich manors, and promised nine more, with thirty marks of gold and twenty pounds of silver, on the condition that if he fell in the battle his body should be brought and buried there. To this gift he also added two crosses of gold and two vestments richly adorned with gold and gems, and a pair of curiously wrought gloves. And so, commending himself to the prayers of the brethren, he went forth to meet the enemy.

" When he met them, undeterred by the multitude of foes and the fewness of his own men, he attacked them at once, and for fourteen days fought with them daily. But on the last day, but few of his men being left alive, and perceiving that he was to die, he attacked them with none the less courage, and had almost put them to flight, when the Danes, taking heart from the small numbers of the English, formed their force into a wedge, and threw themselves upon them. Byrhtnoth was slain, fighting valiantly, and the enemy cut off his head and bare it with them to their own country."

Plainly a prince of men, and the true king of England at that day, though he never wavered in his allegiance to

" Æthelred, my prince." And this last day of the " great dim battle " in the east, more worthy the poet's song than that merely fabulous " battle in the west " which the late Laureate celebrated in such ringing verse, — this last agony of the last vigorous struggle to free England from the ferocious invaders, is the subject of the poem.

True, Byrhtnoth is not so musical a name as Arthur, and Leofsunu and Wulfmær sound harsh compared with Lancelot and Percivale ; but the fantastic chivalry of the Round Table and their phantom-like king are not only historically untrue, but merely impossible, — a bright-hued web of the stuff that dreams are made of, — while these gallant men of Essex and their heroic chief verita-bly lived, and fought, and died where they stood, rather than yield one foot of English ground or forsake their fallen leader ; and they were men of our own race, and it may be that their blood flows in our own veins.

But though they have not been thought worthy the dainty music of Victorian verse, they have not lacked a poet — probably a soldier-poet, for his lines fall like sword-strokes on helmets. He has not written for crit-ics, but for East Saxons, East Angles, Northumbrians, who had looked to Byrhtnoth as their shield, and whose kindred had formed that narrowing ring that circled his corpse, " their mood growing more as their might lessened." We have here no wail of lamentation over the fallen leader ; the poet will not let us see his tears ; yet the eye must have been dim that watched him cast loose his " beloved hawk," knowing that she would never again come to his call, and the hand must have trembled that recorded the hero's dying prayer.

Nay, we hardly are shown the poet's personality at all, intense as his feelings must have been : of the fatal

error that lost the battle, he merely says, " the earl, for
his overmood, left too much land to the hostile people ; "
of the flight of Godric he simply remarks that " more
men fled with him than was right, if they had remembered all the kindness he [Byrhtnoth] had shown them ; "
and when Offa keeps his pledge to his chief to live or
die with him, he breaks into no pæan over his fidelity,
but says simply, "he lay, thane-like, by his lord's
side."

Unflinching courage, personal devotion to the chief,
absolute contempt of death, are matters of course in this
warrior-poet's mind, and need no particular eulogy.   Of
these qualities, two yet abide with the race ; but the
third, the passionate love of the thane for his prince, a
love passing the love of woman — so tenderly sung in
The Wanderer — this we are not likely to see again.
It is much to be doubted whether in that " passage of
society from status to contract," so dear to the political
economist, we have gained any equivalent for the loss.
Men are, as yet, still capable of " falling thane-like ; " but
not of saying, " never shall the thanes reproach me that
I would return to my home, now that my prince lieth
hewn down in fight." [1]]

I have translated two hundred lines of the poem, —
which is a fragment of three hundred and twenty-five
lines in all, without the original beginning or end, —
with special reference to two matters.

(1) In the first hundred lines — being the first hundred of the poem as it stands — I have had particularly in view the send and drive of the rhythm ; and
to keep these in the reader's mind I have made the trans-

---

[1] End of Dr. William Hand Browne's manuscript.

lation, so far as the end of that hundred, mostly in dac-
tyls, which continually urge the voice forward to the
next word, with an occasional trochee for breath and
variety.

(2) But in my second hundred lines — being those
consecutively following the first, up to the hundred and
eighty-fifth line of the poem, when I pass to the last sixteen, with an intercalary account in short of the matter
of the intervening hundred and twenty-five — I have
abandoned the metrical purpose, and changed the para-
mount object to that of showing the peculiar idioms of
Anglo-Saxon poetry : the order of words, the vigorous
use of noun and verb, the parallelisms and repetitions
(like those of Hebrew poetry, as in the lines near the
last, " Ælfnod and Wulfmær lay slain ; by the side of
their prince they parted with life "), and the like. I
have thought that the modern reader might contemplate
with special profit the sparing use of those particles —
such as " the," " a " or " an," " his," " their," and others
— which have made the modern tongue so different from
the old, both in its rhythmical working and in its weight
or momentum. The old tongue is notably sterner, and
often stronger, by its ability to say " man," " horse,"
" shield," and not " *the* man," " *a* horse," " *his* shield,"
etc. ; and it is an interesting question, at least, whether
we might not with advantage educate our modern sense
to be less shocked by the omission of these particles
at need. Without here adducing many considerations
which would have to be weighed before any one could
make up his judgment on this point, I have simply called
attention to these particles, where modern usage required
me to supply them in the translation, by inclosing them
in parentheses.

In both the metrical and the unmetrical portions of the translation I have discarded the arrangement into lines as interfering with the objects in view; the poem showing clearly enough, by the plane of its thought, that it *is* a poem, though presented in whatever forms of prose.

The fragment begins with the last two words of some sentence, " brocen wurde " (was broken), and then proceeds as follows.

Bade then (that is, Byrhtnoth bade) each warrior loose him his horse and drive it afar, and fare thus on to the hand-fight, hopeful of heart.

Then straightway the stripling of Offa beheld that the earl would abide no cowardly thing : so there from his hand he let fly his falcon, belovèd, away through the wood and strode to the battle, and man might know that never that youth would fail from the fight when once he fell to his weapon.   Thereat Eadric was minded to stand by his ealdorman fast in the fight ; forth 'gan bear his javelin foe-ward, manful in mood, whilever that he in his hands might hold his buckler and broadsword ; his vaunt he avouched with his deeds, that there he should fight in front of his prince.

Then Byrhtnoth began to array him his warriors, rode and directed, counselled the fighters how they should stand and steadfastly hold to their places, showed them how shields should be gripped full hard with the hand, and bade them to fear not at all.   When fairly his folk were formed he alighted in midst of the liegemen that loved him fondliest ; there full well he wist that his faith-fullest hearth-fighters were.

Then stood forth one from the vikings, strongly called, uttered his words, shouted the sea-rogues' threat to the earl where he stood on the adverse shore: "Me have the scathful seamen sent, and bidden me say that now must thou render rings [1] for thy ransom, and better for you shall it be that ye buy off a battle with tribute than trust the hard-dealing of war. No need that we harm us, if only ye heed this message; firm will we fashion a peace with the gold. If thou that art richest wouldst ransom thy people, pay, for a peace, what the seamen shall deem to be due; we will get us to ship with the gold, and fare off over the flood, and hold you acquit."

Byrhtnoth cried to him, brandished the buckler, shook the slim ash, with words made utterance, wrathful and resolute, gave him his answer: "Hearest thou, sea-rover, that which my folk sayeth? Yes, we will render you tribute . . . in javelins — poisonous point, and old-time blade — good weapons, yet forward you not in the fight. Herald of pirates, be herald once more: bear to thy people a bitterer message, — that here stands dauntless an earl with his warriors, will keep us this country, land of my lord, Prince Æthelred, — folk and field: the heathen shall perish in battle. Too base, methinketh, that ye with your gold should get you to ship all unfoughten with, now that so far ye have come to be in our land: never so soft shall ye slink with your treasure away: us shall persuade both point and blade — grim game of war — ere we pay you for peace."

Bade he then bear forward bucklers, and warriors go, till they all stood ranged on the bank that was east. Now there, for the water, might never a foeman come to the other: there came flowing the flood after ebb-tide,

---

[1] Rings, that is, of gold, — a favorite form of treasure among our Anglo-Saxon ancestors.

mingled the streams : too long it seemed to them, ere that together the spears would come.[1]

. . . .

[There stood they in their strength by Panta's stream, the East-Saxon force and the ship-host : nor might either of them harm the other, save when one fell by an arrow's flight.

The tide outflowed ; the pirates stood yare, many vikings wistful for war.]

Bade them the Shelter-of-Men [2] a war-hardened warrior hold him the bridge, who Wulfstan was hight, bold with his kinsmen, Ceola's son ; he smote with his spear the first man down that stepped over-bold on the bridge. There stood by Wulfstan warriors dauntless, Maccus and Ælfere, proud-souled twain ; they recked not of flight at the ford, but stoutly strove with the foe what while they could wield their weapons. When they [3] encountered and eagerly saw how bitter the bridgewards were, then the hostile guests betook them to cunning : ordered to seize the ascents, and fare through the ford and lead up the line. Now the earl in his over-bold mood gave over-much [4] land to the foe. There, while the warriors whist, fell Byrhthelm's bairn [5] to calling over the waters cold : —

" Now there is room for you, rush to us, warriors to warfare ; God wot, only, which of us twain shall possess this place of the slaughter."

---

[1] A short gap in the manuscript is here supplied by Dr. William Hand Browne.

[2] Byrhtnoth.

[3] The pirates.

[4] Voluntarily drew back and allowed them to gain the hither bank, in order to bring on the fight.

[5] Byrhtnoth.

Waded the war-wolves west over Panta, recked not of water, warrior vikings. There, o'er the wave they bore up their bucklers, the seamen lifted their shields to the land. In wait with his warriors, Byrhtnoth stood; he bade form the war-hedge of bucklers, and hold that ward firm to the foe. The fight was at hand, the glory of battle; the time was come for the falling of men that were doomed.

There was a scream uphoven, ravens hovered, (and) the eagle sharp for carnage; on earth was clamor.

They let from (their) hands (the) file-hard spears, (the) sharp-ground javelins, fly; bows were busy, shield caught spear-point, bitter was the battle-rush, warriors fell, on either hand warriors lay. Wounded was Wulfmær, chose (his) bed of death, Byrhtnoth's kinsman, his sister's son; he with bills was in pieces hewn. (But) there to the vikings was quittance made; heard I that Edward slew one sheerly with his sword, withheld not the swing (of it), that to him at feet fell (the) fated warrior. For that his prince said thanks to him — to his bower-thane — when he had time. So dutiful wrought (the) strong-souled fighters at battle, keenly considered who there might quickliest pierce with (his) weapon; carnage fell on earth. Stood (they) steadfast. Byrhtnoth heartened them, bade that each warrior mind him of battle that would fight out glory upon (the) Danes.

Waded then (forward) (a) warrior tough, upheaved (his) weapon, shield at ward, and strode at the earl; as resolute went the earl to the carl:[1] each of them to the other meant mischief. Sent then the sea-warrior (a) Southern spear that the lord of warriors[2] was wounded;

[1] The churl, — common person, or yeoman.
[2] Byrhtnoth.

he wrought then with his shield that the shaft burst in pieces and that spear broke that it sprang again. Angry-souled was the warrior; he with (his) spear stung the proud viking that gave him his wound. Prudent was the chieftain; he let his spear wade through the viking's neck; (his) hand guided it that it reached to the life of his dangerous foe. Then he suddenly shot another that his corselet burst; he was wounded in the breast through the ring-mail; at his heart stood the fatal spear-point. The earl was all the blither; laughed the valorous man, said thanks to the Creator for the day's-work that the Lord gave him.

Then some (one) of the warriors let fly from his hand a dart that it forthright passed through the noble thane [1] of Æthelred. Then stood him beside an unwaxen war-rior,[2] a boy in fight; he full boldly plucked from the prince the bloody javelin (Wulfstan's son, Wulfmær the young); let the sharp (steel) fare back again; the spear-point pierced that he lay on the earth who before had grievously wounded the prince. Ran there a cun-ning warrior to the earl; he wished to plunder the prince of (his) treasures, armor and rings and adornèd sword. Then Byrhtnoth drew from sheath his broad and brown-edged sword and smote on the (warrior's) corse-let: (but) too soon one of the pirates prevented him; he maimed the arm of the earl; fell to the ground the yellow-hilted sword; he might not hold the hard blade, not wield (a) weapon. There nevertheless some words spoke the hoary chieftain, heartened his warriors, bade the good comrades go forward; now no longer could he stand firm on (his) feet; he looked towards heaven : —

[1] Byrhtnoth.
[2] That is, a youthful warrior.

" I thank Thee, Ruler of nations, for all the delights that were mine in the world ; now do I own, mild Creator, most need that Thou give good to my ghost, whereby my soul may depart unto Thee in Thy kingdom. Prince of (the) angels, may fare forth in peace ; I am suppliant to Thee that the hell-foes may humble it not."

Then the heathen men hewed him and both the chieftains that stood by him ; Ælfnod and Wulfmær lay slain ; by the side of their prince they parted with life.

And hereupon — as the next hundred and twenty-five lines go on to relate — there was like to be a most sorrowful panic on the English side. Several cowards fled : notably one Godric, who leaped upon Byrhtnoth's own horse, and so cast many into dead despair with the belief that they saw — what no man had ever dreamed he saw before — Byrthnoth in flight. But presently Ælfwine and Offa and other high-souled thanes heartened each other and led up their people, yet to no avail ; and so thane after thane and man after man fell for the love of Byrhtnoth and of manhood, and no more would flee. Finally (at line 309, after which there are but sixteen lines more of the Fragment) we find Byrhtwold, an old warrior, sturdily bearing up his shield and waving his ash and exhorting the few that remained, beautifully crying : —

" Soul be the scornfuller, heart be the bolder, front be the firmer, the fewer we grow ! Here, all hewn, lieth our chieftain, a good man on the ground ; for ever let (one) mourn who now from this war-play thinketh to wend. I am old of life ; hence will I not ; for now by the side of my lord, by the so-beloved man, I am minded to lie ! "

Then Æthelgar's son (Godric) the warriors all to combat urged; oft he (a) javelin let hurl — a bale-spear — upon the vikings; so he among the folk went foremost, hewed and felled, till that he sank in fight; he was not that Godric who fled from the battle.

XI

Chaucer and Shakspere.[1]

The Inter-Relations of "A Midsummer Night's Dream," "Hamlet," and "The Tempest."

I

"I DO not need" — cries Montaigne, protesting against platitude — "I do not need to be told what death and pleasure are ; " and the greatness of Shakspere and Chaucer has come to be so far upon the same scale with death and pleasure that probably every student of those writers must have felt a certain inconvenience when tempted to break forth in that new access of wonder so sure to arise from each fresh contact with their art, in remembering that all general remarks upon them have probably long ago become platitudes.

Never so fairly as at this moment have men beheld that miracle of art which reverses the whole economy of things in favor of the artist and his lover. What with the work of the Chaucer Society, of the Shakspere Societies, and of multitudinous individual laborers from Shirley and Rowe to Blake and Furness ; together with

[1] These three "Chaucer and Shakspere" papers are from the introduction to a text-book with the above title designed by Mr. Lanier, for students of English Literature, but not quite completed, in October, 1880.

a thousand siftings and crystallizations such as can be effected only by the agitations of long debate and the quiet solutions of time, we know Chaucer and Shakspere so much better than their wives Philippa and Anne knew them that we could certainly have given those ladies some useful hints. In this intimacy we find ourselves possessing, indeed, no less than a perfect compensation against that grim bind of the laws of Nature which so wears the tissue of all our spirits. That death destroys, that time dims, that force decreases with the square of the distance : these laws which seem to have jurisdiction everywhere, and to determine every effort of man and Nature, we rejoice to see not only bend, but go backward cap in hand, before the divinity of our dear masters. For the societies and fine labors just detailed are living proofs that death has created these poets better than life did, that time's corrosion has merely etched their features in more relief upon man's heart, and that their power, in defiance of all the mathematics of radiation, has steadily increased with the increasing radius of its sphere.

The figures of Chaucer and Shakspere, in thus escaping the limitations of historic distance, have come nearer to each other as well as nearer to us. Their forms have grown so clear that we seem able to seat them quite palpably side by side in our own room, where a man may kiss both their hands in one and the same reverence.

And, having them in this favorable session, we can draw them on to discuss the same topic, and can take what wisdom we have capacity for in studying their poetic personalities thus sharply relieved upon each other. For instance, a comparative study of *The*

Clerk's Tale (patient Griselda's story) with *The Tempest*, both of which are motived upon Forgiveness, may show us Chaucer very keenly projected upon Shakspere.

There are three singularly representative works of Shakspere which, by their remarkable relations to each other and to three corresponding works of Chaucer,— besides their intrinsic qualities,— are capable of such large and useful applications, in our present system of educational training, to the furtherance of language, of art, and of morals, that it has seemed a plain service to set them forth compactly together, in original and complete forms, and with such helps as a considerable experience has shown necessary to make them available to a large number of readers. These six works are : *A Midsummer Night's Dream* herein studied in conjunction with Chaucer's *Knight's Tale ; Hamlet* with *The Pardoner's Tale ;* and *The Tempest* with *The Clerk's Tale.*

A remarkable set of circumstances and connexions combine about these three plays of Shakspere to make them representative of three great Phases or Periods through which the process of every healthy man's growth naturally passes. If we consider in outline the general cycle of this process, it will become easy to understand the extraordinary manner in which (1) the Moral Views, (2) the Actual Dates, and (3) the Artistic Structure of these three plays converge to illustrate it. If this inquiry involves us for a moment in the commonplace, we need not be surprised ; for it is by virtue of this very commonplaceness that the works named have become typic and of universal attraction. We shall, however, quickly arrive at less open ground.

Let one remind one's self— to begin — how youth, or early manhood, with its debonair waving-off of the more terrible questions of existence in favor of those immediate joys which are rendered possible by the physical luxuriance of this period, succeeds for a while in maintaining toward real life an attitude of nonchalance and irresponsibility. It is, as to the Real, an amateur period.

Life says to the young man, as the artist often says to some *dilettante* painter or musician whom the iron conscience which makes art has not laid under its awful obligations, *very good*, adding under breath, *for an amateur*. Or, from another point of view, youth is a period armed with certain qualities which act toward all facts of Death, of Question, of the Disagreeable, as the large green leaf to the round drops of water which, though falling fairly upon it, do but roll along over it in globules, without breaking, and without wetting the leaf-tissue. To the young man standing at the door, waiting for Angela, of a spring morning, when sun, dew, grass, trees, winding woods, river-stretches, birds, love, delight, call him out like a crowd of gay companions, it is little impressive to insist that the grass there is really in desperate struggle, blade against blade, and grass against tree, for life, and that the very bird now alighting on the sward — picture of innocence! is on a mission of murder to the worm it is swallowing. His ear may hear these words, but they roll off. What if it is? he says; lifts Angela into the saddle, mounts by her side, and these two, riding close together, presently sweep round the curve of the road and are lost among the trees. To him, Life has not revealed its whole self yet; and what is more, cannot reveal it. Is it too much to say that Nature has, of purpose, physically incapacitated youth for the sight of her entire Form?

Or if indeed the sensitive soul of a youth is impressed with the dread revelations of the underlying reality of things, it is so impressed with a saving clause, — namely, with a certain curious doubt which appears to brood beneficially about our dreams. The most painful of dreams affect us but little in comparison with slight actual griefs. We lose our wives, we commit crimes, we are assailed with nameless terrors, in the visions of the night: but it would seem that the soul instinctively takes things with a certain Pickwickian *perhaps*, at these times. No one's heart was ever broken by a dream.

And this dream-relation of youth toward the Real brings us immediately to our point; for it is precisely such a relation which the *Midsummer Night's Dream* expresses in the most ravishing terms of fancy. Death, and the cross of love, and the downward suctions of trade and politics, and the solemn stillness of current criticisms in all ages, and the compromise of creed, and the co-existence of God and misery, and the insufficiency of provision whereby some must die that the rest may live, and a thousand like matters: to these things the youth's senses, made purposely unapprehensive in part, are in a state which is described with scientific accuracy when it is called the state of a dream; and this is the state revealed in the *Midsummer Night's Dream*. Here we have the cross of love — two mad for one, Oberon quarrelling with his wife; but no thought of heartbreak. Here Bottom and his fellow patches show us Shakspere conscious of the fashionable degradations of his art; but there is no mourning over it, as in the later sonnet, " Tired of all these, for restful death I cry," and several others. Here we have the stupid ass-worship of contemporary criticism in all times — Titania, or current applause, doting upon the absurd monster; but it is matter for smiles, only, not indignation. *Certainly, Wrong is abroad, that is clear; but meantime one is young; and this is a dream:* such appears to be the fair moral outcome of this play.

Now, if we examine this work further with reference to the *actual date* at which Shakspere wrote it, and with reference to the quality of the artistic technic he displays in it, we shall find both these particulars bearing out the idea of youthfulness in the most striking manner. But reserving this examination a moment, for the sake of the advantage gained in consecutively tracing Shakspere's advance in moral scope through the other two plays mentioned: let us now inquire how far the attitude of the *Midsummer Night's Dream* toward things has been changed by the time we reach *Hamlet.*

Hamlet, as compared with *A Midsummer Night's Dream* is as much as to say, *ten years later.* Here the ills and wrongs which youth admits in a theoretical sense not at all interfering with one's gayety, have come upon our poet in the shape of actual matters: as they do come, one way or another, to every man soon after his manhood. Immediately in his path young Shakspere finds a grave; it is so real that a voice appears to come out of it, saying, *either explain me or fill me.* Here also, sitting on either side the ugly hole, are the two figures of Sin and Punishment; and a multitude of less definite shapes flit terribly about. No debonair waving away of these now into the vague recesses of youthful

unconcern. Once for all, death and crime and revenge
and insanity and corruption *are*, and I have personal
relations to them. For the first time he realizes the
Real.

Every man of forty, many a man of thirty, knows this
phase. If we call that of youth the Dream Period, we
may designate this as the Real Period. It comes after
one has seen the frightful shifts of his fellow-tradesmen,
or fellow-politicians, or, alas, fellow-artists ; or after
one has deadened to some love, of wife, child, or
mother, found unworthy, and therefore loved by grace
and not by attractive necessity ; or after one has by
turns begged, threatened, and wept in the face of death,
at the parting of one's best-loved, and found oneself
scorned with the scorn of death's imperturbable Nothing ; or from one of a thousand other directions. Turn
which way one will, there is the Devil grinning. The
most familiar references show us the universality of
this phase ; it crops out from all Bibles, histories, biogra-
phies ; the eating of the fruit which brought the knowledge of good and evil ; the giving over of Job into
Satan's hands, the Temptation in the wilderness, the
sequestration of Moses, the hideous groans of Mohammed,
the cry for the actual truth at the Renascence, the rise
of Science : these all occur in each life, and represent
from various standpoints the condition of Shakspere's
mind which expressed itself in the play of *Hamlet*.
Again postponing for a moment the parallel questions of
actual date and artistic advance : let us pursue the matter of moral growth to the third play of our series, *The
Tempest*.

Here the world is resolved. Man — who in the *Midsummer Night's Dream* was the victim of Puck, or

tricksy Chance, and the slave of Nature ; [1] who, in *Hamlet* has advanced only so far from this *status* that he is *inquiring* into Nature, puzzling over death, analyzing revenge, and struggling with fate ; — is, in *The Tempest*, ruler of Ariel (Puck's apotheosis), and lord of the storm, (which here brings good instead of the evil of Titania's freshets). In the Dream Period man is the sport of fate ; in the *Hamlet* period man is still beneath fate, but the thing has gone beyond sport, for man inquires and suffers and struggles; in the *Tempest Period* man is master of the universe. And — what is here essential — this masterhood of Nature is accompanied by a supreme moral goodness to fellow-man. *The Tempest* is motived upon an enormous Forgiveness. The whole plot is, in three words, a *storm* and a *fairy*, used as *servants* by a *man* (Prospero), for a beneficent purpose which embraces in its scope even the man's *cruelest enemy*.

Out of the Real, or Inquiring, or Scientific (these terms become convertible from the point of view herein urged) Period of *Hamlet*, our poet emerges into what we may fairly call, by a nomenclature based on logical extension of the thought started with, the Ideal Period of *The Tempest*.

In comparing these plays, therefore, with reference to the moral scope of the view of life which they present,

---

[1] Compare Titania's speech in Act II. Scene 2, when, after the marvellous picture of the freshets and topsy-turvy seasons, she adds :

> " And this same progeny of evils comes
> From our debate, from our dissension."

But all the details of this preliminary outline of the relations between the three plays will appear in the notes accompanying the representations of them hereinafter made.

we have arrived at a set of inter-relations which may be
accurately summed up in the following scheme :

DREAM PERIOD.	REAL PERIOD.	IDEAL PERIOD.
A MIDSUMMER	*HAMLET.*	*THE TEMPEST.*
NIGHT'S DREAM.		

If, now, advancing to the question of actual dates, we
shall find that all the plays which Shakspere wrote
between about 1590 and 1602 [1] were of a nature to show
clearly the view of life just developed as characteristic
of his first, or Dream, Period, while those written between about 1602 and 1608 arrange themselves, from the
same point of view, under the next, or Real, Period ; and
those written between about 1608 and 1613 (at which
latter date he probably stopped writing, three years before his death) under the third, or Ideal, Period : we
will thus uncover a process of spiritual growth so normal and healthy as to constitute a perfect explanation of
the astonishing universality with which Shakspere ap-
peals to all classes of men, of all nations, in all ages.
For we here discover a complete and simple answer to
that questioning doubt which all persons feel when told
that such and such plays of Shakspere's embody such
and such ideals, or are motived upon such and such cen-

---

[1] Most readers of a work so general as this would find any
detailed discussion of dates exceedingly irksome, and it seems
proper, therefore, to support the chronology here advanced only
by giving such reference as will enable those desiring further research to examine the evidence for themselves. Altogether the
best book for this purpose is the *Chronological Order of Shakspere's
Plays*, by the Rev. H. P. Stokes, Macmillan & Co., London, 1878,
in which the whole body of evidence is admirably collated, and
tables are arranged showing at a glance the conclusions of the
main workers in this field. The dates of the three plays specially
considered will be fully treated in the notes accompanying them.

tral thoughts.   These plays seem to every reader so
natural and spontaneous that instant revolt is excited by
every assertion of special meanings in them implying
deliberate and conscious premeditation on Shakspere's
part. *Pooh!* one is inclined to say, *do not tell me that
Shakspere meant to portray this and that " view " of
things — revenge in " Hamlet," forgiveness in " The
Tempest;" he did not " mean " to portray anything.
The fact was simply that the manager wanted a play
and Shakspere wanted money, and the latter, being called
on by the former, wrote whatever first came in mind;
hence " Hamlet" and " The Tempest" and all the rest.*

Now this is mainly true, and yet, if taken in connection with the dates just advanced and the considerations
preceding them, it is a truth which results very differently from what the hasty thinker would suspect.   For
the outcome of it is to produce a correspondence between every work of Shakspere's and the whole state
of his soul at the moment when that work was produced,
which would amount to a more complete unity of " view "
than any deliberate and conscious premeditation whatever could effect.   It is design that has designed itself.
If we say that *Hamlet* represents the Real period of
Shakspere's growth, we do not affirm that Shakspere
sat down one day and said to himself : *Come now, I
will write a play which shall picture a soul dealing with
dark questions;* but we affirm that Shakspere one day
sat down to write, — incited thereto by whatever personal motive, money or what not, — and that the day
happened to be one of a season when his own mind was
or had been dealing with dark questions ; now, when he
wrote, he wrote with all that was within him, and affected
nothing ; hence *Hamlet.*

Thus the question of Shakspere chronology, which many are at first inclined to class among the driest and most useless of antiquarian discussions, becomes a matter of the freshest living interest, — a matter touching the highest questions of religion and the spirit.

It must be, therefore, that every one who has not before studied this question will feel a certain delightful shock of revelation in finding that a perfectly sober chronology — a chronology lying fairly at the focus of all the numerous rays of evidence uncovered by the loving industry of Shakspere students — authorizes the construction of a scheme like the following, which I have arranged for the purpose of enabling the reader to sweep at a glance along the whole spiral of Shakspere's orbit so far as it was visible from our planet : —

DREAM PERIOD : ABOUT 1590–1602.
   ALL THE LIGHT COMEDIES, such as
      Love's Labor Lost, As You Like It, etc.
   ALL THE HISTORICAL PLAYS, such as
      Richard III., the *Henry* series, etc., except *Henry VIII.*, a
      Forgiveness play, coming in the Third Period. *Romeo and
      Juliet.*

*REPRESENTATIVE PLAY OF THIS PERIOD,
   A MIDSUMMER NIGHT'S DREAM.*

REAL PERIOD : ABOUT 1602–1608.
   ALL THE DARK TRAGEDIES, such as
      Macbeth, Othello, King Lear, and the like.

*REPRESENTATIVE PLAY OF THIS PERIOD,
   HAMLET.*

IDEAL PERIOD : ABOUT 1608–1613.
   ALL THE FORGIVENESS AND RECONCILIATION PLAYS, such as
      Winter's Tale, Henry VIII., and the like.

*REPRESENTATIVE PLAY OF THIS PERIOD,
   THE TEMPEST.*

The most cursory inspection of this scheme shows how completely the plays thus belonging together according to their dates also belong together according to their moral conceptions of life. (*a*) First the sportive comedies explicitly play with life. (*b*) Then the historical plays, even in setting forth wrong and treachery and grief, do not investigate the *why* of them. We have the recognition of Pain in life, but no inquiry into its nature and function in the economy of the world. (*c*) And in *Romeo and Juliet* the darkness of death is used merely as a foil to set off the brilliance of pure young Passion, as jewellers lay a diamond upon black velvet.

In short, all these plays (*a, b, c*), buoyant with youth, recognize the Inequalities of Things only to skip over them, and all the more fun, for who likes the flats? Clearly, in the plays of this time the perplexity and black contradiction of life have not arisen before Shakspere as facts to which he (Shakspere) has personal relations demanding settlement and action. When these facts appear, they appear as in a dream.

It seems therefore a broad and strictly scientific generalization by which all these works from 1590 to 1602 may be classed, to regard them as penetrated with the spirit of youth or young manhood, and as accurately represented by the *Midsummer Night's Dream*.

Thus the First Period, in date, and the Dream Period, in conception, coincide. But, again, if without reference to their plots or conceptions we find that in point of fact *Macbeth* and *Timon* and *Othello* and the others are written all together; and, if upon examining them, we find that they all concur in showing a spirit of scientific inquiry into wrong, superadded to those mere passionate invectives against it which occur in the histories ; we are justified in saying that the Second Period, as to date, and the Real Period, as to conception, coincide.

And so, finally, *The Tempest* and *Winter's Tale* and the others, motived upon Forgiveness and Reconciliation, and written after 1608, put us upon the coincidence of the Third, and the Ideal, periods.

As the mind runs rapidly along the plots of the plays which are here indicated in the briefest possible terms, the proposition grows clear that if — as is highly probable from the evidence which will be hereinafter pointed out in connection with various passages when the plays are separately treated — the *Midsummer Night's Dream* was written about 1593-4 or –5, *Hamlet* about 1602, and *The Tempest* about 1611, then these three plays — so representative, as already shown, of a normal advance in breadth of moral conception — really constitute a historic as well as logical formula of Shakspere's growth. This formula we can embody in an abstract of all the preceding considerations, thus :

DREAM PERIOD:	REAL PERIOD:	IDEAL PERIOD:
1590-1602.	1602-1608.	1608-1613.
Represented by	Represented by	Represented by
A MIDSUMMER NIGHT'S DREAM.	*HAMLET.*	*THE TEMPEST.*

II

HAVING thus established that the moral advance so clear in these three plays is actually the historic advance of Shakspere's unfolding spirit, we may now go on to a third series of considerations which not only support this conclusion but enlarge it into a most striking view of

the symmetry of the poet's growth throughout the whole
mass of his powers. We have seen his growth in moral
compass; let us now see if a growth in *artistic* compass proceeded — as of course it should in every sym-
metrical and healthy development — along with the
other.

This investigation is capable of being conducted with
a scientific accuracy which secures such valuable results
that probably the most cursory reader will not object to
some brief description of the simple apparatus of terms
and principles used for that purpose. To this end, let
us for a moment consider the formal art of the poet in
general from a standpoint somewhat higher than that
usually occupied. It is not difficult to find one com-
manding such a field of view that we can see the moral
and the artistic presenting themselves as really parts of
a continuous line, different enough at the extremes, but
as inseparable at the middle as is plant life from animal
life in certain lower forms of being. This remark is,
however, in anticipation.

Since concrete instances will here be at once more
clear and more interesting than any abstract development of principles, let us obtain familiarity with the apparatus just referred to, by at once beginning to use it.
Selecting two representative passages from the extremes
of the whole period of Shakspere's work, that is, one
from the *Midsummer Night's Dream* (1595?), and
one from *The Tempest* (1612–13), I ask the reader
to utter them aloud and to observe the actual phenomena which occur. For one of such representative passages, let us take the following from the *Midsummer
Night's Dream,* and consider it a moment before its
fellow-passage from *The Tempest.*

> " Love looks not with the eyes but with the mind;
> And therefore is wing'd Cupid painted blind:
> Nor hath Love's mind of any judgment taste;
> Wings and no eyes figure unheedy haste:
> And therefore is Love said to be a child,
> Because in choice he is so oft beguil'd."

Upon reciting this passage aloud, perhaps the first and most striking observation is that between the last word of each line and the first word of the next line the voice made a distinct pause much longer than the pause between any two consecutive words in the body of any one line. The voice, in short, divided off the whole passage into six smaller passages *for the ear* just as the punctuation marks and the verse-method of printing divide it off into six smaller passages — that is, six " lines " —*for the eye.*

What is the effect of this sixfold division? Let it be recalled that in listening to uttered speech, although the primary constituents of that speech are what we may call *alphabetic* sounds, or letter-sounds, yet the ear, at the same time that it pays attention to these letter-sounds individually, also pays attention to them in those little groups or discrete masses called " syllables." For example, in hearing the first word of this passage, the ear consciously hears first the sound of L, then that of o, then that of v; but the whole discrete mass *Love* has nevertheless struck the ear in such quick succession as to be practically simultaneous, and the separate sounds have much the same individual effect with that of each separate tone in a chord of three tones struck on the piano. The ear, therefore, in hearing the sounds of speech, practically hears them in little chords, or groups, each group being that discrete mass of tone called a syllable.

From this grouping, commonplace as it seems, proceed the most remarkable effects. If we analyze the
passage just read by *letter-sounds*, the most hopeless
confusion results : we can trace no law among the
series of sounds. But if we analyze it by syllables, and
agree (for reasons not proper to be detailed here, but
which any curious reader will find detailed in the author's *Science of English Verse*, pp. 59 and following)
to call such syllables " verse-sounds," we will find that
there are in the passage read exactly sixty of these verse-
sounds. The effect of the division into six smaller passages or lines by the pause at the end of each line —
which pause we may here conveniently agree to call the
" end-stop " — may now be clearly seen, when, upon
analyzing the first line by verse-sounds (here easily done
because each word happens to be one discrete syllable
and to constitute, therefore, one verse-sound),

> 1   2   3   4   5   6   7   8   9   10
> " Love looks not with the eyes but with the mind,"

we discover that it consists of exactly ten such verse-
sounds, and, pursuing the analysis, that the second line

> 1   2   3   4   5   6   7   8   9   10
> " And there-fore is wing'd Cu-pid paint-ed blind,"

consists also of exactly ten such verse-sounds, and so
with each of the others. Thus the whole passage reveals
itself from this point of view as a large group of sixty
verse-sounds, divided into six smaller groups of ten
verse-sounds each.

Here the ear has the pleasure of perceiving that in a
great mass of tones — which taken by letter-sounds is
absolutely patternless, relationless, and lawless — there is

nevertheless a definite pattern which runs through the whole mass, a definite law which reduces the whole confusion to a clear and simple order, a set of relations which binds together all the individual constituents of the mass.

Before going on to develop the ear's further management of these patterns, it is worth while remarking that we have here come upon a principle which not only seems to lie at the bottom of all human delight in, and desire for, rhythmic poetry, but which equally inspires every scientific generalization and every formation of moral law. We have just seen that upon presenting to the ear a long series of letter-sounds, the ear, while appreciating them as letter-sounds, eagerly accepts the first indication that this lawless series is capable of an arrangement which is not lawless, eagerly perceives the relations between the verse-sounds just detailed, and traces with delight the pattern of tens and sixes into which it finds the verse-sounds are woven. This stringent search after pattern, relation, law, among confused sounds, this intolerance of chaos (or un-relation), this delight upon discovering a principle which arranges apparently unrelated particulars into an interdependent system, — would seem to be at bottom the same presiding passion which fills the scientific searcher with discontent, when he has accumulated a number of scientific facts, until he finds some pattern, some principle of relation, some law, which binds together those facts just as the patterns of tens and sixes, the relation of ten and six to sixty, the law of grouping by groups of ten verse-sounds into six subordinate groups, bound together the whole mass of otherwise chaotic letter-sounds into the organic and related whole of the verse-structure.

And lastly this same passion appears to act upon moral facts just as upon scientific facts, and to cause the moralist to search eagerly along any accumulation of moral details for some pattern, or relation, or law, which shall dispose them all into order.

We shall presently find this observation of great practical use ; but reserving it for a further stage of the inquiry, let us now proceed with the study of the verse-phenomena.

We found that it was the pause at the end of each line, or "end-stop," which was the active agent in marking off for the ear the six constituent groups into which our sixty verse-sounds were divided. Thus it is easy to see that the "end-stopped line," or line admitting a pause of voice between it and the next line, is a controlling factor in the construction of what we shall have frequent occasion to call the Regular System (for there is, as will presently be detailed, in all musical verse, an equally important series of factors forming an Irregular System) of verse. This function of the end-stopped line becomes perfectly clear upon observing the precisely opposite function of the line which is not end-stopped, the line which, by the close connexion of its last word with the first word of the next line forcibly runs the reader's voice on to that first word, and which from this effect is called the "run-on line." For example, if the following passage from Alonzo's speech in Act II. Scene 1. of *The Tempest* be recited aloud,

> " You cram these words into mine ears against
> The stomach of my sense. Would I had never
> Married my daughter there ! " . .

the sense of the end-word in each of the first two lines is found to be so closely connected with that of the following word at the beginning of the next line that the voice must run on from one to the other ; and thus the ear of a hearer is not advised of the termination of each line by the recurrent pause, or end-stop. Thus the run-on line becomes, in its turn, a controlling factor in what we will have frequent occasion to refer to as the Irregular System, — a system which every maker of verse must construct, to move along with the Regular System and prevent the latter from cloying the ear and from offending the sense of proportion by its stiffness.

Let us now pause for a moment at this point in our study of the phenomena presented by the passage from *Midsummer Night's Dream,* and before going on to observe others, let us inquire how these two great classes of lines — the end-stopped and the run-on — were regarded by Shakspere at the two periods respectively of the *Midsummer Night's Dream* and *The Tempest.* It is evident upon the slightest reflection that the predominance of one or the other of these kinds of lines in a verse-structure would strikingly characterize its nature. If the end-stopped line should largely prevail, the verse would be very rigidly marked off into lines for the ear, and the structure would be simple and clear at the expense of being stiff. If on the other hand the run-on lines should prevail, the structure would be varied and interesting at the expense of becoming less intelligible to the ear in pattern.

Now upon counting the number of end-stopped and run-on lines respectively in Shakspere's earlier plays, and comparing their proportion with the proportion of end-stopped to run-on lines in his later plays, it is found that in the earliest plays he used the end-stopped line (Regular System) almost exclusively, but that he

began very soon to perceive the need of the run-on line
to vary the monotonous regularity of the other, and
thenceforward used it (thus bringing forward the rela-
tive importance of the Irregular System) with increasing frequency until the latest plays. These proportions
have been formulated quite exactly in tables containing
the percentages of run-on and end-stopped lines, which
the reader will probably find most easily accessible in
Mr. Edward Dowden's delightful *Shakspere Primer*
(Macmillan & Co., London and New York). For example, disregarding small fractions for the sake of
brevity: in the *Two Gentlemen of Verona*, an early
play, are but about one-tenth as many run-on as end-
stopped lines; while in *The Tempest*, which we have
seen to be a late play, the run-on lines have increased to about one-third as many as the end-stopped,
and the character of the verse is so changed as to
impress every ear: it has acquired a carriage greatly
larger and more sweeping. Between other plays lying
at the extremes of the periods given, the proportion
is still greater. Thus — in the *Comedy of Errors*, an
early play — the proportion of run-on lines is only about
one in eleven; while in *Cymbeline* — a play of *The
Tempest* period — the proportion has risen to about
one in two and a half: that is to say, there are about
four and a half times as many run-on lines in the late
play as in the early one. Still more striking is the
difference between the early (possibly the first) play,
Love's Labor's Lost, and the late play, the *Winter's
Tale*: for the proportion in the first is one run-on
to 18.14 end-stopped lines, while in the latter it is one
to 2.12: that is to say, *Winter's Tale* contains a
proportion of about nine times as many run-on lines (or

nine times as much of the Irregular System) as *Love's Labor's Lost.*

The increase in the use of run-on lines thus so consistently characterizing Shakspere's later plays holds perfectly good with reference to the two we are specially studying. In the *Midsummer Night's Dream* we find the proportion of run-on lines to that of end-stopped to be greatly less — that is, the verse to be greatly less free — than in *The Tempest.*

Observing only for the present that the advance in Shakspere's artistic technic here indicated is always an advance in the direction of the Irregular System, that is, in the direction of Freedom, Largeness, and Grace : let us now recur to the two passages under study. If we examine that from *Midsummer Night's Dream,*

> " Love looks not with the eyes but with the mind ;
> And therefore is wing'd Cupid painted blind;
> Nor hath Love's mind of any judgment taste ;
> Wings and no eyes figure unheedy haste;
> And therefore is Love said to be a child,
> Because in choice he is so oft beguil'd,"

we will find that three very striking particulars, all connected with the end of each of these lines, call the ear's attention thereto in such a way as to re-enforce the end-stop in its effect, and to make the line division very prominent to the ear. These three particulars are : (1) the Rhyme, which concentrates the ear's attention upon the last word in every line ; (2) the Strong Ending of each line, or important word capable of emphasis in which each line ends, giving a markedly different effect from that of Weak-ending lines, or lines in which the last word is a particle like *and, if, the, but,* and the like, as

> " This is a most majestic vision *and*
> Harmonious charmingly,"

from *The Tempest*, where *and* at the end would be
more likely to deceive, than to advise, the ear as to the
true ending of the line ; and (3) the Single Ending, or
ending in one verse-sound, as opposed to those " Double
Ending," or " Feminine Ending " lines, which end in
two syllables (to be pronounced in the time of one),
like, for example, the second line in the passage first
given from *The Tempest*,

> " The stomach of my sense.   Would I had *never*,"

the line being complete at the syllable " nev ; " or like
the following, also from *The Tempest*, where the double
ending, instead of being two syllables of one word
(" Feminine Ending ") is two words,

> " Why, as I told thee, 't is a custom *with him*,"

a line complete at the word " with " and preserving its
rhythmic structure only through the utterance of the
two verse-sounds " with him " in the same time as one.[1]
We may conveniently formulate these three additional
particulars and their artistic function, as follows :

REGULAR SYSTEM.	IRREGULAR SYSTEM.
Rhymed Lines.	Blank (Unrhymed) Lines.
Strong Ending Lines.	Weak Ending "
Single Ending "	Double ⎰ Ending " Feminine ⎱

Now upon examining Shakspere's plays with reference
to these three particulars, and counting the actual respec-
tive number of rhymes, of strong endings, and of single
endings, with the corresponding numbers of blank-verse

---

[1] A reader desirous of pursuing the subject will find these
phenomena reduced to terms of musical notation and fully explained in the present author's *Science of English Verse*, pp. 201
and following.

(or unrhymed) lines, of weak endings,[1] and of double endings : the same general advance is clear towards freedom and variety; that is, we find all the effects just classified under the head of the Irregular System growing more and more numerous and prominent, and tending more and more to vary the monotony and stiffness of the earlier verse. With the clear conception then that Rhymes, Strong Endings, and Single Endings powerfully fix the ear's attention upon the end of each line and thus powerfully establish the great Line-Rhythmus, while all such departures from this normal type, as Blank Endings, Weak Endings and Double Endings, as powerfully vary the Rhythmic flow and tend to *dis*establish the same great Line-Rhythmus, we find that in the late plays there is a strong and notable tendency to the latter, and that the general proportion of blank or unrhymed verse, of weak endings and of double endings, is greatly larger in the plays of the Ideal Period than in those of the Dream Period. It would be out of place here to trace all these proportions with any detail; and so, referring the reader desirous of going farther to the table of percentages for all these particulars which may be conveniently found in Stokes's *Chronology*, already cited, let us consider only the two extremes of the Periods, and only the two representative plays we have been studying. (1) As to Rhymes : The *Midsummer Night's Dream* presents us with 932 rhymed lines in a total of 2,251, while *The Tempest* presents us

---

[1] The sub-division into "weak" and "light" endings is not of enough importance in the present connection to be worth detailing, in view of the extreme of simplicity desirable in such a demonstration. Readers will find it set forth either in the *Shakspere Primer* or *The Science of English Verse*, already cited.

with only 98 (of which 96 are in songs). It must of course be remembered that this rhyme test might easily be strained out of its province. Special occasion for rhymes might exist and control a general tendency. Of the general tendency, however, to disuse rhymes in Shakspere's growing art, there can be no doubt. (2) As to Weak Endings: The *Midsummer Night's Dream* shows us but one (and therefore is all strong ending, all Regular System in this particular), while *The Tempest*, in a smaller number of lines, has 67. The Weak ending — it may be here remarked — is really but one kind of run-on lines; for every such ending as

> " This is a most majestic vision *and*
> Harmonious charmingly,"

or as

> " It sounds no more ; — and sure, it waits *upon*
> Some god o' th' island,"

which occur so frequently in *The Tempest*, really runs the voice on to the next line, and perhaps there would be little need for distinguishing this particular species of run-on lines were it not for a peculiarity in Shakspere's use of it, which notably separates it from the others. The peculiarity is the suddenness and lateness of its appearance in any numbers. There is here no gradual increase : Shakspere at first seems practically to have considered weak endings inadmissible; in the *Two Gentlemen of Verona* there is not a single weak ending, in the *Midsummer Night's Dream* there is but one, in *As You Like It* but two, and so on; and it is not until we get to *Macbeth* (1606?) that we suddenly find twenty-three weak endings. Having thus fairly started to use them, Shakspere evidently began straightway to rejoice in the long phrasing and sweep

which they render possible in blank verse ; and so in
Antony and Cleopatra (1607, 1608?) we find ninety-
nine weak endings, and in *The Tempest*, which has
but a little over half the total of lines of *Antony and
Cleopatra*, we reach sixty-seven — proportionately equal
to nearly a hundred and thirty.

(3) As to Double Endings : the nature of the variety
with which they relieve the monotony of the single
ending may be seen at a glance on comparing the last
bar of a typic single-ending blank verse line, musically
noted, as

In   maid - en   med - i - ta - tion, fan - cy   free,

— where ♪ is the single ending, — with the last bar of
free
an abnormal double-ending line, similarly noted, as,

The   stom - ach   of   my sense. Would I   had nev-er,

where ♫ — which any one acquainted with musical
nev-er
notation will immediately perceive to occupy exactly the
same time as ♪ in the line above — is the double
free
ending, or feminine ending. Now the form ♪ is the
free
normal form and is what the ear looks for, as part
of the Regular System ; while the form ♫ is ab-
nev-er
normal, and, being a surprise to the ear, belongs therefore to the Irregular System. We naturally expect, then,
to find many more such forms as ♫ at the ends of
nev-er

lines in *The Tempest* than in the *Midsummer Night's Dream*. And we are not disappointed. The advance here toward freedom is so great that, while in the *Midsummer Night's Dream* there are but twenty-nine double endings, there are in *The Tempest* (with a smaller total of lines) four hundred and seventy-six double endings.

For the sake of presenting the sharp contrast of Shakspere's extreme periods, no mention has been made, in this rapid sketch of the metrical tests, of the Middle or Real Period which we found represented by *Hamlet*. But by all the given tests, the position of the play is confirmed. In a total of 3,924 lines, *Hamlet* presents 141 rhymed lines (including the songs), 8 weak endings, and 508 double endings. In comparing the latter number — the 508 double endings — of course the total number of lines in each play is to be considered. *Hamlet* has 3,924, *The Tempest* but 2,058, or slightly over half as many; yet the latter play, in its half as many lines, has nearly as many double endings (476) as *Hamlet;* that is to say, the proportion of double endings in *The Tempest* is nearly twice that in *Hamlet*.

Thus, tried by all the metrical tests proposed, the relations asserted between *Midsummer Night's Dream, Hamlet,* and *The Tempest,* are remarkably confirmed. The four tests here applied, namely, the End-Stop, the Rhyme, the Strong Ending, and the Single Ending (as respectively giving into the Run-on, the Rhymeless or Blank, the Weak or Light Ending, and the Double Ending in the later plays), are not all that might have been used. Without even mentioning several others, it may be useful — as possibly inducing some young worker to make what seems (at least to me) a

desirable contribution to Shaksperean scholarship — to
specify a test which has not yet been pursued. This I
may perhaps properly call the " Rhythmic Accent Test."
In another place (*The Science of English Verse*, p. 213)
I have remarked :

" Perhaps everyone has observed that, particularly in
Shakspere's later plays, he seems absolutely careless as
to what kind of word the rhythmic accent may fall on.
Sometimes it is on the article *the*, sometimes the prepo-
sition *of*, sometimes the conjunction *and*, sometimes the
unaccented syllable of a two-sound word, as quickéns,
instead of quickens, and so on."

The remarkable effect of this freedom, in giving endless
play to the seemingly stiff type of blank verse, is minutely detailed in the author's work cited, and cannot
be entered into here; but the comparative frequency
with which these accentual variations occur, as between
early and late plays, has never been reduced to numbers.
Several reasons may be urged for the belief that this
might prove one of the most valuable of all metrical
tests. In fact, when we consider that this matter of the
rhythmic accent is one which affects *every* bar (that is,
every couplet of verse-sounds; for every normal line of
blank verse not only presents ten verse-sounds, but presents these arranged into five bars, or couplets, by the
five rhythmic accents which are always present or accounted for; see *Science of English Verse*, p. 215) of
each line, while the four tests just now applied affect
only the *last* bar of each line; and when we consider
further that the real result of this freedom in using the
rhythmic accent is to vary the monotonous regularity
of the Regular System with the charm of those subtle
rhythms which we employ in familiar discourse, so that

the habit of such freedom might grow with the greatest uniformity upon a poet, and might thus present us with a test of such uniform development as to be reliable for nicer discriminations than any of the more irregular tests can be pushed to : it would seem fair to expect confirmations of great importance from a properly constructed Table of Abnormal Rhythmic Accents in Shakspere.

We have now pushed over three main lines of inquiry — each, let it be remembered, involving several subordinate lines — to what may surely be called a reasonable certainty. We have applied a Moral Test, an Actual-Date Test, and several Metrical Tests, to each of the three plays, *A Midsummer Night's Dream*, *Hamlet*, and *The Tempest;* and every indication afforded by either has gone to confirm their character as Representative Plays of the three great Periods in Shakspere's life. This is a case, too, when indications confirm at a rate which increases very rapidly ; for each additional proof brings not its own weight alone, but its weight multiplied into that of all the other proofs.

And we may now profitably close this part of our investigation by ascending to a point of view from which what were apparently three lines of inquiry — the moral, the historical, the metrical — really resolve themselves into one, and place the whole matter before us in a holy and reasonable light.

For — as has been hinted already at more than one point, by way of anticipation — a great artist, in growing, grows as a whole, and not by parts nor into monstrosities ; as he grows (1) in his years (historically), he grows (2) in his grasp of the facts of Life (morally), and (3) in his grasp of the facts of Art (in Shakspere's case, "metrically,"[1] though this is a poor term). One of these advances may be said to imply the other, with a great artist; it is, indeed, by virtue of this wholeness in growth that the great artist is great. We may do a service to great art by the sweeping doctrine that in whatever case the artist — whether poet, painter, sculptor, musician — has not become a better artist and a better man and a more aged being, all together, the failure to do so is a note of weakness which simply takes away from *all* his greatness.

For, closely examined, there is a point where what is called the "mere technic" of the artist merges into and becomes wholly indistinguishable from his morality. Not only, at this point, has the knowledge of Pure Beauty become so completely a sense, like the sense of sight or smell, that he cannot do an ugly act (whether the ugliness be moral or artistic, whether the act be a theft, an envy, a jealousy, a hatred, or any of those smaller sins for which men generally consider themselves completely excused by the plea of weakness — or a bit of bad drawing, a weakish chord, a meretricious rhythm or rhyme, a mawkish curve) simply because it is ugly, — that is, because the sense of beauty recoils from it just as the sense of smell recoils from an offensive odor or that of hearing from a harsh noise; not only, I say, has Beauty thus become a sense, guiding the artist away from the morally bad as well as the artistically bad, and performing precisely the functions of our physical sense; but

[1] It ought to be added here that of course a wholly different line of art-tests is also applicable to Shakspere. He was not only verse-wright, but play-wright; and his art in constructing a play, in balancing figures, etc., if similarly examined, is found to advance in precisely the same direction with the verse-art, that is, towards Freedom, towards the Irregular System.

the power of grasping the contradictory details of our physical and spiritual life and of arranging these contradictions into a tolerable proportion, — contradictions which would drive the lesser world of ordinary men and women to instant suicide if these were not protected by partial blindness and by looking the other way, — this power is at bottom the same with that which seizes upon the similar details of verse-structure, which clearly recognizes the contradiction of what is herein called the Regular System as opposed to the Irregular System, and which instead of absurdly fighting the fact of their opposition finds it to be the very basis of music, and employs it to the purposes of formal poetry. To make a moral music out of the antagonistic facts of life; to make a verse-music out of the antagonistic facts of letter-sounds : this is so far one problem as that, when we have passed those limits to which mere cleverness can reach in anything, and beyond which lies the domain of genius and of art, it may fairly be said that a man with an original gift of poetic expression would surely grow in his faculties for both as if both implied one faculty.

It seems at any rate clear — without risking any part of the present case on a theory which may seem to many fine-spun — that, with Shakspere, the larger the music of his verse, the larger became the music of his life, and *vice versâ*.

And, finally, these plays, possessing these peculiar relations to Shakspere's entire growth, are carried to a plane of unique interest by the relations they reveal to each other. The details of these relations will be given in the notes to the passages embodying them, as they occur. But it may be worth while to point out, here, at least three of these in a cartoon outline. Observe, then, that in all our three plays we have certain views of man in his relations (1) to Nature, (2) to his Fellow-man, and (3) to Art.

(1) In *A Midsummer Night's Dream* Nature is a capricious Puck, which is man's superior and plays with him; in *Hamlet*, it is a firm-purposed ghost, which is still man's superior, but instead of playing with him drives him on to terrible ends; in *The Tempest* it is a servant, Ariel, and man has become lord of it, for benevolent ends.

(2) In the *Midsummer Night's Dream* man's Fellow man is the object of Capricious Love or Gentle Satire; in *Hamlet* he is the object of Revenge; in *The Tempest* he is the object of Forgiveness.

(3) All have a play-within-the-play, or anti-masque; that is, a work of art as one of the factors of the plot. In the *Midsummer Night's Dream* this anti-masque is Bottom's Burlesque; in *Hamlet* it is Hamlet's Trap to catch the king's conscience; in *The Tempest* it is Prospero's art, employed for the delight of two young lovers.

These inter-relations exist, of course by no intent, but solely through the wholeness of Shakspere's life. Given a play to write, he wrote it from the deepest of his *then* state of mind. Thus every play not only beats like the bosom of a human being, but beats with the rate of rhythm belonging to the stage of growth at which it was written.

III

The Three Corresponding Works of Chaucer

IF we now compare these three representative plays of Shakspere with three works of Chaucer which are respectively motived upon substantially the same themes,

and thus project Shakspere upon a background of
Chaucer, or Chaucer upon a background of Shakspere,
the tracts and curves of difference between the two men
become very plain.   These will be traced in detail by
the notes hereinafter appended to the special passages
of these works which bring out their relations; but
meantime advantage will be found in beginning with a
view in which the plots of these works are reduced to a
number of lines so small as to be apprehensible at one
glance.   It is proposed to study the first of our plays —
A Midsummer Night's Dream — in conjunction with
Chaucer's *Knight's Tale;* the second — *Hamlet* — in
conjunction with Chaucer's *Pardoner's Tale;* and the
third — *The Tempest* — in conjunction with Chaucer's
Clerk's Tale.

The widest possible generalization of these six works
would perhaps be, using familiar terms :

(1) The plots of the *Midsummer Night's Dream* and
its corresponding *Knight's Tale* are both embodiments
of a conception which may be stated as, *The Course of
True Love never did run Smooth;*

(2) The plots of *Hamlet* and *The Pardoner's Tale* are
both embodiments of a conception which may be stated
as, *The Course of True Hate never did run Smooth;*

(3) The plots of *The Tempest* and *The Clerk's Tale* are
both embodiments of a conception in which the meaning
of the term " love " has undergone a prodigious rectifi-
cation and enlargement since the Dream Period, and
which may be stated as, *In the Course of True Love all
Things run Smooth.*

A slightly sketched anatomy of the special forms assumed in each of these works by these general conceptions
will now be helpful.

The Knight's Tale and The Midsummer Night's Dream.

(1) In the case of the *Knight's Tale* and the *Midsummer Night's Dream* we have a connexion which is not only logical, that is, due to a common underlying basis of idea, but which is also historic, that is, due to an actual use by Shakspere of characters, thoughts, and situations which he found in Chaucer's *Knight's Tale.* I think there can be no doubt that the extent of this connection has not hitherto been appreciated. It is traced in the notes accompanying the works hereinafter given ; but, meantime, I may here remark that the reason for this failure to apprehend the true relations of these works unquestionably lies in the circumstance that the *Midsummer Night's Dream* is an eddy of ideas which, as they whirl, seem confused enough ; but this eddy is produced by the meeting of two currents of thought which, once seen, can be traced along quite unmistakable courses. One, as presently shown, proceeds from Chaucer's *Knight's Tale,* which — as I think can be clearly shown — Shakspere must have read very shortly before he wrote his *Dream.* This current includes Theseus, Hippolyta, Egeus, Philostrate (characters all taken bodily from the *Knight's Tale*), and the fairies, — in fact, all except the action which proceeds from Bottom and his fellow-clowns, culminating in the play-within-the-play, or anti-masque, of Pyramus and Thisbe. *That* current comes — I think — from the Greene-Harvey-Nash quarrel, and can be distinctly traced, — along a number of catch-words and clew-ideas which becomes so large as to make belief the direction of much the least resistance, — to Greene's *Menaphon,* Harvey's *Four Letters,* Nash's *Pierce's Supererogation,*

and Greene's *Groatsworth of Wit*, a body of literature
which must have possessed extraordinary interest for
young Shakspere just at the time he must have been
about to write his *Midsummer Night's Dream*, and with
which he was unquestionably saturated.   This whole
matter of Bottom and that ilk, and of Pyramus and
Thisbe, seems in fact to be a gentle satire upon
Greene and his crew in payment of Greene's fling
of *The tiger's heart wrapp'd in a player's hide* at
Shakspere.   But this cannot be further treated at present, — and remembering this peculiar historic connexion
between the *Midsummer Night's Dream* and Chaucer's
Knight's Tale which is superadded to the merely logical
connection binding *Hamlet* with the *Pardoner's Tale* or
The Tempest with *The Clerk's Tale*, let us outline the
largest processes of this couplet.

In the *Knight's Tale:* (*a*) in contact with Theseus
and Hippolyta come (*b*) two young men (Palamon and
Arcite), who (*c*) love one young woman (Æmilia) ;
(*d*) they quarrel and (*e*) fight about her (*f*) in a wood
(*g*) to which all the characters are brought; (*h*) by
Theseus' gracious arrangement (*i*) a pageant or tourney
is made wherein Palamon and Arcite, each with a hundred companions, wage battle for the lady; (*k*) meantime the supernatural Powers become involved, — Mars,
Venus, Diana, and Saturn; by whose machinations
(*l*) Arcite conquers, but (*m*) in prancing to his bride is
killed by his horse, through a god's jealous working, and
(*n*) finally, after years of tribulation, Palamon, though
beaten, takes all, and wins Æmilia to wife.   Caprice and
criss-cross : this runs through all the *Knight's Tale* of
Chaucer.

In *A Midsummer Night's Dream*, this same caprice

and criss-cross are simply carried to the fantastic point;
and note that along all the points (which are lettered for
this purpose) from (*a*) to (*h*) the circumstances are
identical, letter for letter, with those just given in the
summary of the *Knight's Tale*.   (*a*) In contact with
Theseus and Hippolyta, come (*b*) two young men (Demetrius and Lysander), who (*c*) love the one young
woman (Hermia) ; (*d*) they quarrel, and (*e*) at another
stage of the play attempt to fight, not about this, but
another, her (*f*) in a wood (*g*) to which all the characters are brought ; (*h*) by Theseus' gracious permission
(*i*) a play setting forth how that the course of Pyramus'
and Thisbe's true love ran not smooth, is brought before
him by a company of Athenian clowns; (*k*) meantime,
the supernatural Powers, or Powers of Nature (Oberon,
Titania, Puck, instead of Mars and Venus and Diana and
Saturn) have been at work, whereby Demetrius and
Lysander have been wrought to forget Hermia and as
madly love Helena, while Queen Titania by the same
practice dotes upon a monster, being a man with
an ass's head; (*l*) but the same Caprice which did
these things undoes them, and (*m*) every Jack is re-
stored to his proper Jill, until (*n*) we have Theseus and
Hippolyta, Lysander and Hermia, Demetrius and Helena,
in bliss, Bottom and his fellows snoring with visions of
sixpence a day, while the reconciled Oberon and Titania
with their elf train hover about the three bridal couches
and distribute blessing until daybreak.

The Pardoner's Tale and Hamlet.

(2) Between the following plots no historic connexion exists, and there is therefore no occasion to specify
the steps minutely, as in the last instance.

In *The Pardoner's Tale :* three riotous fellows of
Flanders, seated at drink in a tavern, hear the clink of
a bell go by, and know that a corpse is passing ; inflamed
with anger against Death, of whom they hear also great
complaint, they resolve to slay him ; rushing forth, they
compel an old man to tell them Death's whereabouts,
who informs them that Death has but now been lying
under a certain oak in yonder grove ; hastening to that
tree, they find under it seven bushels of new gold florins ;
fearing accusation of theft, they resolve to wait by the
treasure until night, in order to haul it home unseen ;
and, being hungry and thirsty, send their youngest com-
rade to town for meat and wine ; he, buying the same in
town, buys also certain poison and drops it in the bottle,
that his comrades may be slain and he take the whole
treasure ; in his absence, however, the two comrades
plot to slay him on his return, and they to take that
treasure : all of which plots are indeed carried out, but
in contrary order ; for, on his arrival with the victual the
two instantly slay him ; and, being worn with that work,
drink hard of the poisoned bottle ; whereby presently all
three lie dead under the oak, and the old man is justified
of his saying that they would find Death at that place.

In *Hamlet :* Claudius in secret murders his brother,
the King of Denmark, then seats him upon his
brother's throne and marries his brother's wife ; whereof
young Hamlet, son to the murdered king, is informed
by his father's ghost, and, setting about to perform
the ghost's command of revenge, feigns to become,
or becomes, insane ; to make sure of the ghost's truth,
he causes a play to be played before the king, wherein
the scene of the secret murder is cunningly re-
enacted ; the king's terror confirms the ghost's word ;

Hamlet murders Polonius by mistake for the king; Ophelia, Polonius' daughter and Hamlet's dear Love, is crazed and drowned; Laertes, Polonius' son, seeks revenge; meantime, the king ships Hamlet to England, with command to that king to slay him; but Hamlet in secret changes the commission, and sends on his keepers, Rosencrantz and Guildenstern, bearing their own death-warrant, while Hamlet returns; by plot betwixt the king and Laertes, Hamlet fences with Laertes, this latter having arranged a buttonless and poisoned foil beforehand; therewith he wounds Hamlet, but Hamlet in the struggle exchanges foils, and with the same poisoned weapon wounds Laertes; meantime the Queen, carousing to Hamlet's play, drinks unawares from a flagon the King had poisoned for Hamlet to drink from; which being discovered, Hamlet stabs the King with the poisoned foil; and presently Laertes, the King, the Queen, and Hamlet lie dead together.

The Clerk's Tale and The Tempest.

(3) In Chaucer's *The Clerk's Tale*: the young Marquis Walter, being entreated by his loving people to marry, chooses out of all his land the beggar-maid Griselda, who tends her aged father alone in a hovel; she reigns with her husband thence in marvellous grace and faithfulness, winning all the world to her for wisdom and gentleness; but a madness of assaying her love to the utmost seizes her husband, and he pours upon her injuries frightful to name, sending for her one little child by a grim soldier, and carrying it forth to pretended death under accusation that the people will not have an heir of a low-born mother; which she forgives, even in

lingering over the child, saying that her lord must be wise; and after yet more dreadful wounds, all forgiven heartily, the Marquis, still unsatisfied, puts her away from him, and commands her back to her old father, Janicola, who receives her in sorrow; but presently the Marquis bids that she return and get ready his house for his new bride; which she does, — sweeps and bakes with her own hands, and receives and tends the supposed new bride in all gentleness; whereupon the conquered Marquis reveals all, places in her arms the pretended bride, who is her own daughter, taken from her many years before, and restores her sons also; and a great feast crowns the now-perfect worship of Marquis Walter and the always-perfect forgiveness of his Griselda.

In *The Tempest* Antonio, having artfully usurped the dukedom of his full-trusting brother Prospero, causes the latter, with his infant daughter Miranda, to be set upon the ocean in an open boat for the winds to dispose of; Prospero reaches a desert island, and by long study becomes lord of life and nature; years afterward his brother Antonio, together with Alonso, King of Naples, and Ferdinand, son thereof, with many others, sails by that region from Tunis; Prospero, with help of his fairy servant, Ariel, calls up a tempest, wrecks the ship, brings all parties ashore in groups arranged for his purposes, guides Ferdinand to Miranda, who straightway love each other, involves the others in adventure and deadly conspiracy about the island, and finally brings all to his cave, where he forgives his unnatural brother, reassumes his dukedom, brings several criminals to repentance and better life, and arranges to set sail, over smooth seas, with a new-hearted following, to Italy.

XII

Paul H. Hayne's Poetry

AT a time when the war of secession had left the South in a condition which appeared to render an exclusively literary life a hopeless impossibility, Mr. Hayne immured himself in the woods of Georgia, and gave himself wholly to his pen. Perhaps this was the most convincing method he could have adopted of testifying by acts to his poetic *nascitur*, for it was striking an audacious challenge-blow on the very shield of Fate, and probably none but a poet would have dared it. Doubtless, the struggle which succeeded was passionate, fierce, often bitter, sometimes despairing; one finds traces of all this along the music of these verses. It is pleasant now to open *Legends and Lyrics* with the knowledge that the darkest of his conflict is over, and that in the growing light of appreciation his by-past shadow will show only like a dark calyx through which the poet's rose of fame is bursting.

We wish to ease our mind in the beginning of the only material quarrel we have to pick with Mr. Hayne; and, for the double purpose of setting forth our *casus belli*, and of showing the reader what manner of work Mr. Hayne can do in the most difficult of poetic forms, we quote the sonnet addressed

TO WILLIAM MORRIS.

In some fair realm unbound of time or space,
Where souls of all dead May-times, with their play
Of blissful winds, soft showers and bird-notes gay,
Make mystic music in the flower-bright place,
Yea, there, O poets! radiant face to face,
Keen heart to heart, beneath the enchanted day
Ye met, each hearkening to the other's lay
With rapt, sweet eyes, and thoughts of Old-World grace.
"Son," saith the elder bard, "when thou wert born,
So yearned toward thine my spirit's fervency,
Flamelike its warmth on thy deep soul was shed;
Hence the ripe blood of England's lustier morn
Of song burns through thee; hence alone on thee
Fall the rich bays which bloomed round Chaucer's head!"

This sonnet was written on reading the "L'Envoy" in the third volume of Morris's *Earthly Paradise*. Now — though Mr. Hayne is by no means the only person who has likened William Morris to Geoffrey Chaucer — the enthusiastic belief that the spirit of the older poet has come to shine again in the later one, has never been more tenderly and reverently embodied than in this lovely sonnet; but, protesting that we owe some keen delights to Mr. Morris, we totally dissent from the opinion that there is at bottom any such resemblance betwixt him and Chaucer as to entitle him to any sonship or heirship of the latter. Moreover, we believe that this theory involves far more than a mere critical estimate of the likeness or unlikeness of two poets; nay, we are sure that Mr. Hayne and all modern poets would do well to drink much of Chaucer and little of Morris. For — to indicate briefly some points of contrast — how does the spire of hope spring and upbound into the infinite in Chaucer; while, on the other hand, how blank, world-

bound, and wearying is the stone *façade* of hopelessness
which rears itself uncompromisingly behind the gayest
pictures of William Morris! Chaucer is eager, expectant.   To-day is *so* beautiful, perhaps to-morrow will be
more beautiful: life is young, who knows? — he seems
to cry, with splendid immeasurable confidence in the reserved powers of nature and of man.   But Morris does
not hope: there is, there will be, nothing new under the
sun. To-morrow? that may not come; if it does, it will
be merely to-day revamped; therefore let us amuse ourselves with the daintiest that art and culture can give:
this is his essential utterance.

Again, how openly joyful is Chaucer; how secretly
melancholy is Morris! Both, it is true, are full of sunshine; but Chaucer's is spring sunshine, Morris's is
autumn.   Chaucer's falls upon bold mountain sides
where are rocks, lithe grasses, and trees with big lusty
boughs and juicy leaves; where the wild motions of nature, from spring-winds to leaping fawns, are artlessly
free and unspeakably blissful; and yet where all other
forms, whether of monstrous, terrible, or wicked, are truly
revealed.   Morris's, on the other hand, is a late, pleasant, golden-tinted light (with just the faintest hint of a
coming chill of twilight in it), falling upon an exquisitely
wrought marble which lies half-buried in the sand, and
which, Greek as it is, dainty as it is, marvellous as it is,
is nevertheless a fragment of a ruin.   Chaucer rejoices
as only those can who know the bound of good red
blood through unobstructed veins, and the thrilling
tingle of nerve and sinew at amity; and who can trans-
port this healthy animalism into their unburdened minds,
and spiritualize it so that the mere drawing of breath is
at once a keen delight and an inwardly-felt practical act

of praise to the God of a strong and beautiful world. Morris too has his sensuous element, but it is utterly unlike Chaucer's; it is *dilettante*, it is amateur sensualism; it is not strong, though sometimes excessive, and it is nervously afraid of that satiety which is at once its chief temptation and its most awful doom.

Again, Chaucer lives, Morris dreams.   Chaucer, for all the old-world tales he tells, yet tells them with the mouths and manners of his living time, and so gives us a picture of it like life itself.   Morris stands between his people and his readers, interpreting his characters, who all advance to the same spot on the stage, communicate *per* him in the same language, the same dialect, the same tone, then glide away with the same dreamy mechanism. The *Canterbury Tales* is simply a drama with somewhat more of stage direction than is common; but the *Earthly Paradise* is a reverie, which would hate nothing so much as to be broken by any collision with that rude actual life which Chaucer portrays.

And finally — for the limits of this paper forbid more than the merest indication of a few of the many points of contrast between these two — note the faith that shines in Chaucer and the doubt that darkens in Morris. Has there been any man since St. John so lovable as "the Persoune"? or any sermon since that on the Mount so keenly analytical, so pathetic, so deep, so pitiful, so charitable, so brotherly, so pure, so manly, so faithful, so hopeful, so sprightly, so terrible, so childlike, so winning, so utterly loving, as *The Persoune's Tale*? But where (it is enough to ask the question in such a connection) in all that William Morris has written may one find, not indeed anything like the Persoune and his tale, for that would be too much to ask — there is no

man since Shakspere who has been at all capable of
that, — but anything even indicating the conception of
the possibility of such a being as the Persoune? To this
height, to this depth, neither William Morris nor any
other man has reached since Dan Chaucer wrote. Let
us Shakspere-worshippers not forget that Chaucer lived
two centuries earlier than Shakspere, and had to deal
with a crude poetic language which Shakspere found a
magnificent song-instrument, all in tune and ready to his
hand. Let us not forget that Shakspere is first poet and
Chaucer second poet, and that these two repose alone,
apart, far, far above any spot where later climbers have
sunk to rest. And this adjuration is here made with a
particular and unequivocal solemnity, because of the
conviction that we expressed in the outset of this subject,
that the estimate of these two poets which would have
them like enough to be father and son, involves deeper
matter than mere criticism. For if it be true that
William Morris is Chaucer in modern guise; if it be true
that by virtue of this nineteenth-century dress, Chaucer,
the glowing, actual man and lover and poet and priest
and man's brother, is changed into Morris, the aimless
sunset-dreamer of old beautiful dreams; if Chaucer's
hope is in five hundred years darkened to Morris's thin-
veiled despair, Chaucer's joy to Morris's melancholy,
Chaucer's faith to Morris's blank, Chaucer's religion to
Morris's love-vagueness; if, we say, it be possible that
five centuries have wrought Chaucer, that is life, into
Morris, that is a dream-of-the-past: then, in God's
name, with all reverence, what will five more centuries
do to us? A true Hindu life-weariness (to use one of
Novalis' marvellous phrases) is really the atmosphere
which produces the exquisite haze of Morris's pictures.

Can any poet — and we respectfully beg Mr. Hayne to
think upon this view of the matter, being emboldened to
do so by our regard for his devotion to letters and for
his achievements in that behalf — can any poet, we say,
shoot his soul's arrow to its best height, when at once
bow and string and muscle and nerve are slackened in
this vaporous and relaxing air, that comes up out of the
old dreams of fates that were false and of passions that
were not pure?

In convincing testimony that this question must be
answered in the negative, any careful reader of *Legends
and Lyrics* will observe that it is precisely when Mr.
Hayne escapes out of this influence that he is at his best.
Compare for example Mr. Hayne's treatment of the
Wife of Brittany with the unnamed sonnet on page 55,
which we shall presently quote. The *Wife of Brittany*
is a legend founded upon the plot of the *Frankeleine's
Tale* of Chaucer. Now in Chaucer's time this was a
practical poem; many men had not really settled in
their minds whether it was right to break even a crimi-
nal oath, made in folly. But the plot is only conceivable as a thing of the past, it belongs to the curiosities of
history; and although Mr. Hayne has told the story with
a thousand tender imaginings, with many charming
graces of versification, with rare strokes of pathos, and
with a final flow of lucid and silvery melody, yet the
poem as a whole never reaches the artistic height attained by the sonnet to the mocking-bird. In the *Wife
of Brittany* and in all similar artistic ventures Mr. Hayne
will write under the disadvantage of feeling at the bottom
of his heart that the passion of the poem is amateur passion, the terror of it amateur terror, and the whole business little more than a dainty titillation of the unreal. But

in the sonnet how different ! Here the yellow-jessamine, the bird, the vine-clumps, the odor, the bird-song, all are real; they doubtless exist in their actual, lovely entities around Mr. Hayne's home in the forest, and they have taken hold upon him so fairly that he has turned them into a poem meriting his own description of the mocking bird's song:

> " A star of music in a fiery cloud."

Having thus spoken in the genuine hope of suggesting to Mr. Hayne's mind a train of thought which might be serviceable to his genius, we proceed to remark that in *Legends and Lyrics* we find no polemical discussion, no " science," no " progress," no " Comtism," no rugged-termed philosophies, no devotionalism, no religiosity of any sort. Mindful only of grand phenomena which no one doubts — of fear, hope, love, patriotism, heaven, wife, child, mother, clouds, sunlight, flowers, water — these poems tinkle along like Coleridge's

> " —— hidden brook
> In the leafy month of June,
> That to the sleeping woods all night
> Singeth a gentle tune."

This last word indeed hints at what is one of the distinctive characteristics of all Mr. Hayne's poetry. It is essentially, thoroughly, and charmingly tuneful. In a time when popular poetry is either smug and pretty, or philosophically obscure and rhythmically rugged, this quality becomes almost unique. There is indeed nearly the same difference between poetry and culture-poetry that exists between music and counterpoint-music. Culture-poetry, like counterpoint-music, is scarcely ever satisfactory to the ear; it is not captivating with that indescribable music which can come out of the rudest heart, but which cannot come out of the most cultivated head. This feature alone would suffice to separate the book before us from the great mass of utterances which polished people who are not poets are daily pouring upon the air.

We should like to illustrate Mr. Hayne's faculty by quoting entire his *Fire-Pictures*, a poem which in point of variety and delicacy of fancy is quite the best of this collection, and in point of pure music should be placed beside Edgar Poe's *Bells*. Of course, to one who has warmed his winters by nothing more glorious than coal; to one who has never sate in dreamful mood and watched the progress of a great hickory fire from the fitful fuliginous beginning thereof, through the white brilliance of its prime and the red glory of its decline, unto the ashen-gray death of the same, this poem is unintelligible; but to one who has, its fancies and its music will come home with a thousand hearty influences. We regret that it is too long to quote here. It is a poem to be read aloud; a true *recitativo*. The energy of its movements, the melody of its metres, the changes of its rhythm, the variety of its fancies, the artistic advance to its climax, particularly the management of its close, where at one and the same time, by the devices of onomatopeia and of rhythmical imitation, are doubly interpreted the sob of a man and the flicker of a flame so perfectly that sob, flicker, word, rhythm, each appears to represent the other, and to be used convertibly with the other in such will-o'-wisp transfigurations as quite vanish in mere description,— all these elements require for full enjoyment that the actual music of the poem should fall upon the ear.

Some of the changes of rhythm above referred to merit especial mention, and start some considerations which we regret the limits of this paper will not allow us to pursue. Suffice it here to remark that whenever an English-speaking person grows unusually solemn or intense he instinctively resorts to the iambic rhythm for expression. Note, for instance, how in number II. at the close the change from the trochees to the two iambi "aspire! aspire!" at once represents the intensity of the situation and the broken fitfulness of the struggling flame; or, again, in that fine scene of number IV., where the iambi "dark-red like blood" give the reader a sudden wrench from the trochaic flow as if they plucked him by the sleeve to compel him to stop a second on the thought; or, again, most notable of all, in number VI., where from the words "a stir, a murmur deep" to the close of the picture the iambi present the agony and the glory of the martyr. With these three exceptions the entire poem is in trochees, and is an admirable example of the music which can be made with those elements. Return to number IX. of this poem, from

> "Like a rivulet rippling deep,
> Through the meadow-lands of sleep,"

to its close is, in point of pure trochaic music, of rare excellence. We desire, however, to call Mr. Hayne's attention to a fault of tone which occurs in this picture, and in another of the poems of this book. Where the lines run:

> "Though the lotos swings its stem
> With a lulling stir of *leaves*,
> Though the lady-lily *laves*
> Coy feet in the crystal *waves*,
> And a silvery undertune
> From some mystic wind-song *grieves*,"

"leaves" of course is intended to rhyme with "grieves," four lines down, and "laves" with "waves;" but "laves" is the next rhyme-tone to "leaves," and this proximity renders it obnoxious to two objections. One is, that it leaves the reader for a moment in doubt whether "laves" is really intended to rhyme with "leaves" — a doubt which interferes with the reader's enjoyment as long as it lasts. The other and stronger objection is, that the immediate juxtaposition of the slightly-varying rhyme-tones "leaves" and "laves" gives the ear the same displeasure which the eye suffers from two shades of the same color in a lady's dress,— both tones seem faded.

The faults of *Fire Pictures* are faults which we detect in all Mr. Hayne's poetry; and as they are remediable, we call his attention to them with all the more vigor. They are of two classes. First, we observe a frequently-recurring *lapsus* of thought, in which Mr. Hayne falls into trite similes, worn collocations of words, and commonplace sentiments. To have these hackneyed couples of words and ideas continually popping in upon us out of Mr. Hayne's beautiful things is to suffer the chagrin and the anguish of that hapless man who in the hot summer rushes afar from toil and trouble across the ocean into a distant land, and there in the heavenly weather, while idly wandering down some wild and lovely glen, given up to all tender meditations, suddenly, on pushing aside a great frond of fern, comes bump upon the smug familiar faces of Smith, Jones, and Brown, whom he had left amid the hot grind of the street, and whose presence immediately transports him back to the sweaty moil of stocks, bacon, and dry-goods. Such expressions are : "changing like a wizard-thought," or, "like a charmed thought," or "like a Protean

thought," and others in *Fire Pictures*. More notable
still in this respect is the poem *Renewed*. The first
four lines of this poem are so entirely commonplace that
they are quite sufficient to throw any reader off the scent
and cause him to abandon the piece; yet the very next
four are exceedingly beautiful, with all the clear and
limpid music of Mr. Hayne's style, and with a bright
change in the rhythm which is full of happy effects.
Witness:

RENEWED

Welcome, rippling sunshine!
Welcome, joyous air!
Like a demon-shadow
Flies the gaunt Despair!
Heaven through heights of happy calm
Its heart of hearts uncloses,
To win earth's answering love, in balm,
Her blushing thanks, in roses!

The second fault to which we wish to call Mr. Hayne's
attention is diffuseness, principally originating in a lav-
ishness and looseness of adjectives. Whatever may be
said of Edgar Poe's theory of the impossibility of a long
poem, or that all long poems are merely series of short
poems connected by something that is not poetry, it may
at least with safety be asserted that in a time when trade
has lengthened life by shortening leisure, the ideal of the
lyric poem is a brief, sweet, intense, electric flashing of
the lyric idea in upon the hurrying intelligence of men,
so that the vivid truth may attack even an unwilling
retina, and perpetuate itself thereupon even after the
hasty eyelid has closed to shut out the sight. Now,
either a free or an inexact use of adjectives is a depart-
ure from this ideal, not only because it impairs the
strength of the articulate idea, but because it so far cum-

bers the whole poem as, if the fault extends throughout, to render it too long to be readable by many of those whom all true poets desire to reach. Notable instances of Mr. Hayne's dereliction in this regard may be found in his frequent and often inexact employment of the words " cordial," "weird," and " fairy " in these poems. One can easily trace the manner in which this vice escapes the poet's attention. Busied with some central idea, and hurried by the passion of creating, he will not hesitate for a descriptive in some minor phrase, but dashes down the first term that occurs, if it will but answer tolerably, so that presently, from habit, a certain favored few adjectives come to understand, as it were, that this duty is expected of them, and get trained to stand by and help whenever the poet's mind is fatigued or hurried.

Perhaps the nearest approaches to the ideal of lyric poetry in this book are the invocation to the wife with which it commences — as it were, grace before meat — and the poem called *A Summer Mood*, based on a line from Thomas Heyward : " Now, by my faith, a gruesome mood for summer." From the latter we quote a line out of the third verse and the last three verses : —

> " The sunshine mocks the tears it may not dry,
>
> .   .   .   .   .
>
> " The field-birds seem to twit us as they pass,
> With their small blisses, piped so clear and loud :
> The cricket triumphs o'er us in the grass ;
> And the lark glancing beam-like up the cloud,
>
> " Sings us to scorn with his keen rhapsodies :
> Small things and great unconscious tauntings bring
> To edge our cares, whilst we, the proud and wise,
> Envy the insect's joy, the birdling's wing !
>
> " And thus for evermore, till time shall cease,
> Man's soul and Nature's — each a separate sphere —

Revolves, the one in discord, one in peace,
— And who shall make the solemn mystery clear ? "

The stanza of this poem in which " the field-birds twit
us as they pass, with their small blisses," is a genuine
snatch caught from out the sedges of a Southern field,
where we doubt not Mr. Hayne has often strolled or lain,
companioned only by the small crooked-flighted sparrow,
whose whistle, so keen that it amounts to a hiss, seems
to have suggested the very sibillations of the s's so frequently occurring.

In *In Utroque Fidelis* is beautifully blended a tone
of tranquil description with that of a passionate love-
song. A lover about to be off to the wars has stolen at
midnight to snatch a farewell glance at the home of his
beloved. The following four verses show something of
the art of the poem : —

" I waft a sigh from this fond soul to thine,
A little sigh, yet honey-laden, dear,
With fairy freightage of such hopes divine
As fain would flutter gently at thine ear,
    And entering find their way
Down to the heart so veiled from me by day.

" In dreams, in dreams, perchance thou are not coy;
And one keen hope more bold than all the rest
May touch thy spirit with a tremulous joy,
And stir an answering softness in thy breast.
    O sleep, O blest eclipse !
What murmured word is faltering at her lips ?

. . . .

" Still, breathless still ! No voice in earth or air :
I only know my delicate darling lies,
A twilight lustre glimmering in her hair,
And dews of peace within her languid eyes :
    Yea, only know that I
Am called from love and dreams perhaps to die,

"Die when the heavens are thick with scarlet rain,
And every time-throb 's fated : even there
Her face would shine through mists of mortal pain,
And sweeten death like some incarnate prayer.
　　Hark ! 'T is the trumpet's swell !
O love, O dreams, farewell, farewell, farewell ! "

In the particular of tranquil description, however, some good work occurs in the ode to *Sleep*. Witness the following extracts, which form the beginning and the end of the poem : —

"Beyond the sunset and the amber sea,
To the lone depths of ether, cold and bare,
Thy influence, soul of all tranquillity,
Hallows the earth and awes the reverent air.
　　　.　.　.　.　.　.　.　.　.
Then woo me here amid these flowery charms ;
Breathe on my eyelids, press thine odorous lips
Close to mine own, enfold me in thine arms,
And cloud my spirit with thy sweet eclipse ;
And while from waning depth to depth I fall,
Down-lapsing to the utmost depths of all,
Till wan forgetfulness, obscurely stealing,
Creeps like an incantation on the soul, —
And o'er the slow ebb of my conscious life
Dies the thin flush of the last conscious feeling, —
And, like abortive thunder, the dull roll
Of sullen passions ebbs far, far away, —
O Angel ! loose the chords which cling to strife,
Sever the gossamer bondage of my breath,
And let me pass, gently as winds in May,
From the dim realm which owns thy shadowy sway,
To thy diviner sleep, O sacred Death ! "

We would like to praise *Glaucus* for the fine spirit-of-green-leaves, which makes the poem so dainty and shady and cool. We would like, too, to discuss with Mr. Hayne whether the climacteric point in the tale of the *Wife of Brittany*, — which is the moment when the

Wife meets Aurelian for the purpose of performing her dreadful promise — does not need a more dramatic accentuation to relieve it from the danger of anti-climax to which this wonderfully smooth narrative is liable at that point. We could wish further to commend the admirably harmonized tone of *Prexaspes*, where the words seem at once hot, wan, cruel, and wicked; and the elegant rendering of *Aëthra*, which is quite the most artistically told tale in the book; and the reverent piety which shines in the final offering to the poet's mother; and many other things. But this paper has already reached its limit. We may be permitted in closing it to observe that already since the publication of *Legends and Lyrics*, other poems of Mr. Hayne's have appeared, as for example the two *Forest Pictures* in the *Atlantic Monthly*, which exhibit a growing strength and more vigorous realism in his poetic faculty; and we venture to express the hope that his pen may yet embody the pretty fancy of his poem called

THE NEST

At the poet's life-core lying,
  Is a sheltered and sacred nest,
Where, as yet unfledged for flying,
  His callow fancies rest —

Fancies and thoughts and feelings
  Which the mother Psyche breeds,
And passions whose dim revealings
  But torture their hungry needs.

Yet there cometh a summer splendor
  When the golden brood wax strong,
And, with voices grand or tender,
  They rise to the heaven of song.

XIII

John Barbour's Bruce

I

ABOUT the time when our own Geoffrey Chaucer was working at his *Canterbury Tales*, and John Wyclif and his disciples were translating the Bible into common English, and William Langley was revising his *Piers Plowman;* when Sir John Froissart over in France was writing his *Chronicles;* when, in Italy, Dante had been dead some fifty years, and Petrarch had just stopped singing, John Barbour, in Scotland, was writing that dear and simple Romance which treats — as the old manuscript says at the head, — "of the deeds, wars, and virtues of lord Robert the Brwyss,[1] most illustrious King of Scotland, and of the conquest of the kingdom of Scotland by the same, and of the lord James the Douglas." It was then but a few years since the two heroes of whom Barbour sang had acted, and fought, and loved virtue : about as if Mr. Longfellow should make a poem on the adventures of some soldier in our own War of 1812. Barbour was probably near thirteen years old when Robert Bruce died, in 1329; and the main events of his poem are those wonderful struggles of Bruce during the earlier years of the same century against King Edward I., and after that monarch's death

---

[1] Bruce.

against King Edward II., until the defeat of the latter at Bannockburn in 1314 left the hardy Robert secure on the Scottish throne.

Of John Barbour's life we know little besides the facts that he was Archdeacon of Aberdeen, and that he wrote a metrical account of the Scotch rulers beginning with Brutus called *The Brute,* and a poem on The Lives of The Northern Saints, — besides this poem of *The Bruce.*

But when we read this last work we do not feel that we lack any further knowledge to make us acquainted with John Barbour. About a hundred and fifty years before Barbour a very fervent English poet named Orrmin called his poem *The Ormulum,* or little Orrmin, as if it were a sort of miniature copy of himself; and so we might call Barbour's Romance the Barbulum. It shows him to us over again. We see clearly how simple, how lofty, how clean are all his thoughts; how fervent are his love and admiration of all manful deeds; how keen and intelligent are his ideas of the remarkable degree in which Robert Bruce added perseverance, prudence, ready wit in emergencies, wisdom in hand-ling his resources, to his personal bravery and physical strength; how true is his passion for freedom; and how fine and large is his ideal of manhood as given in his account of James the Douglas.

Here for instance is a tale from the earlier portion of the poem, in which we see not only the valorous deeds and rude hardships of Bruce, but the perfect fellow-feeling of Barbour; and it is easy to believe that the poet would not have fought far from the hero's side if he had been in that trying march when Bruce, single-handed, covered the retreat of his little band from the incessant charges of the Lord of Lorne and his troopers. The poem has told how upon the death of King Alexander III.,

> *The land six years, and more perfaith,*
> The land vi yer, and mayr perfay,
>
> *Lay desolate after his day ;*
> Lay desolat eftyr hys day ;

how the baronage quarrelled as to who should have the kingdom, and finally left the decision to King Edward of England, who at first made a foul proposal to Robert Bruce — grandfather of our Robert —

> *And to Robert the Bruce said he,*
> And to Robert the brwyss said he,
>
> *" If thou wilt hold in chief of me*
> " Gyff thow will held in chayff off me
>
> *For evermore, and thine offspring,*
> For euirmar, and thine ofspryng,
>
> *I shall do so (that) thou shalt be king ; "*
> I sal do swa   thow sall be king ; "

and how Bruce answered —

> *" Sir," said he, "so God me save,*
> " Schyr," said he, " sa god me save,
>
> *The kingdom yearn I not to have*
> The kynryk yharn I nocht to have
>
> *But if (unless) it fall, of right, to me ;*
> Bot gyff   It fall off rycht to me :
>
> *And if God will that it so be,*
> And gyff god will that It sa be,
>
> *I shall as freely in all things*
> I sall als frely in all thing
>
> *Hold it as it behoves a king,*
> Hold It as It afferis to king,

> *Or as mine elders before me*
> Or as myn eldris forouch me
>
> *Held it in freest royalty.*
> Held It in freyast reawte."

Hereupon King Edward, in wrath, decided for Baliol, who had agreed to be King Edward's man; but these two soon fell out, Baliol was degraded, and Scotland lay at King Edward's mercy,

> " All defawtit & wndone,"

in a condition of slavery and ruin which Barbour paints with vigorous strokes. Sir William Douglas, father of Sir James who presently does such heroic deeds, is slain, and the Douglas land given to English Clifford; King Edward has the country

> " Stuffyt all with Inglis men,"

who seize the property, even the wives and daughters, of the Scots, and rob and slay without hindrance. Then

> *This lord the Bruce I spoke of, ere,* [1]
> Thys lord the brwyss I spak of ayr,
>
> *Saw all the kingdom so decay,*
> Saw all the kynryk swa forfayr,
>
> *And so troubl̃d the folk saw he*
> And swa trowblyt the folk saw he
>
> *That he thereof had great pity.*
> That he tharoff had gret pitte.
>
> *But what pity that ever he had,*
> But quhat pite that euir he had,
>
> *No countenance thereof he made,*
> Na contenance thar-off he maid;

[1] Here Barbour forgets that the Bruce he spoke of ere was the grandfather of the famous Bruce. It is the latter he now goes on to speak of.

Till on a time Sir John Cummyn,
Till on A tym Schyr Ihone Cumyn,

As they came riding from Stirling,
As thai come ridand fra strewillyn,

Said to him, " Sir, will ye not see
Said till him, "schyr, will ye nocht se

How that governed is this countree ? "
How that gouernyt is this countre ? "

But as soon as Bruce, touched with pity, signs an
" Indenture " agreeing to take his right place on the
throne and receives the oaths of the barons, treacherous
John Cummyn reveals all to the king at London. Bruce
being soon afterward in that city is confronted by the
king with the fatal Indenture, and only saves himself
by asking, with the readiest wit, that he may be allowed to
compare the seal with his own at his lodging. Here he
stays not for seals, but leaps upon his horse, flies to
Scotland, and showing John Cummyn the fatal Indenture
slays him with a knife even as he stands at the church-
altar.

The ball now opens. Bruce is openly crowned king
of Scotland at Scone, and presently King Edward, in a
rage over the death of John Cummyn, sends an army
into Scotland, which Bruce meets at Methven. Here,
greatly outnumbered, King Robert is defeated and must
fly to the hills. Presently, when the most part of his
" mengye " — that is, his *meinie*, a very common term
in Barbour's time for any troop or band of men following
a leader — was nearly gone, and the men were without
shoes, they go to Aberdeen, where their wives are. But
here is no rest : they must soon flee ; and now, with the
ladies,

That for leal love and loyalty
That for leyle luff and leawte,

Would partners of their pains be,
Wald partenerys off thar paynys be.

. . . . . .

His men in haste he caused be dight (armed),
His men in hy he gert be dycht,

And busked him (got ready) from the town
                                to ride,
And buskyt   of the toune
                                to ryd,

The ladies rode right by his side.
The ladyis raid rycht by his syd.

Then to the hill they rode their way,
Then to the hill thai raid thar way,

Where great default of meat had they.
Quhar gret defaut off mete had thai.

But worthy James of Douglas
Bot worthy Iames off dowglas

Aye travailing and busy was
Ay trawailland and besy was,

For to purchase (procure) the ladies meat;
For to purches   the ladyis mete;

And it on many wise (ways) would get.
And It on mony wiss   wald get.

For (one) while he venison them brought,
For   quhile he venesoun thaim brocht:

And with his hands (another) while he wrought
And with his handys   quhile he wrocht

Gins (snares or traps) to take pike and salmons,
Gynnys,   to tak geddis & salmonys,

Trouts, eels, and also minnows.
Trowtis, elys, and als menovnys.

. . . . . .

And the king oft comforted was
And the king oft confort wes

Through his wit and his business (busy-ness).
Throw his wyt, and his besynes.

On this manner them governed they
On this maner thaim gouernyt thai,

Till they came to the head of Tay.
Till thai come to the hed off tay.

How John of Lorne disconfite King Robert.[1]

The lord of Lorne dwellèd thereby
The lord off lorne wonnyt thar-by,

That was capital enemy
That wes capitale ennymy

To the king, for his uncle's sake,
To the king, for his Emys sak,

John Cummyn ; and thought for to take
Ihon comyn ;   and thocht for to tak

Vengeance, upon cruel manner.
Wengeance, apon cruell maner.

When he the king wist (knew) was so near
Quhen he the king wyst   wes sa ner,

He assembled his men in hy (haste) ;
He assemblyt his men in hy ;

And had into his company
And had in-till his cumpany

The barons   of Argyle also ;
The barownys off Argyle alsua ;

They were a thousand well (full) or more ;
Thai war A thowsand weill   or ma :

And came for to surprise the king,
And come for to suppriss the king,

---

1 This rubric occurs in the Edinburgh manuscript.

That well was ware of their coming.
That weill wes war of thar cummyng.

. . . . . .

The king's folk full well them bore,
The kingis folk full weill thaim bar,

And slew, and felled, and wounded sore.
And slew, and fellyt, and woundyt sar.

But the folk of the tother party
Bot the folk off the tothir party

Fought with axes so felonly,
Fawcht with axys sa [felounly],

For they on foot were every ane (one),
For thai on fute war euir-Ilkane,

That they fele (many) of their horse has slain.
That thai feile   off thar horss has slayne;

And to some gave they wounds wide.
And till sum gaiff thai woundis wid.

James of Douglas was hurt that tide (time);
Iames off dowglas wes hurt that tyd;

And also Sir Gilbert de la Hay.
And als Schyr gilbert de la hay.

The king his men saw in affray (affright),
The [king his] men saw in affray,

And his war-cry began he (to) cry
And his ensenye[1] can he   cry;

And among them right hardily
And amang thaim rycht hardyly

He rode that he them drove back, all,
He rad, that he thaim ruschyt all;

And many of them there made he fall.
And fele of thaim thar gert he fall.

[1] From the French *enseigne*, a sign, or token.

But when he saw they were so fele [1] (*many*),
Bot quhen he saw thai war sa feill,

And saw them such great dints (*strokes*) *deal,*
And saw thaim swa gret dyntis   deill,

He dread(*ed*) *to lose his folk ; for-thi* (*for this, therefore*)
He dred   to tyne his folk, forthi

His men to him he 'gan rally,
His men till him he gan rely,

And said : " Lordings, folly it were
And said : " Lordyngis, foly It War

To us for to assemble mair (*more*),
Tyll ws for till assembill mar,

For they fele (*many*) *of our horse has slain ;*
For thai fele   off our horss has slayn ;

And if we fight with them again
And gyff [we] fecht with thaim agayn,

We shall lose of our small meinie (*following*)
We sall tyne off our small mengye,

And our-self shall in peril be.
And our-selff sall in perill be." [2]

.   .   .   .   .

Then they withdrew them wholly,
Then thai withdrew thaim halely :

But that was not full cowardly,
Bot that wes nocht full cowartly,

For together into a band held they
For samyn in-till A sop held thai ;

And the king him abandoned (*devoted himself*) *aye*
And the king him abandonyt   ay

---

1 Young readers who are studying German will recognize this as from the same stock with the German word *viel*, many.

2 The contrast between this wonderful prudence of Bruce — he never lost his head — and the tremendous personal valor and strength of the deeds next done by him is finely brought out by Barbour.

To defend behind (guard the rear of) his meinie.
To defend behind   his mengye.

And through his worship (worth-ship) so wrought he
And throw his worschip   sa wrouch[t] he

That he rescued all the flee-ers (fleeing men)
That he reskewyt all the flearis,

And stopped so-gate (in such a gate, or manner) the chasers
And styntyt swagat   the chassaris,

That none durst out of battle (out of ranks) chase,
That nane durst owt off batall   chass,

For always at their hand he was.
For alwayis at thar hand he was.

.   .   .   .   .   .

Two brothers were into that land
Twa brethir war [into] that land

That were the hardiest of hand
That war the hardiest off hand

That were into all that countrèe ;
That war in-till all that cuntre ;

And they had sworn, if they might see
And thai had sworn, iff thai micht se

The Bruce where they might him o'erta' (take),
The bruyss, quhar thai mycht him our-ta,

That they should die, or then him slay.
That thai suld dey, or then him sla.

.   .   .   .

Of their compact a third had they
Off thar cowyne the thrid had thai

That was right stout, ill and felon.[1]
That wes rycht stout, Ill, and feloune.

When they the king of good renown [1]
Quhen thai the king of gud renoune

[1] Many words which rhymed in Barbour's time have so changed their
sounds in our day as to seem bad rhymes to his modern reader. Barbour
pronounced these words fel-*òon* and ren-*òon*. This remark applies to

Saw so behind his meinie ride,
Saw sua behind his mengne rid,

And saw him turn so many tide (times),
And saw him torne sa mony tid,

They abode (waited) till that he was
Thai abaid   till that he was

Entered in a narrow place
Entryt in ane narow place,

Betwixt a loch-side and a brae (bank),
Betuix a louchside and a bra;

That was so strait (narrow), I underta' (-take),
That wes sa strait,   Ik wnderta;

That he might not well turn his steed.
That he mycht nocht weill turn his sted.

Then with a will to him they yede (went) ;
Then with A will till him thai yede ;

And one him by the bridle hent (seized),
And ane him by the bridill hynt:

But he reached to him such a dint (stroke)
Bot he raucht till him sic A dynt,

That arm and shoulder flew him fra (from).
That arme and schuldyr flaw him fra.

With that another 'gan him ta' (take)
With that ane othir gan him ta

By the leg, and his hand 'gan shoot
Be the lege, and his hand gan schute

Betwixt the stirrup and his foot;
Betuix the sterap and his fute :

And when the king felt there his hand,
And quhen the king felt thar his hand,

many rhymes which are apparently bad, but which are not explained in detail because I have desired to encumber the young reader's attention with as few notes as possible.

In his stirrups stiffly 'gan he stand,
In his sterapys stythly gan he stand,

And struck with spurs the steed in hy (haste),
And strak with spuris the stede in hy;

And he lanced (leapt) forth deliverly (cleverly),
And he lansyt   furth delyuerly,

So that the tother failed (of) feet (lost his footing),
Swa that the tothir failyeit fete;

And ne'ertheless his hand was yet
And nocht-for-thi his hand wes yeit

Under the stirrup, malgré his (will, spite of him).
Wndyr the sterap, magre his.

The third, with full great haste, with this,
The thrid, with full gret hy, with this

Right to the brae-side he yede (went),
Rycht till the bra syd he yeid,

And leapt behind him on his steed.
And stert be-hynd hym on his sted.

The king was then in full great press;
The king wes then in full gret press;

However, he thought, as he that was
The quhethir he thocht, as he that wes

In all his deeds well-advised
In all his dedys awise (pronounced a-wi-sáy)

To do an outrageous bounté (very great deed).
To do ane owtrageouss bounte.

And then him that behind him was,
And syne hyme that behynd hym wass,

All maugre his will, him 'gan he raise
All magre his will, him gan he rass

From behind him, though he had sworn; [1]
Fra be-hynd hym, thocht he had sworn,

---

[1] That is, with such force that *though* the McIndrosser *had sworn* to prevent it, he could not.

He laid him even him beforn (before).
He laid hym ewyn him beforn.

Then with the sword such stroke him gave,
Syne with the suerd sic dynt hym gave,

That he the head to the harness clave.
That he the heid till the harnys clave.

He rushèd down, of blood all red,
He rouschit doun, off blud all rede,

As he that moment felt of death.
As he that stound feld off dede.

And then the king, in full great hy (haste),
And then the king, in full gret hy,

Struck at the tother vigorously,
Strak at the tothir wigorusly,

That he after his stirrup drew,
That he eftir his sterap drew,

That at the first stroke he him slew.
That at the fyrst strak he him slew.

On this wise him delivered he
On this wiss him delyuerit he

Of all those felon foes three.
Off all thai felloun fayis thre.

When they of Lorne has seen the king
Quhen thai of Lorne has sene the king

Set in himself so great helping,
Set in hym-selff sa gret helping,

And defend him (self) so manlily,
And [defend] him   sa manlely;

Was none among them so hardy
Wes nane amang thaim sa hardy

That durst assail him more in fight;
That durst assailye him mar in fycht:

So dread (ed) they for his mickle might.
Sa dred   thai for his mekill mycht.

There was a Baron Macnaughtan
Thar wes a baroune maknauchtan,

That in his heart great keep (*note*) *has ta'en*
That in his hart gret kep   has tane

Unto the king's chivalry,
[Vnto] the kingis chewalry,

And prizèd him in heart greatly.
And prisyt hym in hert gretly.

. . . . .

Then 'gan the lord of Lorne say:
Then gane the lord off lorn say:

" It seems it likes thee, perfay,
" It semys It likis the perfay,

That he slays yon-gate (*in yon manner*) *our meinie."*
That he slayis yongat   our mengye."

" Sir," said he, " so our Lord me see !
"Schyr," said he, "sa our lord me se !

— To save your presence, — it is not so.
To sauff your presence, It is nocht swa.

But whether he be friend or foe,
Bot quhethir sa [he] be freynd or fa,

That wins prize of chivalry,
That wynnys pryss off chewalry,

Men should speak thereof loyally.
Men suld spek tharoff lelyly.

And surely in all my time
And sekyrly in all my tyme,

I heard never in song nor rhyme
Ik hard neuir in sang na ryme,

Tell of a man that so smartly
Tell off A man that swa smertly

Achievèd so great chivalry."
Eschewyt swa gret chewalry."

Such speaking of the king they made ;
Sic speking off the king thai maid :

And he after his meinie rade (rode),
And he eftyr his mengye raid;

And into safety them led,
And in-till saufte thaim led,

Where he his foes nothing dread (ed).
Quhar he his fayis na thing dred.

And they of Lorne again are gane (gone),
And thai off lorne agayn ar gayn,

Moaning the scath (harm) that they have ta'en.
Menand the scaith　　　that thai haiff tayn.

II

OF KING ROBERT'S PAINS AMONG THE MOUNTAINS, AND HOW THE LADIES AND THE HORSES WERE SENT AWAY.[1]

The king that night his watches set,
The king that nycht his wachis set,
And garred ordain that they might eat,
And gert ordayne that thai mycht et ;

And bade them comfort to them take
And bad [thaim comfort] to thaim tak,
And at their mights (as best they might) merry make.
And at thar mychtis　　　　　　mery mak.

" For discomfort " — then said he —
" For disconford," as then said he,
"Is the worst thing that may be.
" Is the werst thing that may be.

For through mickle disconforting,
For throw mekill disconforting
Men ofttimes falls in despairing.
Men fallis off in-to disparyng.

---

1 These headings are fuller than those in the manuscript.

And fra (soon as) a man despairèd be,
And fra   A man disparyt be,
Then utterly vanquishèd is he.
Then wtraly wencusyt Is he.

And fra the heart be discomfit(ed),
And fra the hart be discumfyt,
The body is not worth a mite.
The body is nocht worth A myt.

" Therefore" — he said — " above all thing,
" Tharfor," he said, " atour all thing,
Keep you fra despairing:
Kepys yow fra disparyng:

And think, though we now harms feel,
And thynk, thouch we now harmys fele,
That God may yet relieve us weel (well).
That god may yeit releve ws weill.

Men reads of many men that were
Men redys off mony men that war
Far harder stead (bestead, pushed) than we yet are;
Fer hardar stad   then we yhet ar;

And since (afterwards) our Lord such grace them lent
And syne   our lord sic grace thaim lent,
That they came well to their intent.
That thai come weill till thar entent.

. . . . . .

Thus gate them comforted the king;
Thusgat thaim confort[yt] the king;
And, to comfort them, 'gan in-bring
And, to confort thaim, gan Inbryng

Old stories of men that were
Auld storys off men that wer
Set into hard assays (trials) ser (several),
Set in-tyll hard assayis   ser,

And that Fortune contraried fast,
And that fortoun contraryit fast,

And came to purpose at the last.
And come to purpos at the last.

. . . . . .

He *preachèd them on this mannèr*
He prechyt thaim on this maner;
And feignèd to make better cheer
And fenyeit to mak bettir cher,

Than he had matter to, by far
Then he had matir to, be fer :
For his cause went from ill to waur (worse).
For his causs yeid fra ill to wer.

They were aye in so hard travail,
Thai war ay in sa hard trawaill,
Till the ladies began to fail,
Till the ladyis began to fayle,

That might the travail dree (endure) no mair (more):
That mycht the trawaill drey   na mar ;
So did other also that were there.
Sa did othir als that war thar.

The Earl John was one of tho (those)
The Erle Ihone wes ane off tha,
— Of Athol — that when he saw so
— Off athole, that quhen he saw sua

The king be discomfit(ed) twice
The king be discumfyt twyss,
And so fele (many) folk against him rise,
And sa feile   folk agayne him ryss ;

And live in such travail and doubt,
And lyff in sic trawaill and dout,
His heart began to fail all-out.
His hart begane to faile all-out.

. . . . . .

The king saw that he so was failèd,
The king saw that he sa wes failyt,
And that he eke was for-travailèd (worn-out).
And that he Ik wes for-trawaillyt.

He said: "Sir Earl, we shall soon see,
He said: "Schyr Erle, we sall sone Se,
And ordain how it best may be.
&   ordayne how It best may be.

Wherever you be, our Lord you send
Quhar-euir ye be, our lord yow send
Grace, from your foes you to defend!"
Grace, fra your fais yow to defend!"

.   .   .   .   .   .

Then among them they thought it best
Then amang thaim thai thocht It best,
And ordained for the likeliest
And ordanyt for the liklyest,

That the queen, and the Earl also,
That the queyne, and the erle alsua,
And the ladies, in hy should go
And the ladyis, in hy suld ga,

With Neil the Bruce[1] *to Kildromy.*
With Nele the bruce, till kildromy.
For them thought they might securely
For thaim thocht thai mycht sekyrly

Dwell there, while they were victuallèd well;
Duell thar, quhill thai war wictaillit weile:
For so stalwart was the castlè
For swa stalwart wes the castell,

That it with strength were hard to get
That It with strenth war hard to get,
While that therein were men and meat.
Quhill that thar-in war men and mete.

As they ordained, they did in hy:
As thai ordanyt, thai did in hy:
The queen and all her company
The queyne, and all hyr cumpany,

1 Nigel Bruce.

Leapt on their horses and forth they fare(d).
Lap on thar horss, and furth thai far.
Men might have seen, who had been there,
Men mycht haiff sene, quha had been thar,

At leave-taking the ladies gret (weep)
At leve-takyng the ladyis gret,
And make their face with tears wet :
And mak thar face with teris wet :

And knights for their loves' sake
And knychtis for thar luffis sak,
Both sigh, and weep, and mourning make.
Baith sich, and wep, and murnyng mak.

They kissed their loves, at their parting,
Thai kissyt thar luffis, at thar partyng,
The king bethought him of a thing :
The king bethocht him off A thing;

That he from then on foot would go,
That he fra-thine on fute wald ga,
And take, on foot, both weal and woe,
And tak, on fute, bath weill and wa,

And would no horsemen with him have.
And wald na horss-men with him haiff.
Therefore his horses all   he gave
Tharfor his horss all haile he gaiff

To the ladies that need had.
To the ladyis, that mystir had.
The queen forth on her ways rad (rode),
The queyn furth on hyr wayis rade;

And safely came to the castlè
And sawffly come to the castell,
Where her folk were receivèd well
Quhar hyr folk war ressawyt weill;

And easèd well with meat and drink.
And esyt weill with meyt and drynk.
But might none ease let (prevent) her to think
Bot mycht nane eyss let   hyr to think

On the king that so sore was stad (bestead)
On the king, that sa sar wes stad,
That but two hundred with him had.
Thot bot ij.   C. with him had.

.   .   .   .

How the King and his Men passed over Loch Lomond in a Little Boat.

The king saw how his folk was stad (bestead),
The king saw how his folk wes stad,
And what annoys that they had.
And quhat anoyis that thai had;

He thought he to Cantire would go
He thocht he to kyntyr wald ga,
And so long sojourning there make
And swa lang soiowrnyng thar ma,

Till winter weather were away.
Till wyntir weddir war away;
And then he thought without more delay
And then he thocht, but mar delay,

Into the mainland to arrive
In-to the manland till arywe,
And to the end his weirds (fates) drive.[1]
And till the end hys werdis   dryw[e].

And for (because) Cantire lies in the sea,
And for   kyntyr lyis in the Se,
Sir Neil Campbell before sent he
Schyr Nele Cambel befor send he,

For to get him navy (boats) and meat.
For to get him nawyn   and meite:
And certain time to him he set
And certane tyme till him he sete,

---

1 That is, after wintering in Cantire, he thought he would come back
to the mainland and pursue his destiny — *dree his weird.*

When he should meet him at the sea.
Quhen he suld meite him at the se.
Sir Neil Campbell with his meiniè
Schyr Nele cambell, with his mengye,

Went his way without more letting (hindering)
Went his way, but mar letting
And left his brother with the king.
And left his brothir with the king.

.   .   .   .   .   .

The king, after that he was gane (gone),
The king, eftir that he wes gane,
To Loch Lomond the way has ta'en,
To lowchlomond the way has tane,

And came there on the third day.
And come thar on the thrid day.
But thereabout no boat found they,
Bot thar-about na bait fand thai,

That might them o'er the water bear.
That mycht thaim our the watir ber.
Then were they woe on great mannèr,
Than war thai wa on gret maner:

For it was far about to go (to go around,)
For It wes fer about to ga;
And they were in (to) doubt also
And thai war in-to dout alsua,

To meet their foes that spread were wide.
To meyt thar fayis that spred war wyd.
Therefore, along the loch's side
Tharfor, endlang the louchhis syd,

So busily they sought, and fast,
Sa besyly thai socht, and fast,
Till James of Douglas at the last
Tyll Iamys of dowglas, at the last,

Found a little sunken boat
Fand A littill sonkyn bate,
And to the land it drew foot-hot (quickly).
And to the land It drew, fut hate.

But it so little was, that it
Bot It sa littill wes, that It
Might o'er the water but three-some [1] *flit.*
Mycht our the wattir bot thresum flyt.

They sent thereof word to the king
Thai send thar-off word to the king,
That was joyful of that finding,
That wes Ioyfull off that fynding;

And first into the boat is gane ;
And fyrst in-to the bate is gane,
With him Douglas ; the third was ane
With him dowglas ; the thrid wes ane

That rowed them o'er deliverly (cleverly)
That rowyt thaim our deliuerly,
And set them on the land all dry ;
And set thaim on the land all dry :

And rowed so oft-times to and fro,
And rowyt sa oft-syss to & fra,
Fetching aye o'er two and two,
Fechand ay our twa & twa,

That in a night and in a day
That in A nycht and in A day,
Come out o'er the loch are they.
Cummyn owt our the louch ar thai.

For some of them could swim full well
For sum off thaim couth swome full weill,
And on his back bear a fardel (pack).
And on his bak ber a fardele.

So with swimming and with rowing
Swa with swymmyng, and with rowyng
They brought them o'er, and all their thing.
Thai brocht thaim our, and all thar thing.

The king, the whiles, merrily
The king, the quhilis, meryly
Read to them that were him by
Red to thaim that war him by,

1 With three in it.

Romance of worthy Ferambrace
Romanys off worthi ferambrace
That worthily o'ercome (n) was
That worthily oer-cummyn was

.   .   .   .

The good king upon this mannèr
The gud king, apon this maner,
Comforted them that were him near,
Comfort[yt] thaim that war him ner ;

And made them games and solace
And maid thaim gamyn [and] solace
Till that his folk all passèd was.
Till that his folk all passyt was.

.   .   .   .

HOW THE EARL OF LENNOX, WHO HAD RETIRED TO THESE
HILLS THINKING THAT THE KING WAS DEAD, JOYFULLY
RAN TO MEET HIM WHEN HE HEARD HIS HORN BLOW.

They had full great default of meat,
Thai had full gret defaut off mete,
And therefore, venison to get,
And tharfor venesoun to get

In two parties are they gane.
In twa partyss ar thai gayne.
The king himself was in to ane,
The king him-selff wes in-till ane ;

And Sir James of Douglas
And Schyr Iames off Dowglas
Into the t'other party was.
In-to the tothir party was.

Then to the height they held their way,
Then to the hycht thai held thar way,
And hunted longwhile of the day,
And huntyt lang quhill off the day ;

And sought shaws (woods) and traps set ;
And soucht schawys and Setis set ;

But they got little for to eat.
Bot thai gat litill for till ete.

Then happened at that time per case (by chance)
Then hapnyt at that tyme percass,
That the Earl of the Lennox was
That the Erle of the Leuenax was

Among the hills near thereby:
Amang the hillis, ner tharby;
And when he heard so blow and cry,[1]
And quhen he hard sa blaw & cry,

He had wonder what it might be ;
He had wondir quhat It mycht be ;
And on such manner speerèd (tracked, spyed) he
And on sic maner spyryt   he,

That he knew that it was the king:
That [he] knew that It wes the king:
And then, without (en) more dwelling (hesitating),
And then, for-owtyn mar duelling,

With all them of his company
With all thaim off his cumpany,
He went right to the king in hy,
He went rycht till the king in hy,

So blythe and so joyful that he
Sa blyth and sa Ioyfull, that he
Might on no manner blither be.
Mycht on na maner blyther be.

For he the king weened (thought) had been dead ;
For he the king wend   had bene ded ;
And he was also will of red[2]
And he wes alsua will off red,

That he durst rest into no place ;
That he durst rest in-to na place ;

---

1 That is, the horn-blowing and crying of the king's people, in hunting.
2 " Will of red " is an idiomatic phrase meaning *wild of rede or counsel,*
that is, *at a loss what to do.*

Nor, since the king discomfit(ed) was
Na, sen the king discumfyt was

At Methven, he heard never thing,
At meffan, he herd neuir thing
That ever was certain, of the king.
That euir wes certane off the king.

Therefore, in (to) full great dainty (fond delight,)
Tharfor, in-to full gret daynte,
The king full humbly greeted he;
The king full humyly haylist he;

And he him welcomed right blithely,
And he him welcummyt rycht blythly,
And kissèd him full tenderly.
And [kyssyt] him full tendirly.

And all the lords that were there
And all the lordis, that war thar,
Right joyful of their meeting were,
Rycht Ioyful off thar meting war,

And kissèd him in great dainty.
And kissyt him in gret daynte.
It was great pity for to see
It wes gret pite for till Se

How they for joy and pity gret (wept)
How thai for Ioy and pite gret,
When that they with their fellows met
Quhen that thai with thar falow[is] met,

That they weened had been dead; for thi (for this)
That thai wend had bene dede ; forthi
They welcomed him more heartfully.
Thai welcummyt him mar hartfully.

And he for pity gret (wept) again,
And he for pite gret   agayne,
That never of meeting was so fain.
That neuir off metyng wes sa fayne.

Though I say that they gret, soothly
Thocht I say that thai gret, sothly,
It was no greting properly.
It wes na greting propyrly:

.   .   .   .   .   .

But I wot well, without lying,
Bot [1] I wate weill, but [1] lesyng,
Whatever men say of such greting,
Quhat euir men say off sic greting,

That mickle joy, or yet pity,
That mekill Ioy, or yeit pete,
May gar (cause) men so a-movèd be
May ger   men sua amowyt be,

.

That water from the heart will rise,
That watir fra the hart will ryss,
And wet the eyne (eyes) on such a wise.
And weyt the eyne   on sic a wyss.

.   .   .   .

The Earl had meat, and that plenty,
The Erle had mete, and that plente,
And with glad heart it them gave he,
And with glaid hart It thaim gaiff he;

And they ate it with full good will,
And thai eyt It with full gud will,
That sought none other sauce theretill (there to)
That soucht [nane othir] salss thar-till

But appetite, that oft men takes;
Bot appetyt, that oft men takys;
For well scoured were their stomàchs.
For weill scowryt war thar stomakys.

.   .   .   .

And they full piteously 'gan tell
And thai full pitwysly gan tell

---

1 With Barbour, "bot" is the modern *but*, and "but" is the modern *without*.

Adventurès that them befell,
Auenturis that thaim befell,

And great annoys and poverty.
And gret anoyis, and powerte.
The king thereat had great pity,
The king thar-at had gret pite :

And told them piteously again
And tauld thaim petwisly agayne
The annoy, the travail, and the pain
The noy, the trawaill, and the payne,

That he had tholed (suffered) since he them saw.
That he had tholyt,   sen he thaim saw.
Was none among them, high nor low,
Wes nane amang thaim, hey na law,

That he not had pity and pleasance
That he ne had pite and plesaunce,
When that he heard make remembrance
Quhen that he herd mak remembrance

Of the perils that passèd were.
Off the perellys that passyt war.
For, when men aught at ease are,
[For] quhen men oucht at liking ar,

To tell of pains passèd by
To tell off paynys passyt by
Pleases to hearing wonderly.
Plesys to heryng [wonderly].

And to rehearse their old dis-ease (pain)
And to reherss thar auld disese
Does them ofttimes comfort and ease,
Dois thaim oft-syss confort and ese ;

So (provided) that thereto follow no blame,
With-thi   thar-to folow na blame,
Dishonor, wickedness, nor shame.
Dishonour, wikytnes, na schame.

.   .   .   .

How King Robert was chased with a Sleuth-hound in
Galloway; and how he fought alone against Two
Hundred, at a Ford.

And when the Gallowese [1] *wist soothly*
And quhen the gallowais vist suthly
That he was with a few meinie,
That he wes with a few menyhe,
They made a secret assembly
Thai maid a preue assemble

Of well two hundred men and ma (*more*).
Off weill twa hundreth men & ma.
A sleuth-hound with them 'gan they ta' (*take*)
Ane sluth-hwnd vith thaim can thai ta;

    .   .   .   .

They shaped them (*intended*), *in an evening*
Thai schupe thame,   in ane evynnyng,
Suddenly to surprise the king,
Suddandly to suppriss the king,

And to him held they straight their way.
And till him held thai straucht thar way,
But he, that had his watches aye
Bot he, that had his vachis ay

On each side, of their coming
On ilk syde, of thar cummyng,
Long ere they came — had wittering (*knowledge*);
Lang or thai com, had vittering;

    .   .   .   .

And went him down to a morass,
And vent hym doune till a marrass,
On a water that running was;
On a vattir that rynand was;

---

[1] The men of Galloway. Bruce, after many adventures by sea and land
— omitted in these brief extracts — has come over into his own earldom of
Carrick, and wanders about there, having but sixty men as his meinie.

And in a bog he found a place
And in a bog he fand a place
Full straight (very narrow), that well two bowdraught was
Veill strate,   that well twa bowdraucht was,

From (where) they the water passèd had.
Fra thai   the vattir passit had:
He said " here may ye make abode (stop)
He said, "heir may yhe mak abade;

And rest you all a while and lie.
And rest yow all a quhile and ly.
I will go watch you privily
I will ga vach yow preuely,

If I hear aught of their coming ;
Giff I heir oucht of thar cummyng;
And if I may hear anything
And gif I may heir ony thyng,

I shall gar warn you, so that we
I sall ger varn yow, sua that we
Shall aye at our advantage be."
Sall ay at our avantage be."

.   .   .   .   .   .

Sir Gilbert de la Hay left he
And schir gilbert de [la] hay left he
There, for to rest with his meinie.
Thar for to rest with his menyhe.

To the water he came in hy,
To the vattir he com in hy,
And listened full intently
And lisnyt full ententily

If he aught heard of their coming :
Gif he oucht herd of thare cummyng;
But yet then might he hear no thing.
Bot yeit than mycht he heir na thing.

Endlong (along) the water then went he
Endlang   the vattir than yeid he

On either side great quantity (distance);
On athir syde great quantite ;

He saw the braes (banks) high standing,
He saw the brayis   hye standand,
The water all through mire running,
The vattir holl throu slike rynand,

And found no ford that men might pass
And fand na furd that men mycht pas
But where himself o'er passèd was.
Bot quhar hymself [our] passit was.

And so straight (narrow) was the up-coming[1]
And sua strate   wes the vp-cummyng,
That two men might not together thring (throng).
That twa men mycht nocht sammyn thryng,

. . . .

His two men bade he then in hy
His twa men bad he than in hy
Go to their feres (mates) to rest and lie.
Ga to thair feris   to rest and ly ;

" Sir " — said they — " who shall with you be ? "
Schir," said they, " quha sall vith yow be ? "

" God " — he said — " withouten ma (more).
" God," he said, "forouten ma ;
Pass on, for I will it be sa."
Pas on, for I will it be swa."

They did as he them bidden had,
Thai did as he thame biddin had,
And he there all alone abade (abode).
And he thar all allane abaid.

When he a while had bided there,
Quhen he a quhile had biddin thare,
And harbored (waited lurking), he heard as it were
And herbryit,   he herd as it war

[1] The ascent up the bank from the ford.

A hound's questing (hunting) upon far (afar)
A hundis quhistlyng   apon fer,
That aye came to him near(er) and near(er).
That ay com till him ner   & ner.

He stood still for to hearken mair (more)
He stude still for till herkyn mair,
And aye the longer while he was there
And ay the langer quhill he wes thair,

He heard it near(er) and near(er) comand (coming);
He herd it ner   and ner   cumand;
But he there still thought he would stand
Bot he thair still thoucht he vald stand,

Till that he heard more tokening;
Till that he herd mair taknyng;
For, for a hound's questing
For, for a hundis quhestlyng,

He would not waken his meinie.
He wald nocht walkyn his menyhe.
Therefore he would abide and see
Tharfor he walde abyde and se

What folk they were, and whether they
Quhat folk thai war, & quhethir thai
Held toward him the right way
Held toward him the rycht vay,

Or passèd another way far by.
Or pas[syt] ane othir way fer by.
The moon was shining right clearly,
The moyn wes schynand rycht cleirly,

And so long stood he harkenànd (harkening)
And sua lang stude he herkynand,
Till that he saw come at his hand
Till that he saw cum at his hand

The whole rout in full great hy.
The haill rowt, in full gret hy;
Then he bethought him hastily
Than he vmbethocht him hastely,

If he went to fetch his meinie
Gif he yeid to feche his menyhe,
That ere he might repairèd be (come back)
That, or he mycht reparit be,

They should be past the ford, each ane.
Thai suld be passit the furde ilkane.
And then behooved he chose him ane [1]
And than behufit, he chesit him ane

Of these two, either to flee or die.
Of thir twa, outhir to fle or de.
But his heart, that was stout and high,
Bot his hert, that wes stout and he,

Counsellèd him alone to bide
Consalit hym allane to byde,
And keep them at the ford's side
And kep thame at the furdis syde,

And defend well the up-coming,
And defend weill the vp-cummyng,
Since he was provided with arming (armor)
Sen he was varnysit of Armyng

That he their arrows need not dread.
That he thair Arravis [thurt] nocht dreid.
For if he were of great manhead (manhood)
For gif he war of gret manheid,

He might stonish them every ane
He mycht stonay thame [euir] ilkane
Since they could come but ane and ane (one at a time).
Sen thai mycht cum bot ane and ane.

    .   .   .   .

Therewith he to the ford 'gan go
Thar-vith he to the furd can ga;

And they upon the t'other party,
And thai, apon the tothir party

---

[1] And then it was necessary (behooved) that he should choose one of these two, either to flee or die.

That saw him stand there one-somely (alone),
That saw him stand thair anerly,

Thronging into the water rade (rode) ;
Thryngand in[-till] the vattir raid ;
For of him little doubt they had (sure they had him)
For of him litill dout thai had,

And rode to him in full great hy.
And raid till him in full gret hy.
He smote the first so rigorously
He smat the first sa rygorusly

With his spear, that right sharply share (sheared, cut),
Vith his spere, that rycht scharply schare,
Till he down to the earth him bare.
Till he doun to the erd hym bare.

The lave (rest) came then in a randoun (at random),
The laif   com than in a randoune,
But his horse that was borne down
Bot his hors, that wes born doune,

Cumbered them the up-gang (ascent) to ta' (take).
Cummerit thaim the vpgang   to ta.
And when the king saw it was sa (so)
And quhen the kyng saw it wes sua,

He stickèd the horse, and he 'gan fling
He stekit the hors, and he can flyng,
And then fell at the up-coming,
And syne fell at the vpcummyng.

The lave (rest), with that, came with a shout,
The laif   with that com [with] a schowt,
And he, that stalwart was and stout,
And he that stalward wes and stout,

Met them right stoutly at the brae
Met thame rycht stoutly at the bra,
And so good payment 'gan them ma (make)
And sa gud payment can thaim ma,

That five-some in the ford he slew.
That fiff sum in the furd he slew.
The lave then some-deal (somewhat) them withdrew,
The laif than sumdeill   thaim vith-drew,

That dread(ed) his strokes wonder sore,
That dred   his strakis voundir sare;
For he in no thing them forbare (spared them not).
For he in na thing thame forbare.

Then one said " certes (certainly) we are to blame:
Than ane said " certis,   we ar to blame;
What shall we say when we come hame (home),
Quhat sall we say quhen we cum hame,

When one man fights against us all ?
Quhen a man fechtis agains vs all ?
Who wist ever men so foully fall
Quha vist euir men sa fouly fall

As us, if that we thus-gate leave !"
As vs, gif that we thusgat leif ! "
With that all whole a shout they gave
With that all haill a schout thai [geve],

And cried " On him ! He may not last."
And cryit " on hym ! he may nocht [last]."
With that they pressèd him so fast
Vith that thai presit hym so fast,

That had he not the better been
That had he nocht the bettir beyn,
He had been dead withouten veyn (doubt).
He had beyn ded forouten veyn.

But he so great defence 'gan make
Bot he sa gret defens can mak,
That where he hit with even strake (stroke)
That, quhar he hit, with evin strak,

There might no thing against it stand.
Thar mycht no thing agane it stand.
In little space (while) he left lyànd (lying)
In litill space   he left lyand

So fele (many) that the up-come was then,
Sa feill   that the vpcom wes then
Stopped up with slain horses and men,
Dittit with slayn hors and men;

So that his foes, for that stopping,
Swa that his fayis, for that stopping,
Might (could) not come to the up-coming.
Micht   nocht cum to the vp-cummyng.

Ah, dear God! who had been by
A! deir god! quha had beyn by,
And seen how he so hardily
And seyn how he sa hardely

Addressèd him against them all,
Adressit him agane thame all,
I wot well that they should him call
I wat weill that thai suld him call

The best that lived into his day;
The best that liffit in-till his day;
And if that I the sooth (truth) shall say,
And gif that I the suth   sall say,

I heard never in no time gone
I herd neuir in na tyme gane
One stint (stop) so many, him alone.
Ane stynt   sa mony hym allane.

.   .   .   .

Till he such martyrdom there made
Till he sic martirdome thair maid,
That he the ford all stoppèd had,
That he the furde all stoppit had,

That none of them might to him ride.
That nane of thame mycht till him ryde.
Then thought them folly for to bide,
Than thoucht thame foly for to byde,

And wholly the flight 'gan ta' (take)
And halely the flicht can ta,
And went hameward where they came fra.
And went hamvard quhar thai com fra.

For the king's men with that cry
For the kingis men with that cry
Wakened, and full affrightedly
Valknyt, and full affraitly

Came for to seek their lord the king.
Com for to seik thair lord the king.
The Galloway men heard their coming
The galloway men herd thair cummyng,

And fled, that durst not bide no mair.
And fled, that durst nocht byde na nair.
The king's men, that dreading were
The kingis men, that dredand wair

For their lord, full speedily
For thai lord, full spedaly
Came to the ford and soon in hy
Com to the furde and soyn in hy

They found the king sitting alane,
Thai fand the kyng sytand alane,
That off his bassnet (helmet) then had ta'en
That of his basnet   than had tane

To take the air, for he was hot.
To tak the air, for he wes hate.
Then speered (asked) they at him of his state,
Than sperit   thai at him of his stat;

And he told them all whole the case:
And he told thaim all haill the cass,
How-gate that he assailèd was,
Howgat that he assalyeit was,

And how that God him helpèd sa
And how that god hym helpit sua,
That he escapèd whole them fra.
That he eschapit haill thame fra.

Then lookèd they how fele (many) were dead,
Than lukit thai how feill   war ded,
And they found lying in that stead (place)
And thai fand liand in that sted

Fourteen that slain were with his hand.
Fourteyn that slayn war vith his hand.
Then praised they God fast, all-willdànd,[1]
Than lovit thai god fast, all-veldand,

That they their lord found whole and fair (sound),
That thai thar lord fand haill and feir;
And said: " them behooved in no mannèr
And said: " thai[m] byrd on na maner

Dread their foes, since their chieftain
Dreid thair fais, sen thair chiftane
Was of such heart and of such main (strength)
Wes of sic hert and of sic mane,

That he for them had underta'en
That he for thame had vndirtane
With so fele folk to fight, him ane."
With sa feill folk to fecht him ane."

[1] All-wielding, that is, almighty.